Management for Growth

Management for Growth

Richard Normann

Scandinavian Institute for
Administrative Research, Lund, Sweden

A Wiley–Interscience Publication

JOHN WILEY & SONS
Chichester · New York · Brisbane · Toronto

Translated from the Swedish by
Nancy Adler

Original version: Skapande företagsledning:
Aldus, Stockholm 1975.

Library of Congress Cataloging in Publication Data:

Normann, Richard, 1943–
  Management for growth

  Translation of Skapande företagsledning.
  Originally presented as the author's thesis, Lund.
  1: Management.   I. Title.
HD37.S84N5913   658.4   77–2839

ISBN 0 471 95513 4

Photosetting by Thomson Press (India) Ltd., New Delhi
and printed and bound in Great Britain at The Pitman Press, Bath

Contents

Foreword

This book has been written under the auspices of SIAR (Scandinavian Institutes for Administrative Research), an organization that combines in its activities both clinical research and consultation. I have tried here to interpret clinical material and to use it to develop the conceptual framework which is the basis of the Institute's attempts to help companies and other large organizations with their development problems.

It is therefore natural that a book of this kind should be the product of teamwork. I owe a great debt of gratitude to all those members of SIAR who have previously worked on the development and formulation of our ideas, as well as to all my colleagues—and at present there are about 60 of us—who have worked with me on the projects without which this book would not have been possible. I am equally grateful to all those clients who have provided me with material and with the personal encouragement necessary to bring the work to fruition.

It would be difficult—and perhaps also unjust—to try to pick out the people who have given me the most impulses. Instead I would like to name those who have had a more or less direct influence on this book.

Eric Rhenman has been my chief source of inspiration for many years, and it has been my ambition to carry on where he left off at the end of *Organization for Long-Range Planning*. Gabor Bruszt has also been a major influence, both as regards the clinical orientation of the present work as well as on my understanding of the political processes of companies. I discussed the manuscript, while still only half finished, chiefly with Christian Junnelius, who has done his best to help me sift the wheat from the chaff, and with Carsten Dahlman, who made me aware of certain weaknesses in my conceptual scheme. Rolf H. Carlsson helped to correct some misconceptions about growth in conglomerates, as well as supporting me in many other ways. Magnus Hallberg and Henry Lundbergh have contributed to the final editing of the manuscript, at the same time persuading me to make some improvements in the scientific content.

I am afraid that I have not managed to satisfy all their requirements, and naturally I alone am responsible for the interpretations of the data presented in this book and for everything in the following pages.

Many research workers and others outside SIAR have also meant a great deal to me during my work on this book. Jay W. Lorsch and Larry E. Greiner arranged for me to spend some time during the autumn of 1971 as a guest researcher at the Harvard Business School, where I had the opportunity to work undisturbed on the fundamental theoretical framework of the book. At that stage Larry Greiner helped me very much by strongly criticizing my conceptual framework, thereby—among other things—reinforcing my determination to go on and see where it would lead me. I received other major impulses during my stay in the USA, particularly from Walter Buckley, Harry Levinson and the late James D. Thompson.

In particular I would also like to thank Lennart Strömberg for his continuous and unwavering moral support.

The manuscript has been translated from the Swedish by Nancy Adler. Inga-Britt Aggeklint and Eva Jonson of SIAR Dokumentation AB have worked on the final manuscript, while Birgitta Fritsch, Inger Karlsson and Ingrid Nilsson have typed out innumerable working papers for me over the last few years. Astrid, Anja and Torvald have coped with the trials that accompany authorship—at least according to my method.

A grant from the Bank of Sweden Tercentenary Foundation has made the writing of this book possible.

To all those mentioned here, and to many more whom I have not been able to name, I would like to offer my warmest thanks.

RICHARD NORMANN

... the valuing of consistency that leads to competence; the valuing of inconsistency that leads to learning; and both that lead to increased effectiveness...

(Argyris and Schön, 1974, p. 109)

PART I

Points of Departure

The mainspring of Progress is the accumulation
of knowledge ...
(Sir Geoffrey Vickers, 1968, p. 3)

The first part of this book consists of two chapters. In Chapter 1, starting from a broad frame of reference, we describe the practical problems which we are trying to highlight and the theoretical basis of this study.

We start by discussing the situation of the large corporations, explaining that unless these companies can succeed in two important ways, they are going to find it increasingly difficult to survive. First, they must readjust to the task of developing new knowledge. In this way they can contribute to the creation of quality in society, thus fulfilling a role that is potentially within their reach. Secondly, they must provide a better working environment, in the broadest sense of the term, for the individuals who work in them. We are looking for the truly entrepreneurial organization.

Some fundamental ideas and concepts are presented in Chapter 2 where, in conclusion, we introduce an idea that is pivotal to our argument: that 'growth problems' often spring essentially from a lack of adjustment between on the one hand a company's 'dominating ideas' or values and the associated social structure in which these values are embodied, and on the other the new situation calling for new strategies in which the company finds itself. The process that shapes and changes values and ideas is a process of absolutely fundamental importance to any company; it is discussed in more detail in the last part of the book.

CHAPTER 1

The Problem—Practical and Theoretical

1.1 In quest of the entrepreneurial organization

This book is about processes of renewal in business companies.

Most of us spend a considerable amount of our active life within the bounds of fairly large companies and other formal organizations. These same organizations also supply us with the greater part of the goods and services which we consume. The technology of production has become so complex, and different parts of society so inextricably interdependent, that the large organizations alone appear able to command the resources and the ability to satisfy our demands.

Intrinsically there is nothing negative about this. But the situation has placed a very great responsibility on those who lead the large organizations which provide the variety of things we consume and the environment in which we operate as individuals.

It has often been claimed that the growing predominance of large, complex organizations has destroyed the possibility of individual initiatives; the age of the entrepreneurs is over. It seems to me, however, that this conclusion is based on some serious misunderstandings. To begin with, it can be shown that even the 'old' type of entrepreneurs operated to a very great extent within organized systems; it was above all their ability to exploit and combine different resources which, within the relevant systems, turned them into innovators (Burns, 1968). Greater resources, advanced technologies and more complex needs in society should in fact serve to encourage rather than inhibit a spirit of innovation and enterprise.

Furthermore, there is also a significant tendency—or a discontinuity— in the way society is developing which suggests that the need for genuine renewal and the possibility of achieving such renewal are both increasing. The industrial revolution has had its golden age, and has found its purest expression in the technology of mass production and the consumer society. During its final period the problem of business enterprise has customarily been seen as a matter, chiefly, of technology and logistics, focusing not so much on what is being done as on the ability to do it efficiently and rationally. The results of these efforts have been remarkable, far beyond what could have been imagined even a few decades ago.

Perhaps it is for this very reason that certain myths have been able to flourish.

The businessman as the rational decision-maker has become a hero, and success has been guaranteed by advanced information systems and complicated logistics. But the prescription for success is in the process of changing, at least in the industrialized or developed countries. Here the idea of the post-industrial society, in which the greater part of man's fundamental needs are satisfied, is no longer new. Much has also been heard of the new knowledge technology (Bell, 1974; Thompson, 1974). The difficult challenge that faces large companies—and, notably, the major public institutions—today is to create *quality* to the same degree as *quantity*. This is a job quite unlike the one these organizations have been doing, namely, building the mass production society. And it will not be possible to succeed in it by applying the major management techniques to be learnt from the study of companies successful in the past. Two examples can serve to illustrate this point.

- Perhaps one of the most striking cases is the failure of the building industry to create quality—striking, because houses are not commodities (as was obviously thought), but very much an ingredient in the quality of life. In recent years it has been possible for the Swedish building industry—protected by an artificially created demand and believing that its main problem was to learn a variety of production and management techniques and generally to industrialize itself more—to create environments for living which, while admittedly cheap, are often of such frighteningly poor quality that even quite hardened—or modest—consumers are refusing to live in them. It is also extremely illuminating to look at recent attempts in the USA to encourage successful companies from other branches of industry—companies known for their advanced management techniques and rational methods—to enter the building business in order to speed up the process of efficiency improvement there. The discouraging results can be seen in Figure 1.1.

  The reason for this, it seems to me, is that the people involved have to a very great extent misunderstood what the building industry is all about; advanced management principles alone could not help in a bewildering situation where success depends so much on the ability to create a complex 'quality' of life.

- Interesting growth patterns can also be discovered in the distribution and retail trades. The companies which succeeded best in the period of the most rampant mass production and mass consumption (in Sweden this was during the first half of the 1960s) have the biggest headaches today. They try to tackle their problems by pushing their distribution systems and planning routines to further heights of refinement, but this is not a strategy to bring success. The companies which do cope are those which combine reasonably rational operations with a more differentiated structure, those which allow for local initiative and, above all, those which try to adapt their services to new market segments—segments that they cannot even identify today.

BIG LOSERS IN LAND AND SHELTER			
Company	Lines of business	indicated losses (including reserves)	Current losses (fiscal 1973)
		Millions of dollars	
Alcoa	Residential and commercial development, apartments, low-income housing	N.A.	$7·4*
American Cyanamid	Apartments, offices, and shopping centres in planned unit developments	$10·7	5·5
American Standard	Planned unit and recreational developments, modular housing, foreign housing	16	2·9
Avco	Planned communities, land sales, mobile-home parks	3	6·1
Bethlehem Steel	Residential, offices, construction management, modular homes		15·7**
Boise Cascade	Land sales, recreational development, home building, modular housing	257	N.A.
CNA Financial	Home building, mortgage banking, real estate investment trust, recreational land	12·9	4·5 (profit)
Dart Industries	Land sales, recreational development	None	6
International Paper	Community development, home building, land sales, shopping centres, resorts	30·5	N.A.
ITT	Home building, land development, rental apartments, modular homes	57	14
Potlatch Forests	Land development, residential construction, modular housing	3·5	1·7 (est)*
Westinghouse Electric	Land sales, military and low-income modular homes	30	N.A.

*After tax   **First half of 1973   Data Company reports. BW est

Figure 1.1. Some Major American Companies' Losses when Trying to Enter the Building Industry (from *Business Week*, February 16, 1974)

How can rigid bureaucratic bodies be transformed into enterprising organizations—in the fullest sense of the term? How can business managements be persuaded to 'unlearn' some of the effective management techniques which were so successful in dealing with the problems of yesterday but which can actually represent the greatest obstacle to coping with the tasks of today? How can they be made to learn, instead, the new management methods which will be required but which are still diffuse and only vaguely understood? How can we open up our present limited social debate about the working environment, and go in for creating organizations designed to satisfy the ambition and the need of individual people to be able to develop and grow— now when the realization of these needs appears to accord so well with the new business challenge, with the call for the creation of quality?

These fundamental questions provide the broader frame of reference within which this book will, it is hoped, make a contribution. Personally, however, I am not at all certain that any total transformation of society is needed to realize these visions. I believe very strongly *in companies as an instrument for creating quality in society*. But the chances of companies being able to function in this way depend on a basic reappraisal of the prevailing management tradition. If there must be a revolution, then this is the one that is needed. I also believe that efficiency—albeit in a broad sense—is extremely important and must be required of any company trying to create quality; in the same way I am convinced that the companies which will succeed best in being genuinely innovative will also be—and should also be—those which generate the biggest profits. It is a serious misconception that there is any necessary contradiction between the creation of quality and the generation of profit.

Thus, starting from the empirically known real world, we shall try to plumb and to understand the problems of innovation and growth in business companies. I must naturally start from my own experience, i.e. as a clinical researcher working with business managements, seeking to help them with the problems of growth in their companies. I shall try to benefit from my experience of situations in which these problems have been concerned with true innovation, and from my experience of less spectacular situations—less spectacular, that is, in terms of quality creation. The following are some of the typical problems which, in a variety of guises, are most frequently met:

- The traditional large company, perhaps raw-material oriented and with a stable tradition in local manufacturing (in Swedish, *brukstradition*), whose established operations are just about played out and in need of fundamental renewal from within or the addition of new operations of another type. Companies of this kind often sink gradually into inertia and bureaucracy, not least because they were once successful. They may also have been operating in the shelter of industrial cartels and various other kinds of artificial protection. These companies thus often find themselves operating in relatively stable industries, where 'zero sum games' predominate—I win, you lose.

    There is no genuine renewal which could increase the size of the whole cake; one company grows only if some others contract. There is a striking example of the artificial creation of this win-or-lose structure in the building industry in Sweden: a certain quota of apartments is allocated to a municipality by the central authority, after which the different clients receive their given share of the cake, regardless of how competent or incompetent they are.

- The company which, despite many attempts, has failed to generate interesting ideas for new lines of business or to renew its established operations.

- The company with original ideas and the embryo of new activities, which has nevertheless failed to develop these, despite good resolutions.

- The company with several lines of business, often in different industries, which has failed because it has tried to impose uniform management principles on all parts of its organization, failing to understand the special and unique character of each separate growth problem.

The reader will find that these problems, in my interpretation, are not in the first place intellectual problems. Intelligence and rational problem-solving may be important to innovation, but more is required: to create the entrepreneurial company, fundamental philosophies have to be changed.

1.2 A note on terminology

In the following pages I shall be using terms such as development, renewal, growth and innovation, without distinguishing very clearly between them. I would like to stress that, regardless of which of these expressions I choose, I am primarily concerned with processes by means of which quality is created. It is the *growth of knowledge or the process of knowledge development* that is the central process in growth as I interpret it below.

This approach has of course been dictated by personal interest; it is also a question of ethics. Ideologically, it seems to me infinitely more urgent to tackle problems connected with the creation of new quality rather than with the splitting up among companies of a given cake. The 'plus sum game' where everyone can win is more attractive than the demoralizing game where you win at the expense of others.

Naturally, however, we cannot simply ignore quantitative growth. On the contrary, provided that superior competence in developing knowledge is exploited in the right way, the right kind of quantitative growth will—and indeed should—follow. There are a great many links between quality, size, quantitative growth, and efficiency, which it would be wrong to ignore and which we shall be discussing in this book.

1.3 Some theoretical problems and starting-points

In terms of established disciplines, the theoretical problems which I shall be trying to tackle here fall within areas such as 'growth processes in companies', 'situation-oriented organizational design' and 'theory of social learning'.

An important theoretical problem concerns the dilemma 'to control or not to control'. On the one hand, I shall be claiming that established control theory does not function for a large number of the processes we shall be discussing, especially not for the development of knowledge or the learning process itself. This is confirmed by an ordinary empirical observation, namely, that many successful lines of business have pushed their way up 'through the tarmac', despite attempts to stifle them, while attempts to control and encourage growth very often fail. On the other hand, however, I am trying to establish guidelines of some kind to help companies which want to generate development processes. Is it possible to speak of control at all in this context? And if so, how can we distinguish between different kinds of control?

It has been necessary for those of us involved in this study to try to understand the very essence of the process of knowledge development—what is unique to it, what distinguishes it from other processes in a company. Only by developing a suitable language for describing the process can we begin to understand something of the ways in which it can be influenced. One of the basic assumptions underlying the whole of the study has been that it is possible to distinguish a number of stages in a company's development process and that these stages differ fundamentally from one another; they therefore call for different types of organizational structure and different 'management philosophies'.

On the theoretical side, one of our main purposes has been to clarify some crucial links between stages in the development process, various characteristics of the company, and company efficiency. In this respect the study has points of contact with contingency theories of organization which have begun to emerge in recent years, but it adds a kind of time dimension to the situational factors that other researchers have studied. We have also tried, which is not perhaps so usual, to understand the way in which a company's system of ideas—the values and assumptions that prevail in it—must be adapted to different situations. Thus, the difference here in relation to most existing organization theory is that we have added a time dimension and introduced the concept of the dominating ideas of the company.

I shall try to illustrate more clearly how the present book stands in relation to the work of several well-known researchers and to various current theories. I present no systematic survey of the literature on company growth; it would in any case be difficult to improve on the survey in Starbuck (1971). Instead I shall simply indicate a few important ways in which my present frame of reference differs from previous research in this field, and refer briefly to some of my major sources of inspiration.

Relation to some classical researchers

We shall be touching on an area which is often called 'company policy' or 'strategy formulation'. First, we can examine our relation to a well-known representative of this field, namely, Ansoff (cf. Ansoff, 1965). We deviate from Ansoff's view primarily in three respects:

1. Ansoff regards the choice of strategy and the formulation of policy chiefly as a decision process: first, goals are established, after which (using

a series of analytical techniques) alternatives are evolved and (still using analytical techniques) a choice made among them, possibly after some adjustments in the original goals. For such complex questions as choice of strategy and formulation of policy, I reject this type of 'rational' decision model, suggesting that processes of this kind can be controlled and understood better if they are handled as *learning processes*.

2. My present argument also has *deeper roots in organization theory* than Ansoff's, since in this and other studies we have found that the design of the organization structure—including the organization's control system—has a profound effect on the way in which learning takes place and decisions are made. This applies perhaps more than anything else to such overriding decisions as how, and in what direction, the company is to grow. Further, we find it unreasonable to try to steer, describe, or understand a company's growth process without taking into account the effects of the values and assumptions embraced by the leading actors. These values and assumptions are not mentioned by Ansoff. Thus, in my view, it is not possible to wrest the analytical problem of formulating a strategy out of the context in which the process has to take place—because this is the context which must be exploited by anyone wanting to influence the process.

3. Finally, I find Ansoff's description too generalized. He describes a decision process or 'checklist' which would fit some of the situations I have experienced fairly well, but which would fit others poorly indeed.

By differing from Ansoff on these admittedly fundamental points, I do not mean to imply that many of the analytical techniques employed by Ansoff and other members of the decision-theory planning school cannot be extremely valuable if used in a suitable situation.

A major source of inspiration has been Chandler's description of the growth of some large American companies (Chandler, 1962). I found it equally important to understand the points on which I disagree with Chandler as to establish the points on which we agree. Chandler's central thesis is that a company first formulates a strategy and then designs a structure adapted to this strategy which makes it possible for the company to grow in accordance with the strategy. The importance of a match between 'structure' and 'strategy' is a fundamental ingredient also of my frame of reference. On the other hand, I do not altogether agree with Chandler about the relationship in time between design of structure and formulation of strategy. According to our observations, the reverse relation—i.e. with strategy as a function of structure—is every bit as valid as the idea that structure should agree with a previously formulated strategy. The structure is a basic decision variable in any attempt to influence policy-making.

According to our way of looking at it, strategy is dependent on structure primarily in two ways. First, it is often natural that as a result of existing operations and structures certain types of ideas and the embryos of new lines of business are spontaneously generated, and this in turn has considerable implications for the kind of strategy that will be desirable or possible to formulate. Secondly, to a great extent, the organizational structure governs the type of learning which can take place—i.e. what knowledge can be created in a company—and is consequently a major determinant of the possibility of finding a strategy. For instance, organizational structure often reflects an old strategy, making it more difficult to unlearn this and to learn a new one.

It should also be noted that, throughout, Chandler regards a new strategy as something given; he does not really discuss strategy formulation at all. We, on the other hand, regard the strategy—and the structure that reflects the strategy—as the result of a learning or knowledge-development process, which is in fact the most crucial of all the subprocesses in a company's growth.

One of the classical works on company growth is Penrose (1959). The approach is on the whole that of the economist. Starting mainly from parts of microeconomic theory, Penrose presents an elegant analysis of the forces that act on a company's development and of the way these forces determine the direction and the rate of its growth. Penrose holds, among other things, that a major growth mechanism is the drive to reach full exploitation of all the company's production resources; in practice this cannot be achieved because of the inevitable and regular occurrence of bottlenecks and excess capacity in various parts of the company, so that growth is directed, for instance, towards coping with problems of shortage and surplus. Penrose also analyses growth forces outside, in the company's environment; here she starts from ideas about different kinds of competition on the market.

In Chapter 5, under the heading 'Natural driving forces', I have tried to describe growth mechanisms of this kind, both the external and the internal. My terminology differs somewhat from Penrose's, and in making my description I have a slightly different purpose from hers. However, the basic idea is the same: to understand the mechanisms that arise more or less naturally and which generate growth and growth opportunities.

Quite rightly, Penrose's most renowned thesis concerns the existence of a connection between these driving forces (the ones I call 'natural') and the management-cum-entrepreneurial resources in the company. These resources determine whether or not the natural driving forces will be exploited. On the other hand, Penrose does not discuss the conditions that determine whether these entrepreneurial driving forces are available and whether they function. On this point I have tried to go a little further. I was able to do this because, unlike Penrose, I have adopted an organization-theory approach; furthermore, I was specifically intending to formulate a theory aimed not only at explaining growth but also at providing guidelines for leading actors in the company.

Links with organization theory

Organization theory is the theory about the relations—in a wide sense—between organizational structure, the processes that take place in the organization, and some kind of functional indicators—for example, efficiency in some particular respect. For anyone with roots in organization theory, it seems unfruitful to try to understand such a central process as strategy formulation— or, indeed, to try to generate and deal with change problems in a company— without taking into account that the whole organizational setup has great influence on the process.

Within organization theory two schools in particular have influenced me. The first is the school which has concentrated on trying to understand the difference between situations, rather than on finding universal laws or general prescriptions for success. From the beginning this appears to have been a European or more specifically a British tradition, particularly in the Tavistock School, for example Burns and Stalker (1961) and Woodward (1965). However, the tradition has also recently been applied in the USA, particularly by Thompson (1967) and Lawrence and Lorsch (1967). This 'situation-oriented' school—the contingency theory of organization—has been a frequently recurring source of inspiration to me during the present study.

The other tradition in organization theory that has especially influenced me is less well known and less widespread, although it is older and goes back to the works of Weber. I am thinking of the school that has tried to understand organizations as products of history, and which for me is represented chiefly by Selznick (1957) and Crozier (1964). If we regard the ideas or the social reality existing in an organization as one of the most important things to understand, and if we bear in mind that this social reality cannot be understood or even observed except against a background of critical events often far in the past, it will be obvious how important the historical perspective must be. Only by going back to a company's history is it really possible to understand the world of ideas that constitutes a significant set of restrictions on the way the company's management can act. Historical studies also provide the best way of charting the growth mechanisms operating in the particular company and industry. As a result of concrete events and experiences, mechanisms are developed in the company for dealing with difficult situations and growth problems. Whether or not these mechanisms will be effective depends on how well company members have succeeded in interpreting external and internal events. An historical analysis can therefore often reveal any lack of consonance (and its origins) that may exist between the driving forces operating in the company and its environment, and the company's way of dealing with its growth problems.

Depth psychology theory

Two other important sources of inspiration have been Freudian depth psychology and existentialist philosophy. In the course of collaborating with a number of companies, I have sometimes been able to observe how change processes in companies have involved difficult personal readjustments, and how the personal situations of individual people affect the situation of the company in various ways. The position of the business leader is both unique and problematic. The idea of the 'lonely leader' has its roots in a very real situation, and in fact applies to the occupants of many top positions. The chief executive's way of dealing with this existentially unique situation has, in most cases, a profound influence on the company's problems and on its ability to deal with them.

There are two theoretical orientations in this branch of psychology which I have found particularly valuable, namely, that concerned with the individual's growth and self-actualization (e.g. Maslow, 1962; Hampden-Turner, 1970), and that concerned with the individual's way of dealing with and reacting to tension, conflict, etc., in his environment (e.g. Laing, 1961; Zaleznik, 1966).

Traditional planning theory called in question

The practical experience and the research undertaken by myself and my colleagues have made us question very seriously the relevance to the complicated problems and situations that our subject encompasses of traditional planning theory based on decision models. In Chapter 4, I shall describe in greater detail how the study of product development and innovative ability in a number of companies (Normann, 1971) led me to a couple of important conclusions. The planning model of decision theory—the means-end model—appeared to be applicable even to very complex development processes, provided these took place within the frameworks represented by the company's existing field of operations and, consequently, on the whole within the framework of the existing organization structure and value systems. On the other hand, the model did not function in the case of more fundamental changes in the company's operations. This was not only because knowledge about the new areas was lacking, but also because the whole established system of criteria of relevance and rationality, which is so necessary to the means-end model, ceased to apply in such cases. The art of understanding and controlling fundamental changes appears to tie up to a great extent with concepts such as forces and counterforces, tension and conflict, power and values, ambition and anxiety, creating and learning.

Does this mean that we must give up hope of being able to plan change processes that involve genuine innovation? Must we simply put up with the inadequate rational decision model and its applications and variants? I do not think so. The reader can perhaps regard this book as an attempt to develop an alternative planning philosophy adapted to situations in which the development of knowledge is the central process. While I have been working on the development of this planning concept, I have tried to amalgamate three main ingredients: first, a general learning or 'process' view, which was a tentative outline of a methodology for research into complex societal problems (Normann, 1970); secondly, the new and fascinating theory of learning in social systems that is in the process of emerging (represented mainly by Schon, Kuhn, Buckley, and Dunn, and presented here in Chapter 6); and, thirdly, elements of organization theory.

Our attempt to develop an alternative planning philosophy has not led us to reject the rational means–end planning model. Instead, we claim that there are different classes of situations in which one or the other planning philosophy should be employed. In this respect the two planning concepts are of equal value. This leads us on to the question of whether there is some kind of overriding planning philosophy that fulfils a regulatory function by interpreting the needs of the situation and adapting the chosen planning philosophy to these. This third kind of planning philosophy—the 'statesman philosophy'—is outlined in the last chapter of the present book.

1.4 Practical foundation

The small 'cases' I am using for purposes of illustration come from sources reflecting the practical foundation of this work.

First and foremost, I have drawn on my own *clinical experience* from assignments with organizations geared to the resolution of growth problems. In the kind of research I am undertaking here, this kind of solid empirical basis is absolutely essential. In the main I have used projects which I myself have been engaged on from 1969 onwards; sometimes, however, I have taken cases where I have played only a subsidiary role, or cases with which I have had contact through colleagues.

There are about a dozen projects where it has been possible for me to gain considerable insight into the companies concerned as a result of intensive collaborative efforts often lasting several years at a time. I have also collaborated, to varying degrees, in a whole series of other projects. In this clinical work both analytical techniques and the change techniques used by process consultants have been employed. Through our long interaction with the companies, we have not only become familiar with their situations in terms of 'hard data' but have also been able to penetrate their cultures, the subjective worlds in which the leading actors live their lives.

A second source is *research projects* in which neither I nor my colleagues (at SIAR) have been involved. I have not always indicated in the text whether the material is from my own or my colleagues' clinical experiences or whether it is from these other sources.

A third source is published (or otherwise available) *case descriptions* which are sufficiently penetrating to allow an outsider to draw conclusions from them. Among these are two cases in particular, each of which describes developments in a large American corporation as seen by the leading actors concerned (Sloan, 1963; Dessauer, 1971).

Finally, to illustrate specific points, I have sometimes used a variety of *statistics and official material*, such as the annual reports of some listed Swedish companies.

These are the sources of the 'minicases' I shall be using in the following chapters. The examples are intended to sharpen, to illustrate, to simplify and to provide a little relief in the presentation of my argument. On the other hand, they are naturally not intended to be statistically representative of the material available, since I don't regard this as important. If my purpose had been to test isolated hypotheses, naturally such questions as representativeness, selection, etc., would have mattered very much. But my purpose here is to present a consistent conceptual framework, in which every separate concept must be seen and judged as part of a larger system; the only thing that can really be evaluated is the whole system of concepts. Research whose aim is to develop a new language or a new frame of reference rather than to develop and refine relations within an existing frame of reference cannot be verified or falsified; it must be compared in its entirety with another frame of reference altogether. The important questions to ask are therefore of the following type: what kind of understanding do we achieve by looking at things in this way? what problems can this frame of reference help us to solve? in what way does it help the actors in business companies to act?

In conclusion, I would like to say a few words about the anonymity of the material. The illustrative examples are presented anonymously out of consideration for our clients, who, in doubtful cases, have also been consulted before publication. We have tried very hard to maintain complete anonymity without breaking the link with real life.

CHAPTER 2

Basic Organization Model

2.1 Some fundamental concepts

Exchange process and development process

Companies can be regarded as open systems which interact with their environment. Different types of inputs (raw materials and various sorts of energy) are transformed into outputs (products and systems). We shall call this process the *exchange process.*

Efficiency in the exchange process can be obtained by achieving a relation, as favourable as possible, between the cost of what goes into the process and the revenue from what comes out of it. Furthermore, the company must develop mechanisms to protect the exchange process against disturbances, variations and other threats which can lead to a reduction in its efficiency. Administrative systems such as production control, budget review and co-ordination committees are also geared to improving the efficiency of the exchange process. Areas of responsibility, information channels and problem-solving resources are designed in such a way as to provide the best possible support for the exchange process. We shall subsume all such arrangements—the shape of the formal organization, the various kinds of control systems, the kind of resources and the pattern in which they are arranged, etc.—under the single heading *the company's organizational structure.*

Thus the efficiency of the exchange process is determined by the conditions the company has managed to achieve in its *task environment*, i.e. that part of the environment with which the company has continuous exchange relations, and by the degree of success with which the company's structure has been designed to support the exchange process.

However, the exchange process is not the only central process that takes place in the company. Internal conditions and relations with the task environment change more or less continually. The exchange process changes in quality, the company extends its task environment, new lines of business—with new exchange processes—are started in task environments where the company has not previously had any dealings, etc. The process by means of which the company changes its structure and its environmental relations will be called here the *development process* or the growth process.

Among important features in the development process can be mentioned

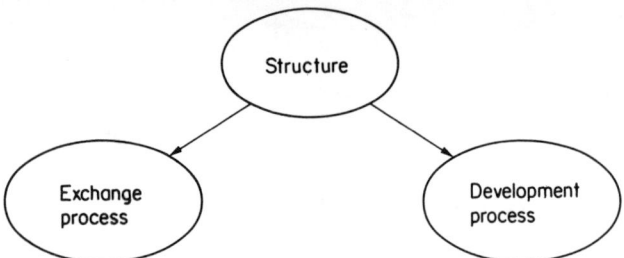

Figure 2.1. The Organizational Structure Affects the Exchange
Process and the Development Process

the discovery of new business opportunities, internal technological innovation, and the learning of new patterns for effecting exchange processes. Most companies try to control and influence the development process by means of routines and organizational arrangements, for example long-range planning systems, development departments, or systematic information-seeking. Thus the structure also influences the development process, and it is a well-known problem that those features of the organizational structure that encourage an efficient development process are not always the same as those that support an efficient exchange process.

In Part II we shall discuss the major conditions of efficiency in the exchange process. In subsequent chapters we shall concentrate mainly on the development process, and on ways in which the organizational structure can be regulated, bearing in mind the apparently contradictory demands made upon it by the two main processes.

The principle of consonance

The company's structure can be seen as a number of interdependent subsystems. The subsystems chosen for closer study depend upon the purpose of the particular study. Some examples of subsystems that we shall be discussing later are: economic control systems, production systems, reward systems, power systems, status systems, and cognitive systems, i.e. systems for information-processing and problem-solving.

The division into subsystems fulfils an important analytical function, making it possible to describe relations between subsystems in a way that explains the existence of efficiency or inefficiency. We are going to describe relations between subsystems in terms of their degree of *consonance* or *fit*.* If subsystems support one another's functions, we say that there is 'fit' between them; if not, there is a 'misfit'.

In formulating the conditions of efficiency in a company we can now use a partly new language: an efficient exchange process is achieved if the designs

---

*In future we shall use the expressions 'consonance' and 'fit', and the expressions 'lack of consonance' and 'misfit', synonymously. The concepts of 'fit' and 'misfit' are taken from Alexander's book *Notes on the Synthesis of Form* (1964).

of the different subsystems are consonant with the specific demands made upon them by the exchange process. The conditions of an efficient development process can be formulated analogously.

The 'principle of consonance' can perhaps best be illustrated by an example of lack of consonance or misfit.

- An investigation of the exchange process in the Special Retailing Company showed that in this company the exchange process should have been characterized by a high and even use of capacity and an optimal stock level for the company as a whole. However, it was emphasized in the company's economic control operation that stocks should be kept within prescribed limits. Stocktaking took place every quarter in the stores, at times well known to all. The store managers knew that they could expect a pat on the back—and perhaps in the long run better promotion opportunities—if they kept within these limits or, even better, a little bit under them.

  A few weeks before stocktaking, it was therefore usual to reduce orders from central stocks; it often happened that goods demanded by the customers were not available at these times. Immediately after stocktaking, however, central stocks were overwhelmed with orders, which meant that they had to maintain a much larger workforce and distribution apparatus than would have been necessary if the internal flow of goods had been more even.

  What was the problem? Was the system of economic control and the informal reward system (the 'pat on the back' system), with the dual emphasis on stock size as a measure of efficiency, really consonant with the exchange process? And, obviously, there were misfits between the unsatisfactory division of responsibility for total stocks, the economic control system, and the system of goods distribution (including the order system). All these misfits resulted in a series of problems and inefficiency.

However, we cannot assume that a good fit is advantageous in all situations. We shall see later, in fact, that the kind of fit and harmony that marks the company whose exchange process is operating effectively can sometimes obstruct or even conflict with the development process.

Dominating ideas and significant actors

In every organization there is a set of values, of norms, creeds, concepts, assumptions, etc., that together constitute an important part of the reality in which the actors operate—a part of what we shall call the *system of ideas*. Among the elements usually incorporated in the system of ideas are ideas— more or less consciously held—about the company's role and tasks, assumptions about the kind of organizational structure that will encourage efficiency in the company, various types of more or less formal 'goals', ideas about what constitutes an efficient leadership style, ideas about individual motivation, and so on.

Not all the ideas belonging to the company's system of ideas will have a decisive influence on the way the company functions and the way it will develop. On the contrary, most companies are characterized by a more or less continuous 'struggle' about which ideas should be guiding action in the company. In future I shall refer to the victors in this struggle as the company's *dominating ideas*.

By *significant actors* I mean persons with sufficient power and influence to be able to affect the dominating ideas. A rough generalization from the experiences I am drawing on here is that there are usually very few people in a company who possess this ability—seldom more than five.

The dominating-ideas concept refers to the psychological–social reality prevailing in groups of significant actors in the company. This very formulation reveals that the dominating ideas are not only the products of values and intellectual processes, but also of power games and politics. We shall therefore often return in the following pages to the interplay between the dominating ideas and the company's power system.

Perhaps, with the concept of dominating ideas, I am trying to penetrate a field somewhere between the sphere of psychoanalysis—the inner or psychological reality of the individual—and that of phenomenologically oriented theories of knowledge as represented by Berger and Luckmann (1967)—the social reality common to a group. The group of significant actors in a company is sufficiently small for the inner, subjective reality of certain individuals to have a far-reaching influence on what happens in the company. At the same time the group is often so large and so well incorporated in an established and relatively stable structure that it is possible for a common social reality to emerge for the group as a whole, for example in the interactions involved in joint problem-solving or in the power game. On the whole, however, it seems that the greater the concentration of power, the more important it is to penetrate the inner, subjective reality of the power centre in order to understand problems and processes in the organization as a whole.*

I would like to emphasize that the phenomenon to which I refer by the concept of dominating ideas is not the same as 'management philosophy', 'company X's way of doing things', or 'executive Y's formula for success'. The concept of dominating ideas is broader and more comprehensive than any of these, and in fact can be said to embrace them all.

2.2 Basic scheme for the analysis of misfits

The organizational structure is management's tool for influencing the exchange and development processes and for achieving efficiency. How manage-

*In the last part of this book we shall elaborate the subject of the dominating ideas as an historical product and as a reflection of the personal situation of the significant actors. We shall also show how these two properties, in their different ways, often make it much more difficult to change or adapt the dominating ideas to prevailing situations.

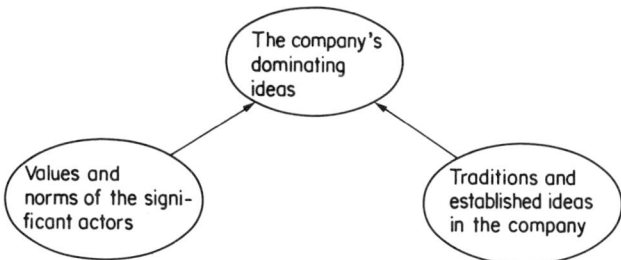

Figure 2.2. The Dominating Ideas are a Product of the Company's History and of the Personal Development of the Significant Actors

ment acts will depend on the dominating ideas and on how the particular situation is perceived. There are many opportunities here for management to fail in its task: the relevant situation may be misinterpreted, the dominating ideas may be inadequate for coping with a complicated situation, the right tools may not be available although the right diagnosis has been made, etc. This is the basis for the fundamental paradigm or scheme for analysis of misfits which will be a recurring theme throughout the rest of this book. This basic scheme is reproduced in Figure 2.3.

The figure can be seen as a structural arrangement of major factors or variables, but it is also—and this is perhaps its most important feature—a representation of an ongoing process. Traditionally it is assumed that this process proceeds 'clock-wise': after reviewing the company's situation, management designs strategies and then manoeuvres the structure to fit—and thereby making possible the realization of—the strategies. In reality, however, the process is far more complicated than this, which is unlucky for most long-range planning theorists. For instance, the system of ideas cannot be looked at in isolation, separate from other parts of the organization. The company's power structure has considerable influence on the ideas that are able to catch on, and *vice versa*. The organizational structure—in the shape of routines, resources, channels of communication, etc.—is also in many ways a determinant of which ideas and notions can take shape at all.

From Figure 2.3 we can deduce some important kinds of misfits, all of which will be illustrated in various ways in subsequent chapters. At a very general level they are as follows:

- misfits between the system of ideas and the (growth) situation
- misfits between the system of ideas and the organizational structure
- misfits between the structure and the (growth) situation
- misfits between different parts of the system of ideas
- misfits between different parts of the organizational structure.

To be able to describe and understand these types of misfits, and to say something about how they can be avoided, we must have some kind of initial

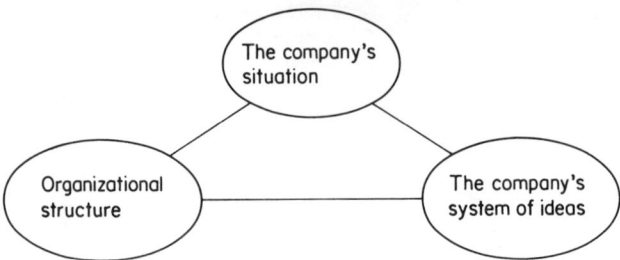

Figure 2.3. Basic Frame of Reference for Interpreting the
Company's Growth Problem

description or frame of reference for each of the three spheres in Figure 2.3.

We have already touched briefly on the *organizational structure* and the system of ideas. The organizational structure, at least theoretically, is perhaps the best known of the three spheres. As we have already seen, the chief elements here are such factors as areas of responsibility in the company, budget system and other economic and administrative control systems, rewards system, channels of communication, degree of differentiation and integration between units, degree of formalization, etc.

When it comes to describing the *company's situation*, the literature is more meagre. However, a few studies have succeeded in throwing some light on the relation between different situational factors and their implications for the structural design:

• Most progress has perhaps been made concerning the influence of techno-logy and the company's situation. One pioneer was Woodward (1965), who distinguished between different types of technologies, mainly the process production, mass production, batch production, and unit produc-tion. Thompson (1967) has elaborated various ideas about technology, particularly as regards different types of dependencies between sub-processes and the consequences of these on instruments of coordination in the structure. Burns and Stalker (1961) have demonstrated the situational factor 'degree of variability in the environment' and its implications for the company's structure; Lawrence and Lorsch (1967) and Thompson (1967) have continued working on these ideas. Rhenman (1973) has described the relationship between various kinds of values in the external environment and the company's choice of strategy and structure. Another interesting contribution is Crozier's study of the influence of the external 'cultural environment' (Crozier, 1964).

To recapitulate, the aim of the present study is to develop a frame of reference which can help us to understand and handle growth processes and growth problems. For this purpose, however, the ideas outlined above about *situation types* are hardly sufficient. We shall therefore develop below, step by step, something of a typology of the growth situations of business companies.

2.3 Doctrine of the fundamental cause of growth problems

If, as clinical consultants, we discover misfits of the type described earlier, what are we to do and which of the misfits should we try to get rid of first?

The usual strategy is to make changes in the organizational structure, at best changes bringing the structure into agreement with the growth situation. In my opinion this approach is inadequate. *It is, in fact, misfits between the company's dominating ideas (and in particular what we shall later term its growth idea) and its growth situation which, in turn, lead to other misfits and which must therefore be eliminated first if we want to effect really permanent changes.* If this basic misfit is not eliminated, we cannot expect measures imposed on the organizational structure to be adequate. A clinical consultant cannot assume that once certain problems have been solved and the organizational structure changed, he can simply go away. *The dominating ideas and the organization's problem-solving ability are what have to be adapted to the situation; they are what must be functioning properly.*

The most crucial process that takes place in the company is therefore the process through which the dominating ideas arise, and by which they are changed and adapted to the prevailing situation. This leading process will be discussed chiefly in Part IV.

PART II

The Efficient Exchange Process

Indeed, this ability to deal with several layers of form–context boundaries in concert is an important part of what we often refer to as the designer's sense of organization. The internal coherence of an ensemble depends on a whole net of such adaptations. In a perfectly coherent ensemble we should expect the two halves of every possible division of the ensemble to fit one another. (Alexander, 1964, p. 18)

In Chapter 1 we discussed the need for development and growth—especially knowledge development—in light of the fact that society is in the process of changing in many respects, and that in future the 'knowledge technologies' will become increasingly important.

In Part II we shall start from another base, namely, one geared entirely to economics and efficiency. We shall study more closely the conditions of efficiency in the mature company, more specifically in the company's exchange process. Starting from a theory of efficiency, it can be claimed that the purpose of development and growth in a company is to create or maintain a satisfactorily functioning exchange process.

An efficient exchange process presupposes that the company has a *business idea*. We shall investigate more closely the constituents of a business idea, and this in turn will give us a better basis for our subsequent analysis of the growth process.

CHAPTER 3

The Company's Business Idea

3.1 Dominance of a territory

Companies interact with their environments, and the conditions of their survival and success are to be found in the establishment of a favourable balance in their relations with the surrounding world. This balance can be achieved by a kind of specialization: the company selects a certain segment of the external environment—the task environment—and carries out certain types of transactions with it.

The choice of task environment, and of the type of transactions to undertake there, must be approached with great care and in such a way that the company can learn to handle what it takes on. If the task environment is too large, the organization's resources will not be able to master it, and the balance will be unfavourable; and the result will be the same if other competitors choose the same task environment and the same type of transaction and develop a superior competence there. If the task environment is too narrow, it will not be sufficiently rich in resources to keep the organization going.

The proposition that companies can achieve success and can be efficient only by *developing superiority (a superior system) in order to handle a certain segment of their task environment* will be a basic assumption in the argument that follows. Obviously it is easy, on a purely intuitive level, to claim support for this statement. Businessmen and marketing researchers have both been acknowledging it in different forms for a long time, as the common use of terms such as 'market segmentation' and 'niche', derived from biology and ecology (Alderson, 1965), bears witness. Among organization theorists we can mention Selznick (1957), Thompson (1967) and Rhenman (1973).*

Some interesting empirical data are presented in Chevalier (1972). The following are some of the conclusions Chevalier draws:

> ... corporate size does not always indicate profitability. (p. 63)
> First, it is not so much overall size that seems to matter, but size in a given market segment. Second, it is not only the firm's size in a segment, but its relative size in comparison with other competitors. (p. 64)
> Only at the level of a market segment can we discover a relationship between size and profitability ... (p. 66)

*The theory on the efficiency of the company that I shall be describing in this chapter is based in part on ideas presented in Rhenman (1973).

The Boston Consulting Group also puts great emphasis on the importance of 'dominance', i.e. of having a large market share. By means of empirical data from the semiconductor industry and the automobile industry among others, they are able to show how the companies which have become market leaders were also those with the highest profitability not only in absolute terms but also in terms of profitability margin in relation to turnover and return on invested capital. They choose to explain this in terms of what they call the experience effect:

> The longer you keep producing it, the less it will cost you. This is the experience effect...
> (Moose and Zakon, 1971, p. 23)

The conclusion is obvious: a company that enters a new market must strive to dominate its market segment, to become a market leader.

Rhenman (1973) comes to much the same conclusion from a somewhat different starting-point. While Moose and Zakon clearly see high internal efficiency—in the first place cost efficiency—as a *result* of market dominance and long production series, Rhenman starts from the other end of the argument. He sees market dominance rather as in *indicator*: it shows that the company has succeeded in creating a superior system that generates efficiency. The superior business idea enables the company to influence its environment by imposing its structure upon its surroundings, which in turn makes long production series and so on possible.

Thus, according to Moose and Zakon the company should aim in the first place at achieving a large market share, while according to Rhenman its first concern should be to develop a superior system. Perhaps these two views are not so far removed from one another, but the difference in emphasis is interesting. However, the significant point for us at present is that both approaches assume a close link between company efficiency and dominance over a market segment.

But in defining 'market segment' we must use caution. Chevalier (1972) gives as his example the automobile firm BMW, which is small in comparison with many other companies in the industry but which is nevertheless very successful and profitable. This is explained by the fact that BMW has a very large market share in a fairly restricted market segment, i.e. the market for relatively sporty family cars. The Swedish sewing-machine company Husqvarna is another example. Although in terms of the industry as a whole it is a small company on the American market, it has managed to become very profitable by dominating the market segment 'exclusive hobby sewing-machines'. In Sweden, on the other hand, the same company has succeeded in dominating the segment 'standard sewing-machines' with exactly the same product.

The Swedish building industry provides examples of companies which have managed to acquire dominance in a variety of ways. The traditional way of achieving success in this industry is through local affiliations: by developing

Product \ Market	Sweden Builders	Sweden Retailers	Denmark	Norway	Finland
Refrigerators/Freezers	11	15	—	—	—
Cookers	39	41	15	11	6
Washing machines	13	33	29	15	—
Dishwashers	25	37	31	33	41
Fans	6	16	41	11	8

Figure 3.1. Example of a Company's Territory (from Rhenman, 1972)

a substantial network of contacts, and as a result of employment policy and other factors, one builder comes to dominate in one place or in one region. Other companies, however, have gradually become more dominating in market segments such as 'very large construction projects', 'large housing projects on total contract', 'power plant construction in northern Norrland', 'large housing projects for municipal housing companies in social-democrat boroughs', and so on.

The part of the task environment that a company dominates represents that company's *territory*. The product–market matrix in which data regarding turnover, market share, contribution, and possible return on invested capital can all be combined is an aid which can be used to identify a territory. If we disregard the difficulty of actually defining products and markets, we will usually find that the company's total profitability—often more than 100 per cent of its contribution—comes from the few boxes in the matrix representing segments with a large market share.

Figure 3.1, which is a schematic and anonymous example of a product–market matrix, shows the market shares of a company in different product–market segments. The segments which the company dominates—its territory—have been indicated according to the basic rule-of-thumb that market-oriented companies should have a market share of about 30 per cent at least before it is possible to speak of 'dominance' or 'territory'.

In the following pages we shall try to discover what lies behind this picture. If it is true that the company earns money by acquiring and dominating a territory, why is this so?

3.2 Business idea or system for dominance

Behind the conditions that the product–market analysis can reveal, there is often some kind of *superiority*, for example superior knowhow or superior competence, which is built into the company's organizational structure or embodied in the people who work there. An expression which can designate this often very complex and rather undefinable knowhow is the *company's business idea*.

To begin with, however, it must be noted that the word 'idea' may be misleading on two counts. First, our term 'business idea' refers not only to conditions in the world of ideas but also to definite concrete conditions in the material world. Secondly, the circumstances that we wish to describe have in most cases a very complex character, and this is something that the word 'idea' barely even suggests.

Some examples of business ideas

Before we analyse the fundamental elements in the business idea in greater detail, we should perhaps give a few examples of such ideas in operation.

● The first Swedish hypermarkets were based on the realization that the sale of consumer goods could be carried out in a new and more efficient way. As the density of motor-car traffic increased, a location in the centre of the city was no longer necessary. On the contrary it was sometimes a disadvantage. Instead it became possible to locate stores outside the city and to provide them with extensive parking facilities. An essential aim was to keep prices below those of any competitors. But since this could not be done by reducing the quality or range of the products, some other way had to be found.

To maintain a broad and relatively rich assortment, the hypermarket had to be very large; it also had to aim at a wide range of consumers. In this it was helped by the general levelling of incomes and the increasing frequency of motor-cars, but the effect could be reinforced by the location of the store. The combination of a large customer flow and a total absence of any stocks other than those on the shelves permitted a high rate of turnover, which meant that capital costs were low. Moreover, it was easier to finance expansion. Most goods were sold for cash before the buyer had been paid. Since no stocks were held except in the store, heavy investment was avoided. Stocktaking was a relatively easy matter, and it was possible to use very simple systems of information and goods-handling. Central staff could be kept at an absolute minimum.

The central buyers made general agreements with the suppliers. It was then left to the staff 'on the floor' to make their own orders and to be responsible for certain product groups, in accordance with order lists within the terms of the general agreement. This had the further advantage of increasing the staff's feeling of commitment and responsibility. By abandoning any ambition to provide special service for the customers and, as far as possible, by engaging suppliers in various specialized activities, it was possible to cut down the number of trained specialists on the staff. This meant, in turn, that it was possible to have a cheap and simple system of engagement and training and it was easy to move people around between tasks.

Another example of a niche being opened in the market and invaded by a company is provided by Tools & Machines Ltd. This company, which traditionally sells tools to ironmongers and industry, developed a new business idea.

- In the middle of the 1960s a new market opened for this company, when the system whereby school materials were bought centrally and at the national level was wound up. This meant that sellers could now go direct to the various schools around the country, since these were no longer obliged to buy through a central purchasing organ in order to receive a state subsidy for the purpose.

  To be able to offer the schools the same service that the central purchasing organ had done—namely, providing complete equipment for school activities—the company's existing knowledge and product range needed developing. With this in mind, several people who 'knew about wood' (school benches, cupboards, etc.) were engaged on the 'tools' side. On the 'machines' side, the company extended its range by means of an advanced system of collaboration with the suppliers. Knowledge of the political and bureaucratic system (state-subsidy calculations, etc.) was incorporated into the organization through the appointment of persons who had held key posts in the central purchasing organ.

  After attending various school committee meetings all over the country at the end of the 1960s, people in the company became aware of the problems caused in the schools by the actual installation of the various equipments. The teachers were either incapable or unwilling to undertake the work of installation, while the way the budget system was designed made it easier for the municipality to finance this job by using help from outside. The result was that all the equipment stood in a heap on the floor at the beginning of term. The company's installation operations solved the problem for both parties—the schools and the municipalities—while their own installation engineers were able to unpack the equipment and correct any faulty or incomplete deliveries.

  As a result of a reform of the Swedish school system at the beginning of the 1970s, the amount of vocational training in the state schools was cut down, leaving teachers with less time to spend with individual pupils. Tools & Machines Ltd developed various tapes and instructions as teaching aids. To do this properly, it was necessary to have some special competence in the areas that the various instructions concerned, and this was incorporated into the company through the engagement of specialists. A complete catalogue supports these operations. Lists of all the necessities for a particular function, for example for teaching in the sheet-metal workshop, provide ready-made tenders for complete sets of equipment. The computer system also plays an important part here.

'Problems and changes' in the company's environment	Action taken in the company
Central purchasing of school material at the national level ceases	New appointments—new competence introduced
	Agreement with machine suppliers
No resources in the schools for installation	Installation operations
The reforms in the 'Gymnasium' schools leave the vocational teachers less time for the pupils	Tapes and AV-material
	Incorporation of special competence
Different norms and values in the school system	Close contact with 'feeler organs' in the industry
Need for quick, complete tenders with up-to-date prices	Lists of equipment on computers

Figure 3.2. The Business Idea Emerges—Various Elements in the Environment are Matched in the Structure of the Company

Information about the current school system is obtained at special teacher-training days, from school committee meetings, from journals, and in daily contact with teachers. In our terminology, all these activities provide opportunities for the industry to put out feelers.

This is a particularly clear example of how an organization successively 'mapped' the structure of the new niche in its own structure (Figure 3.2).

Consonance between three main components in a business idea

These two examples illustrate the theoretical content of the concept of the business idea. In both cases we see that there are several factors inside and outside the company that fit (or are consonant with) one another. These factors are interwoven into complicated pattern and form a *system for dominance*.

One way to see some structure in this pattern is to identify the degree of consonance between a market segment, the product that the company has on offer, and the company's internal organization and control system; there must also be consonance between different subelements at each one of these three levels (Normann, 1971). Figure 3.3 illustrates this *principle of consonance*.

Examples of abortive business ideas

Perhaps the principle of consonance can best be illustrated by some examples of cases where consonance is lacking ('misfits'), with the result that a business idea or a system for dominance is less efficient than it should be.

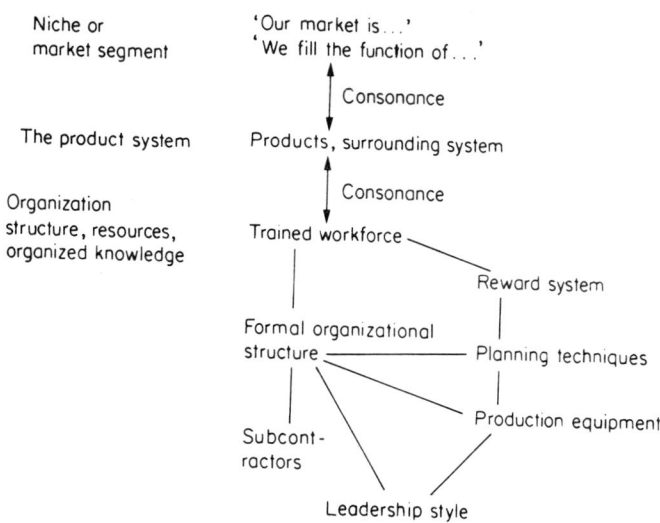

Figure 3.3. Three Main Ingredients in a Business Idea

- A classical example of misfit between a niche and a product is represented by the model T Ford, which was so extremely successful for its first twenty years. But, as a result of various changes in the market and in social conditions, towards the end of the 1920s this product was no longer at all what the consumers wanted. By 1927 things were so bad that Ford had to close the plant, and no cars were manufactured at all for almost a year while the production apparatus was completely reorganized.

- The Military Electronics Company manufactured equipment of a very complicated technological nature. For various reasons it was decided to enter the market for simpler electronic products, such as radios, etc. But this move was a total failure, partly because it proved impossible to launch a new approach involving a reduction in quality standards in a company which had for so long been striving to build up an advanced level of highly qualified technical excellence. The new products manufactured were far too expensive and complicated; what the company really needed was a different type of production apparatus and a different production team geared to different technical norms. Also, the whole of the company's 'marketing' side had always been more or less adjusted to a single customer (defence), and neither the knowhow nor the resources were available for entering civil markets, for example, where competition and customer structure were of a more conventional kind.

Europharma gives us another example of a company misjudging the character of a niche.

- Europharma tried to break into a new market, namely, the market for advanced psychopharmaceuticals. The company even managed to build up a research team and to develop a couple of preparations which, to all appearances, had good effects within the intended therapy. However, what had not been understood was that in this new line it was not enough just to supply the products; it was necessary to provide as well a whole supportive system of clinical trials, contacts with opinion-leaders, etc. The system produced—i.e. the product—had been defined too narrowly in relation to the very complex structure of the niche.

In the Convenience Goods Distribution Group (CGD) a lack of consonance grew up between the company's traditional structure and new demands for products and services which had arisen as a result of changes on the market.

- CGD, which had a foreign principal, had traditionally three equal but independent affiliated companies in Sweden. However, over a ten-year period the market had been undergoing a series of changes; the previous regional customer structure had been replaced by a structure in which a few nationwide customers came to dominate exclusively. In this situation it gradually became increasingly clear that the Group's old structure with the three regional subsidiaries—companies which were sometimes even played off against each other—no longer accorded with the character of the market.

  Another change that took place at the same time was that the new customers made increasingly heavy demands for individual 'fit' in the services they bought. The industry as a whole was changing more and more from supplying pretty well standardized systems to offering a kind of individual bespoke tailoring. By the time we were called in as consultants, this was beginning to be understood, and it soon became clear that the type of structure and resources which would make this kind of bespoke tailoring possible were simply not there. To get the company's operations to agree with the new niche, it was going to be necessary to make serious efforts to build up a new structure.

Misfits between any of the three *main components or levels* in the business idea—the market segment, the product system, and the organizational structure—are not the only ones which can spoil the efficiency of the system of dominance. Business ideas can also be thwarted by *misfits between different subcomponents on the same level.*

- In Medical Products Ltd, which had traditionally been manufacturing fairly sophisticated products, discussion had been going on for some time about various aspects of the design and marketing of a new simple skinfood, which for various reasons the company had decided to manufacture and sell. Generally speaking, the idea was to give the product a 'non-medical' image by advertizing it in the weekly press, selling it without a doctor's prescription, and so on. At the same time, however, it was decided in accordance with company tradition to market the product through chemists' shops only, although this obviously conflicted with the image that had otherwise been aimed at. Gradually the company was ousted from the market by a competitor which was manufacturing a technically equivalent product, but which was more successful in harmonizing the different parts of its product's total character.

A very common type of misfit occurs when different parts of a company's internal structure and control system fail to agree with one another and therefore also fail to provide a consistent picture of the business idea.

- For Swedish Building Materials Ltd it was obviously of paramount importance in competition to maintain a good, even quality. In one production line, facing slabs were checked as they came from the machines and were then divided into two piles: one for defective slabs and one for slabs proceeding to stocks. However, a certain proportion of the wages of the controller depended on the proportion of slabs that went direct to stocks, i.e. on their quality, and this was something that the controller had no chance of influencing. The result, naturally, was that too high a proportion of defective slabs went into stocks, leading ultimately to complaints and claims. Clearly the remuneration system was not consonant with the 'system for influencing quality'.

3.3 The concept of the business idea has a deeper meaning

The concept of the business idea, as we employ it here, is related to a number of other similar concepts. Before going further we should perhaps discuss some of these links.

As we have already mentioned, the question of market segmentaion and the identification of niches in the environment occupies a central position in modern marketing literature. The definition of a niche requires a combination of access to facts and creativity. Examples of the way people have come to use increasingly complicated definitions can be found in a recently published book on 'life-style marketing' (Hanan, 1972). Techniques are described for defining market segments on a basis of differences in the 'life style' of the consumers.

However, the man who has done more than anyone to publicize the idea of the creative definition of the niche is Theodore Levitt, with his famous declaration that the American railroad companies lost their customers because they thought they were in the railroad business, while really they were in transportation (Levitt, 1960). We have seen several almost pathetic examples of companies in a particular line of business—say, the X trade—which have tried to demonstrate their up-to-date approach by proclaiming proudly 'we are really in the Y trade and not in the X trade at all'. Such proclamations often have no effect at all, either on these companies' business activities or on their organization. It is simply that Levitt has made all too easy an impression.

Instead of describing any cases of this sort, however, I will let another author comment on Levitt's thesis, without trying to hide his rather malicious slant.

> Levitt's thesis sounded very plausible, although it did raise certain questions. Would dumb-headed railroad proprietors have been any brighter at managing truck companies or airlines? And what if the buggy-whip had decided that, instead of being in transport accessories or guidance systems, it was in flagellation?
>
> But managers love a new panacea: so companies all over the world turned, as the American railroads didn't, into the business of defining their businesses...
>
> The search for definitions led off in strange verbal directions. Of all odd results, Britain's Cube Investments had the most alliterative and meaningless one—'metal manipulation'. This fine phrase can cover everything from the tubes which provide most of TI's profits to hairpins, which it doesn't make: but the company's products include some which use no metal, and others, like gas heaters, in which manipulating metal is about the least important factor.
>
> (Heller, 1974, pp. 44–45)

However, we must not let ourselves be carried away by these well-founded but perhaps rather facile comments. Many managers have in fact found it useful to start rethinking and debating the whole question of what 'business' they are in. But what certainly can be criticized is the naive belief that a new 'business' can be forged as the result of the intellectual exercises of a management group. The 'definitions' which we have sometimes come across have been wordy and generally rather superficial, but the number of times they have found any expression in immediate concrete action or in structural reorganizations has been strikingly small. In most cases the act of defining has been nothing more than a pleasant and elegant ritual.

Let us return to market segmentation, which is not really a new idea at all—except possibly to the theorists. Thus, for example, the product policy that was formulated and carried out by General Motors at the beginning of the 1920s provides a fascinating account of a consistent segmentation of the market, whereby every segment was 'matched' by products of a suitable price and quality (Sloan, 1963). Between Cadillac in the 'highest' segment and Chevrolet in the 'lowest', there was a make of car for everyone.

The idea of identifying one's own niche or line of business has given birth to expressions such as 'concept of the firm's business', 'strategy', etc. There is one major difference between concepts of this kind as they are generally employed and our concept of 'business idea' in the sense of 'system for dominance'. We want a concept which includes not only ideas about the market and the role of the company in the external environment (i.e. *what* is to be dominated), but also *what is to be done* to transform these ideas into concrete arrangements. It is not enough to say 'we are in the transportation business' (and whether such a remark could ever have much point is anyway doubtful); there is no business idea until a formula for 'earning money in the transport business' has been found, and until this formula has been translated into organizational and other arrangements.

Perhaps the writer who (although he is not always easy to understand) has described the relationship between external mission and internal structure with the greatest insight is Selznick in his book on institutional management (Selznick, 1957). Management's first task is to define some kind of role or mission in the external environment—a task that demands not only creativity but also a high degree of realistic insight into the organization's 'distinctive competence' and an understanding of the nature of the commitments and obligations *vis-à-vis* the various power groups inside and outside the organization. The values related to the mission or role then have to permeate all parts of the organization; they must in some way be 'embodied' there through what Selznick calls the process of 'institutionalization'. This is not only a technical process but also a social one: the overriding values linked to the company's role must penetrate and stamp its social structure. Selznick frequently emphasizes that the external mission and the internal attributes of the organization are inextricably connected and must be brought into harmony with one another. The following is one of many possible quotations that demonstrate this argument.

> Beyond the definition of mission and role lies the task of building purpose into the social structure of the enterprise, or, to repeat a phrase used earlier, of transforming a neutral body of men into a committed policy. In this way, policy attains depth. Rooted in and adapted to the daily experiences of living persons, policy is saved from attenuation and distortion as lines of communication are extended.
> (Selznick, 1957, pp. 90–91)

It is also interesting to see that much the same point has been made by a discerning and successful business leader, the former president of General Motors, Alfred P. Sloan.

> . . . Mr Ford, whom no-one had dared seriously to challenge in the low-price field since 1907, was tightening his grip while we were losing in unit volume as well as in the profitability of most of our divisions. All in all, with no position in the big-volume low-price field and no concept to guide our actions, we were in a bad situation. It was clear that we needed an idea for penetrating the low-price field, and for the deployment of the cars through the line as a whole; and we needed a research-and-development policy, a sales policy, and the like, to support whatever we did.
> (Sloan, 1963, p. 62)

The rest of Sloan's book demonstrates that GM's special structure—with its combination of strong decentralization and strong centralization—did not have its roots in any general principles of organization, as has often been claimed. Instead it was a strict and skilful pragmatic translation into organizational terms of the very special requirements of making money in the motorcar business.

But Levitt, too, has suggested that the 'concept of the firm's business' must be matched in the firm's structure. In a section headed 'Goals are not enough', he says that companies must have an effective 'full-time marketing vice-president', and mentions other demands on the company's structure. However, there is one element in Levitt's argument with which I cannot entirely agree. We can look at the following quotation.

> Balance between the requisites of the various functional departments must be provided by the corporate balance wheel—the chief executive or his first lieutenant. He must decide what is finally right in order to work toward the desired markting posture. But he cannot be effective in that decision and he cannot get proper support and understanding for it unless all functional departments have indeed developed some capacity to appreciate that the corporation's ultimate mission is marketing—that its function is to create and keep a customer in a profitable fashion. Unless everyone fully appreciates this, and understands what this means in an operating sense, there will be a great deal of recrimination, hostility and ineffectiveness.
>
> (Levitt, 1969, p. 250)

Although Levitt does not exactly say that all business ideas are the same, it is obvious from the above that he wants to provide general prescriptions for organizational structure, and that he assumes a similarity between all successful 'concepts of the firm's business'. In contrast, let us once again turn to Sloan, who is equally discerning here. He declares that GM's strength obviously lies in its capability as a manufacturing company: it is superior in the effective mass production of relatively expensive and complex articles. Here we are clearly talking of a kind of business idea that is different from Levitt's. Sloan recognizes that business ideas differ, and that it is important in the case of any new departure to understand which idea represents a company's strength. The following quotation illustrates this view.

> The automobile constitutes 90 per cent of our business, but each operation or potential operation is considered as a separate problem. We have no inflexible policy on products that we might manufacture, but motors are at the center of the business. Our product decisions must, of necessity, be in part empirical, and actual experience with some products may suggest that they are not well suited to our managerial skills. In such cases we withdraw from the activity.
>
> For example, in 1921 we found it best to withdraw from the agricultural

tractor business, because we did not believe that we could make a special contribution in that field. Since then we have built up and subsequently disposed of interests in companies which manufactured airplanes, household radios, glass, and chemicals.
(Sloan, 1963, pp. 442–443)

Experience has taught us the vital importance of understanding the unique quality of every individual business idea; at the same time, many business ideas naturally resemble each other more or less closely in their main attributes. The Levitt type of approach can therefore cause a great deal of trouble, since it tries to force the concept of the business idea into a compartment that is both standardized and too narrow.

In companies where several business ideas are all on the go at once, it is particularly important for corporate management to recognize the differences involved and understand their consequences; different business ideas call for different ways of working. Sometimes it may be difficult to spot that there really are different business ideas in operation, with the result that some of them may not receive the special support they require in order to be able to grow.

● The original core of operations at Swedish Building Materials Ltd was the highly streamlined mass production of standard articles. During the 1960s various new products and lines, to a great extent deviating from traditional operations, were introduced. A mixture of business ideas was emerging.

   But production—including now both standard articles and specialized items—was still subject to the original control system geared to mass production. Norms expressed in terms of high plant utilization, efficiency measured in tons and manhours, degree of mechanization, production for stock, etc., fitted traditional operations but often raised problems for developing the special lines. The 'ton' measure, for instance, was often totally irrelevant to the new products with their different materials. Nor did the 'batch production' approach suit the new and more refined special products.

3.4 Some characteristics of the business idea

We can now summarize some of the fundamental characteristics of a company's business idea as follows:

 1. The business idea is a system, an aggregate of elements which form a complex pattern. Or perhaps it would be more accurate to say that the business idea expresses the unifying principle of such a system.

 2. A description of the business idea involves description of:

● the niche in the environment dominated by the company, in other words the company's territory

- the products or the 'system' that are supplied to the territory
- the resources and internal conditions in the company by means of which dominance is acquired

3. The business idea is an expression of concrete conditions existing in a company; it describes the company's actual way of functioning—as it is sometimes rather disrespectfully put, its 'way of making money'. The business idea does not exist until it has been realized; an untried idea about where or how money can be earned is no business idea; it may possibly be an idea about a business idea.

4. The business idea represents 'superior knowledge' or a 'superior skill'. This skill or ability should be built into or, to use Selznick's expression, 'embodied' in the company's organizational structure and in its significant actors. (In some cases, for example in an estate agency, most of this knowledge may be 'embodied' in one person.)

5. The business idea is an historical product which would be difficult to imitate on account of its complexity. Territory that has once been conquered therefore tends to remain fairly intact. At the same time, though, this very complexity may make a business idea very difficult to learn and to 'embody' in the organization. (This is the type of learning process or knowledge-development process which we shall be discussing below.)

6. 'Harmony' and 'consonance' are two words that spring to mind when we try to capture the essence of the business idea. A business idea can be compared to a piece of complicated and well-oiled machinery, where all the parts fit neatly in with one another, making their contribution to the whole.

These are the dimensions which make it possible for us to understand the *uniqueness* of every single business idea. In the real world you will never find any combination of market, technology, product, competition and so on which is exactly like any other. There is therefore no one general way of conducting business, of constructing control systems or of designing organizations. And this is the main reason why all attempts to apply uniform principles to organizations or to build integrated systems for 'management information' and long-range planning have failed and will always fail.

Rather, in the world of business ideas—as in the vegetable kingdom, where every flower is unique—it is possible to distinguish species, families and classes. In a later chapter we shall be distinguishing, for instance, between production-oriented and market-oriented business ideas. This is an important distinction to make, since the two types of ideas are also subject to different kinds of growth problems.

We mentioned above that the smoothly functioning business idea evinces a high degree of stability. This statement may require some explanation, and in examining it we may also come closer to understanding certain important differences between various types of business idea. The notion of the stability of the business idea is not difficult to understand in a case such as the mass-producing chemical company, where the flow of raw materials, the physical production process, and often even the customer structure are all pretty well given. Quite different, however, is the situation that usually characterizes companies engaged in the slaughter, carving up and partial processing of animals.

- In this case the supply of raw materials cannot be altogether predicted or controlled in either the short or the long run, partly because the producers are a number of small marginal organizations. Thus, each morning, a largely unpredictable mixture of animals of different ages, breeds and qualities all enter the production process. On the consumer side, too, there is a whole series of factors which can have a quite unpredictable effect on demand: a new general price list affects the relative prices between cuts and qualities of meat; export subsidies are changed; one retail chain launches a drive promoting a particular type of product; the cookery column of a weekly magazine arouses suspicion about the purity of meat balls, while another persuades all housewives to demand lamb chops on Thursday for a new wonder recipe, and so on. The company tries to avoid all these pitfalls by hurriedly introducing new cuts, altering the proportion of processed to unprocessed products, sending animals to export instead of cutting them up, trying to influence demand by steering the marketing and gearing it to production, altering the formula for the processed products within permitted bounds, etc.

Looking at such a company, it is easy to get the impression that its 'way of making money' is anything but stable; instead it appears to be characterized by extreme flexibility in the face of changing situations. Admittedly this is true at one level, but appearances are deceptive. In such a company stability and efficiency consist of a 'programme' which makes possible the immediate recognition and diagnosis of every situation and a quick choice between a number of alternative action strategies—or 'subprogrammes'—which have been developed in advance. The 'main programme', which enables the company to choose an action strategy suited to the situation, together with the 'subprogrammes', provides a stable and hard-won structure allowing for great flexibility. But this flexibility is no more improvised than that exercised by a concert violinist in a cadenza, where the improvisation is governed by the rules of the game and by established aesthetic norms. However, the existence of rules and norms does not necessarily make the cadenza easy to play.*

3.5 Protection and maintenance of the company's business idea

Since companies achieve high efficiency as a result of realizing a business

*On the other hand, it should perhaps be emphasized that what we are saying here about business ideas applies to large 'corporations' but hardly to 'marginal organizations' (to use the classification suggested by Rhenman, 1973). The latter achieve success by being generally flexible and grasping opportunities as they arise, but without aiming at the conquest of a territory or the creation of any permanent knowhow in their structures.

idea and dominating a market segment, they also strive to protect and maintain their territories. There are two main ways in which companies fulfil this purpose: by successively refining their business ideas or by influencing power relationships in the surrounds of their territory.

Refinement of the business idea is effected basically by means of 'product variation', i.e. continual marginal improvements in products and structures within the framework of the business idea (Normann, 1971).

- In Provisions Ltd, the 'maintenance' of products was a continual concern. Labels were changed, formulas altered slightly, products removed from the range and replaced by others, etc.

- Through its ability and its skilfully composed range of products, the Trading Company had gradually succeeded in dominating a large sub-range among the largest and most progressive retailers in the particular line of business. Naturally, however, this development was not greeted too enthusiastically by the company's competitors. The Trading Company's main strategy for protecting its territory was to embark on further systems development, among other things extending its computer system so as to provide customers with new and useful services as an aid to their own operations. In this way customers became even more closely committed to the company.

Among organization theorists, Thompson (1967) has described different strategies for protecting a territory by influencing the power structure. From our own fieldwork we have gleaned many examples of how the desired stability in a territory can be achieved as a result of the skilful handling of institutional contacts.

- Processing Ltd, a small company, was a customer of the much larger Raw Materials Corporation, which had almost total control of the raw materials and was even responsible for most of the processing. As a result of skilful handling of the public authorities and the Raw Materials Corporation on the part of the managing director of Processing Ltd, the smaller company was gradually able to secure its own raw materials supply. In fact, in the end the Raw Materials Corporation came to regard Processing Ltd as a partner—and as a partner which was doing the Corporation a service by preventing it from monopolizing the processing side as well.

PART III

Growth and the Development of Knowledge

The belief in Progress, in its short life, has embraced several mutually inconsistent ideas; it is hard to find any which is shared by every version of the faith. All, however, seem to me to proceed on one common assumption, which might be called the 'faith in Process'.
(Sir Geoffrey Vickers, 1968, p. 3)

In Part II we discussed the character of the company or the individual branch of operations in its mature state. In Part III we shall examine the way in which it reached this state.

We have already introduced the concept of *business idea* to help us to describe the conditions of an *efficient exchange process*. My aim now is to describe— or rather, to construct—another tool, this time to help management to generate growth and to achieve an *efficient growth process*. In analogy with the business idea, I shall call this tool the *growth idea*.

The members of a perfectly successful company may never have heard of the 'business idea' or the 'growth idea'; or even consciously practised the theories behind these terms. The concepts can therefore best be described as tool concepts whose purpose transcends the distinction between descriptive and normative. I would briefly like to discuss two features of such a tool concept.

To begin with, the concept must capture the very essence of the process which it is trying to describe; in this way it is essentially empirically based. I believe that one way of penetrating to this essence is to study the really successful and the really unsuccessful or pathological cases. Secondly, the concept must be able to promote action, which means that its relevance must be grasped by certain actors—in our case probably management—and that it must contain action variables which can be influenced by these actors. Thus, our concept must supply a specially constructed bridge between the descriptive and the normative, in order to be able to help the actors concerned to understand and handle a particular type of situation.

At this point I would like to mention something that the reader may at first find rather paradoxical. In the following pages I shall be arguing that the kind of quality-oriented growth which we are discussing here, i.e. growth that is based on the development of knowledge, cannot be planned. At the same time, however, I shall be trying to construct frames of reference for doing just exactly that. In reality, though, there is no contradiction, since we are working with two entirely different concepts of planning. If some kind of theory for the planning of growth is possible, it will have to build on quite different assumptions from those that underpin traditional planning theory. It is a case of two quite different logical systems. The differences between the two planning theories will be discussed in greater detail in Chapter 4.

I shall examine and analyse individual growth processes from several angles before trying to hammer out our comprehensive tool—the growth idea. First, in Chapter 4, I shall describe a theory of the different stages involved in the development of a line of business. This will help us to see how the nature of the planning problems changes in the course of a growth process. In Chapter 5 we shall examine a little more closely the types of driving forces which are incorporated in a natural way in the company's environment and in its technology, and which help us to understand how and why growth often appears to occur spontaneously without having to be actively generated. In Chapter 6 we shall review the state of knowledge about 'learning'—how individuals and social systems learn. By Chapter 7 we should be in a position to formulate the principles of a 'planning-for-growth philosophy', and to identify and describe a number of important components in the concept of the growth idea. Finally, we shall return in Chapter 8 to our basic organization model, showing how the different growth situations we have identified can be matched in the company's structure and reflected in its dominating ideas.

CHAPTER 4

The Growth Cycle of a Business Idea

4.1 Product variations and reorientations

In an earlier book (Normann, 1971), in which I studied product-development projects in a variety of companies, I tried to show that the course of the projects followed two completely different patterns. It was possible to divide them into two groups.

We have already briefly mentioned one type of change process in our discussion of the defence and maintenance of a territory. This consists of the introduction of modifications and improvements within the framework of the company's existing business ideas, but does not involve any essential change in prevailing product–market relations. We can call this kind of change a *product variation*. The other type of change represents the development of new products falling outside the scope of the established business ideas and representing the inception of new business ideas or lines of business. We shall describe this type of project as a *reorientation*. Reorientations generally, although by no means always, require more financial resources than product variations and they involve very demanding processes of an entirely different kind.

Behind the distinction between product variations and reorientations lies far more than a superficial division between developments that take place within existing product lines and developments that take place outside these limits. The two patterns of change differ fundamentally in several ways. We shall frequently have cause to return to these differences in the following pages; here we shall mention only a few.

Perhaps the most obvious difference is the purely technical one, connected with the knowledge content. Product variations do not generally require anything outside the company's existing resources of knowledge and technology; reorientations call for new types of resources, knowledge and skill. There is generally a reasonably good chance of being able to plan product variations in a rational way, but this does not seem to be so in the case of reorientations. Product variations and reorientations appear, for several reasons, to require different *planning philosophies*. Rationality always has to be evaluated against a known, well-defined background. An established territory or business idea, whose structure is known and which company members have learnt to handle, can represent such a familiar and bounded context, where it is often possible to judge with reasonable certainty what is 'wrong', 'right' or 'rational'. But in the case of changes and choices connected with some new and different business idea, it is no longer a question of optimizing within given or known limits. Unlike product variations, this type of change process is greatly affected by expressions of will and the manifestations of creative entrepreneurial activity rather than by norms relating to rationality. At the end of this chapter we shall discuss in a little more detail the planning philosopies required by the two types of change process and the ways in which they differ from one another.

But a reorientation process requires more than mere changes in the company's resources, its production or its marketing resources. The emergence of a new line of business also involves *changes, often of a far-reaching kind, in the company's power system and internal political processes.* Since the values and ideas around which the company has been built (its value system) are in consonance with its existing business ideas, there is a natural—and in most cases a healthy—tendency to regard changes in the value system as illegitimate. Incipient reorientations are thus weeded out. The opposition to any fundamental change is reinforced by the ideas or 'images'* that the various members of the company have of the fundamental relations between their company and its environment.

In Figure 4.1 we have summarized some of the differences between product variations and reorientations. Our provisional conclusion is that the two problems of growing within the framework of existing business ideas and of developing new business ideas are of a fundamentally different character and therefore require different types of knowledge, different planning techniques, different leadership styles, and so on.

Type of product development	Part of the organizational structure		
	Nature of the resources	Value and power structure	Information-processing and problem-solving— the cognitive system
Product variations	Marginal changes only	Can be executed within the existing value and power structure	Existing value criteria and heuristics are used. Direct feedback from traditional territory
Reorientations	Far-reaching changes. New types of specialist knowledge and resources are demanded	Related to new goals and values. Changes in the supportive power system are required	The existing cognitive structure is insufficient. New value criteria, interpretation criteria are needed. Indirect feedback from new market segments

Figure 4.1. Dependencies Between Product Variations/Reorientations and Some Subsystems in the Organizational Structure (Normann, 1971)

*This is the term used by Boulding (1956).

4.2 Bridge between two theories

The discovery that companies grow sometimes as a result of product variations and sometimes as a result of reorientations leads us directly to another observation: every company tends to pass through growth cycles, in which the two types of growth pattern succeed one another and generate subprocesses. New lines of business arise as the result of a reorientation process; these lines then grow and are further elaborated, to increase efficiency, in a process which resembles a series of product variations.

From this observation the idea was born that the theory about the different demands that face a company's management and organization in different situations could perhaps be extended to include a new situational dimension: *a description of different stages of growth along a time axis*. Rhenman (1973) has given us a classification of situations based on the argument that companies and lines of business generally pass through various stages in a cycle of growth. First a new business idea is born and grows (this corresponds to a 'reorientation stage'); the business idea then spreads, it is further refined, it is stabilized and exploited (all this corresponds to a 'product-variation stage'). I shall briefly describe Rhenman's argument and supplement it with a few points of my own.

4.3 A typical growth cycle

As we have described in Chapter 3, the end result of a successful growth cycle is the company's domination of a territory resulting from the development of some form of superior skill—a business idea. But a great deal has to happen before this state can be reached. First, there has to be some sort of idea about the direction in which growth should go. Products or systems that are superior enough to generate dominance then have to be developed. Further, financial resources must be found with which to build an organizational structure capable of penetrating the market, i.e. to conquer the territory. Finally, the conquered territory has to be defended and exploited.

The first stage in the growth cycle can be called the *feeler stage*.* There must be some kind of vision, or some sort of direction guiding the search; but this alone is not enough. If the vision is to inspire any practical action, it must be supported by power centres, so that commitment to the vision and active search along the lines it suggests can be developed. All too often this first stage is misunderstood. It is thought to be mainly concerned with problems of knowledge (cognitive problems), whereas the real difficulty may be that the vision fails to fit into the company's general orientation. If the vision is a real innovation in some fundamental way the company's existing power structure will probably regard it as at least partly illegitimate. Generally speaking the number of possible visions, and the number of directions in which a company could grow, is very great. And, as we pointed out at the beginning

*The names for the different stages of development have been taken from Rhenman (1973).

of this chapter, there aren't really any rational criteria on which to base a choice between them. However, we have often noticed that the successful company tends to send out a number of feelers that are continually exploring in different directions. The company thus develops a state of preparedness; it is continually learning about new areas.

Once a feeler has been dispatched and a hypothesis for growth been formulated, and once interest has been channelled into the given direction, the requisite knowledge can be collected, and a new stage in the growth cycle—the *development phase*—takes over. This stage is concerned with the further development of knowledge about the intended business idea and the shape it may assume; at the same time, concrete products and systems are being developed to help in the conquest of the territory. Once the company has a clear idea about the territory to be conquered, and about how the conquest is to be achieved, this stage can be said to be complete. The products and systems to be incorporated in the business idea have now been developed and possibly tested on a minor local market. By now the company should also have a reasonably good idea of what resources will be needed, and how these should be organized in order to conquer the territory.

The third stage is *market penetration*. This involves building up resources and creating an organization suitable for conquering the territory. It is an extremely difficult phase, calling for knowledge and a brand of leadership quite different from that required in the earlier phases. Often, too, the market-penetration stage makes great demands on the company's financial resources.

Once the territory has been conquered, a fourth stage begins—a period of *exploitation* and *stabilization*. This is a less dynamic but no less important stage. It is now that the company should be taking a firm hold of its territory and harvesting the fruits of the laborious and expensive work that has gone before. At the end of Chapter 3 we discussed some of the methods for defending a territory.

Finally, of course, a business idea may enter a *termination* stage, or—perhaps more frequently—a period of successive redefinition of the business idea. This latter process will be analysed in greater detail in the next chapter.

Although this description is already rather abstract, its basic idea can perhaps be caught even better in a yet simpler description. We can identify two fundamental stages in the development of a new business idea: *learning* and *extension*. In the earlier stages—the learning stages—new aspects of the environment must be mapped or in some way reflected in the company, by changing or extending the organizational structure. Once the company has developed a superior system and superior knowledge of the environment, the extension process takes over; the company conquers and defends its territory by mapping its own structure on the environment in ever widening circles.

In our clinical work we have found a description in terms of *growth stages* extremely valuable. But it should be stressed that the above description has been unrealistically streamlined. In fact, of course, growth stages overlap,

Trucks & Machines Ltd make their own hydraulic motors, among other things for the mining machinery which they make. However, there is over-capacity on the motor production side. Their technical manager has been going round looking for ideas. He's been in contact with shippers and the marine transport people. Certain properties of the motor would make it suitable for use on certain kinds of winch. Loading problems are being considered a little more closely; the idea of a ship's crane starts to emerge. An inventor actually puts the idea forward, but 'the point is that we should exploit this hydraulic motor to the maximum'. There is even a surplus of financial resources. The market is judged to be rapidly growing.

More and more resources are allocated to the project; a special project group is established on the technical side, receiving strong support from the technical manager (with some opposition from the fully occupied sales and production departments). A couple of new, highly qualified engineers are engaged. The quality of the new cranes is tested against that of earlier models. Weight, safety, etc., are judged to be superior. A strategy emerges vis-à-vis the dominating company in the field. Gradually the importance of building up a worldwide service organization is understood, and a conscious effort is made to study the decision processes of the shipbuilding yards and the shippers; how do they purchase their equipment, what are their informal channels of communication, how is news of innovations spread? Preparations are also made for selling the project internally—among others to the president, who was not particularly keen to begin with. Various technical ancillary systems are developed.

The first cranes (after several more or less fundamental reconstructions of the prototype) are sold by the technical manager to a strategic point in the marine system. The project is then handed over to a newly appointed presidential candidate, a marketing man. He establishes a separate sales department. Several people are taken on. This means that lots of resources are needed, but—mainly thanks to the high status and decisiveness of the technical manager—these quickly appear as soon as the market response shows signs of being good. Many details in the product are improved, which means appointing a number of specialists. Various sizes are successfully produced. The marketing and service organization expands and is consolidated. The company's production of electric motors (which are used by other companies for deck cranes) is sold to the major competitor on that side. The company is very successful on the market; operations are very profitable. But some of the people who were involved in developing the crane and selling it during the first period sometimes complain that the work is getting too bureaucratic.

Axis labels (bottom to top): Stabilization · Market penetration · Systems development · Feelers

Figure 4.2. Stages in the Development of the New Line of Business 'Marine Deck Cranes' in Trucks & Machines Ltd

and their relative importance depends on the line of business in which the company is operating. Figure 4.2 illustrates an attempt to identify the different growth stages in a concrete case.

4.4 The goal view and the process view—two planning philosophies

It is traditionally assumed that in planning the decision-maker first formulates his goals, then breaks these down into subgoals and designs what is known as a means–end hierarchy; after this he seeks for alternatives, weighs the alternatives against the goals and decides whether they satisfy the requirements or not. He then chooses the most satisfying alternative, or the alternative with the highest degree of goal-fulfilment. If there is no satisfactory alternative, he can embark on a new cycle of seeking for alternatives and, possibly, lower his level of ambition.

This planning technique is based on the model of the rational decision-maker—a model that has been successively refined and modified, above all by the 'Carnegie Tech' school (Simon, 1947; March and Simon, 1958; Cyert and March, 1963). The great contribution of this school is that it has made the model of the rational decision-maker much more realistic. Instead of the super-man of economic theory, these writers have described a decision-maker who, although admittedly rational, also has his limits. This is a crucial point in their theory—the limits of rationality.

But even the 'Carnegie Tech' school's modified version of the goal-formulating and alternative-seeking decision-maker has met with some opposition. Lindblom, with political science as his frame of reference, has described planning as 'the science of muddling through'. Hirschman, with experience of growth processes in developing countries and the planning of major techno-logical development projects, has noted that the results of goal-formulation and planning according to a means-end hierarchy are often poor. Hirschman and Lindblom (1969) recommend a planning process with freer goal formula-tion, which allows for 'unbalanced growth', in which the idea is to exploit gradually acquired knowledge rather than to follow a pattern drawn up in advance.

Although in many people's minds he has come to stand for the means–end view of planning, Simon actually represents quite a different approach, at least in one context: when he discusses future planning in the American educational system.

> ... I have ignored the term of reference instructing me to make specific recommendations for action in 1970 and various subsequent dates. I see no point in recommendations for actions that are not to start now, or very soon, unless they require preparatory actions—in which case the latter should be recommended. Hence, all the recommendations in this paper are for action now.
>
> (Simon, 1968, p. 380)

We too have viewed with considerable doubt the idea of planning as a decision process in which the decision-maker first formulates goals and then generates alternatives. This view seems particularly unsuitable in cases where companies or other organizations are especially anxious to inaugurate some kind of planning and guidance for a complex future (Rhenman, 1963; Normann and Rhenman, 1975).

How, then, shall we formulate our alternative to the traditional planning philosophy, to the 'goal view'? I have tried elsewhere (Normann, 1970) to describe a different or at least supplementary planning philosophy, the 'process

The goal view	The process view
The decision-maker first formulates goals and then (alternative) plans, which are evaluated in terms of their estimated goal-fulfilment	Planning is a learning process in which the perspective continually shifts between visions and immediate actions
Man (and management) as rational decision-makers	Man (and management) as learning and knowledge-developing systems
Suitable in clearly delimited and well-known planning environments, or when the strength of the organization is so superior that there is no need to take account of the environment in any planning	Suitable in complex environments (causal relationships, restrictions and opportunities, systems boundaries—all partly unknown)
Mature stages in the company's growth cycle	Early stages in the company's growth cycle
Tensions and misfits are not desirable and are eliminated by means of planning	Tensions and misfits are to a great extent desirable and represent planning resources; sometimes attempts are even made to create tension

Figure 4.3. Some Differences Between the Goal View and the Process View in Planning Philosophy

approach'. Characteristically, according to this view, the planner does not formulate his goals as future states he wishes to achieve; instead he formulates a *vision* of a future state, a vision based on insights at present available. Starting from this vision, he decides upon one or two *first steps in a process*. When these steps have been taken, the experiences they generate should be evaluated and the vision adjusted in light of the new state of knowledge. Further steps in the process can then be decided upon.

Naturally the process view of planning is not, *ipso facto*, superior to the goal view. But it does seem to me that the two planning philosophies suit *different kinds of situations*. However, the process approach is the more misunderstood of the two planning philosophies, so that the goal approach is often used—usually with discouraging results—in situations where the process view would have been better.* Thus, the leaning towards rational behaviour that so noticeably marks our society, and which has made the goal approach so widely accepted, often leads to a sort of quasi-rationality only.

The goal view seems to suit situations where the planning environment—that is, the technology, the causalities, and the external factors in the company's environments—is reasonably well known and well structured, although the situation itself may well be complicated. The goal approach suits systems that are in the main 'closed', in the sense of being well charted.

*We have frequently found this to apply in the case of complex planning problems in the public administration (Normann and Rhenman, 1975).

The process approach, on the other hand, suits situations where the planning environment is in part unknown, and where flexibility and innovative ability are important preconditions of success. Such situations—resembling 'open' systems, exposed to uncertain factors in the environment and subject to little-known causalities—characterize the environment of many companies concerned with long-range planning and strategy formulation. Thus we have the paradox that *genuine* long-range planning is always short-range in the process view sense.

Figure 4.3 summarizes some of the differences between the goal view and the process view. A pattern emerges, suggesting that the two planning philosophies match the theoretical problems of different stages in the growth cycle of a line of business. While the goal approach is suitable to the mature growth phases following the exploration and definition of a territory, the process approach is better suited to the earlier stages concerned with the creation of new boundaries rather than with optimization within given limits. The goal view is also linked to the idea of harmony and consonance, while the process view exploits tensions and inconsistencies in the cause of efficiency.

We can therefore expect a situation-conscious business management to use the goal approach in planning operations at a mature stage of development, and the process approach for operations at earlier stages of development.

4.5 Note on the diagnosis of different stages of growth

The differences between stages of growth (especially the transition from one stage to another) can usually be identified by examining the historical develop-

	Feeler stage	Systems-development stage	Market-penetration stage	Stabilization stage
Development costs	?	H	M	L
Market investment costs	?	M	H	L
Equipment investment costs	?	M	H	L–M
Growth in terms of volume	L(?)	L–M	H	L–M
Return on invested capital	L(?)	L	M–H	M–H
Capital requirements	L(?)	M	H	L
Self-financing	No	Seldom	Sometimes*	Yes†

Figure 4.4. Typical Changes in Key Figures During a Growth Cycle. H, High; M, Medium; L, Low;* Depends on how Quickly the Market and/or the Company's Own Resources Grow;+ Should Generate Capital

	1968	1969	1970	1971	1972
Turnover —Mill. Sw. kr —Relative increase	37·5	40·7 8%	44·0 8%	57·8 31%	94·1 63%
Sales costs*		19%	24%	26%	23%
Development costs*		19%	17%	14%	9%
Return on working capital		−5%	8%	8%	34%

Figure 4.5. Some Changes in the Course of Transition from a Successful Period of Systems Development to a Period of Market Penetration in an Advanced and Highly Technological Company. * as a % of Turnover

ment of a particular line of business. Figure 4.4 shows how certain costs and other key figures generally change during a growth cycle. Figure 4.5 shows how a very advanced, very specialized and highly technological company suddenly surged forward after a successful period of systems development.

Thus an important conclusion to emerge from the arguments above is that the development of a line of business goes through certain specific stages and that these stages can be identified; also, they require different types of organization, of planning and of control. However, although it is possible to identify the transition from one stage to another in an *historical* growth cycle, it is often very difficult to distinguish and identify growth stages in an *ongoing* growth process and still more difficult to readjust accordingly. Later we shall see that growth problems are often linked to this kind of inability to adjust organizational structure and leadership style to different situations.

CHAPTER 5

Natural Driving Forces and Problems of Growth

A company's management cannot simply invent a growth problem *a priori*. Factors in the nature of the company itself and in its external environment also to some extent determine the types of growth situation in which the company will land. It is not always possible for management to influence such factors directly. Generally they have to be regarded as given or, to use the technical term of the model-builders, as exogenous. We shall use the expression *natural* driving forces* to refer to the impetus that arises without any active initiative on the part of the company's management; they are to be distinguished from the driving forces which, in the main, result from a direct expression of management's will and its striving for growth. This chapter will be devoted to an analysis of some typical natural driving forces, and the type of growth patterns and growth problems which they generate.

We have often noticed that if management is unable to analyse the cause of a particular situation, then the specific problems and the specific opportunities of the situation may both be grossly misjudged. Also, since growth and growth problems can often be handled most efficiently by going along with the natural forces, the particular character of these forces has to be recognized.

5.1 Some causes of naturally generated growth patterns

As far as possible most growing companies seem to follow a kind of principle of least resistance. Using their established business ideas, they try to extend over ever larger but still similar areas; their growth is really a form of repeated reproduction (Nilsson, 1971). Seldom, however, can growth operate altogether in this simple way; growth patterns are modified by a series of factors that are built into the company's environment or into its technology.

Various *barriers and restrictions* are the most usual obstacle to continued homogeneous expansion. A company has been successful and has conquered a territory, but then finds that the growth opportunities for the established business idea are blocked; the whole market has already been conquered, or as much of it as is reasonable in view of the marginal utility of further expansion.

---

*The reader should note that 'natural', in the meaning we give the term here, has nothing to do with laws of nature. Although some natural driving forces might be rooted in natural laws, this is not the point here.

- The Continental Construction Company had landed in just such a situation. It had been extremely successful on its own domestic market, carrying out a particular type of construction job, and had succeeded in conquering almost the whole market. The president, who was personally committed to the idea of growth, was nevertheless dissatisfied with the situation. The successful exploitation of the territory had generated a great deal of capital which was available for financing further growth. But this new growth would have to assume a different shape, since there was no more market to conquer—and in any case he felt that the company's territory was dangerously sensitive to fluctuations in the business cycle.

Scarce resources—perhaps a limited supply of raw materials—can also impose restrictions on further homogeneous expansion. The Swedish forest industry, for instance, is in this kind of situation today. Or we could take the example of a company which had developed a very interesting business idea in optical retailing, but which was having growth problems because there was a short supply of authorized opticians.

Another kind of restriction may be connected with the particular production technology. It may not be possible for a certain chemical process, for example, to give a return on capital above a certain level within the bounds of the existing technology. Or, to take another example, a plantbreeding company is restricted by the fact that the rate at which new strains can be developed and reproduced depends on biological and genetic laws.

Nor are barriers and restrictions necessarily only physical or technological: they may also be legal, social or cultural. New legislation, for instance, may prevent the further spread of established business ideas. One way of revealing the institutional restrictions is to study what has happened when actors have tried to bring about change by going beyond traditional boundaries.

- The function of the Swedish Forest Service in the industry is to administer the country's forests in an economically acceptable manner. However, the Forest Service has little chance of growing in the way that is typical of the industry, i.e. by integrating forwards into the sawmill and pulp industry for example, since institutional regulations have declared this to be the field of another state-owned organization, the National Swedish Forest Industries.

Growth is also governed by various kinds of *interdependency*. These, too, may appear as technical or other restrictions that regulate the relations between subcomponents in a larger system. For example, a slaughterhouse which buys a large number of pigs before Christmas knows that it cannot restrict itself to marketing hams; there will also be other cuts to sell—one loin of pork for every ham, for example. Furthermore, certain subprocesses or subcomponents on the customer side may be closely interrelated. Thus, for example, it was discovered at IBM that the hardware for information-processing on the one hand and the client company's information and decision processes in general on the other were very intimately connected, and this circumstance has greatly influenced IBM's growth and the development of its business idea.

A third type of driving force is *disturbances and variations*. As we shall see later, production-oriented companies tend to grow by absorbing and dominating any sources of disturbance or other uncertainty, in order to ensure a high and regular use of production resources. In fact, however, disturbances and variations may well provide an important driving force to the generation of new business ideas directed towards this very activity, i.e. the elimination or exploitation of disturbances. The development of cold-storage and refrigeration techniques, for example, sprang from the need to cope with differences between the pattern of food production and the pattern of food consumption. In other words, the refrigeration plant provides a buffer between two systems with different and irregular kinds of disturbance. In the same way, fluctuations on the domestic market have pushed many a company into export operations whose original purpose was simply to iron out certain troublesome variations.

The existence of disturbances and variations may also be interesting for another reason: it often suggests that somewhere in the system there is, at least temporarily, some sort of overcapacity. This kind of situation has been exploited by companies selling foreign-language travel to schoolchildren. These companies have been able to arrange travel on weekdays at lower rates than those required for ordinary charter travel, since the charter companies are normally fully loaded at weekends but have surplus capacity during the week. The language-school organizers have also been able to use school premises that would otherwise have been empty during the summer holidays and teachers on leave for the summer. In future we could expect these companies to try to grow at least partly by exploiting the internal surplus capacity which they generate themselves in the same way.

Thus we have seen that restrictions, interdependencies, and variations in technology and in the environment can all affect a company's growth patterns. But these driving forces are closely linked to—and to a great extent modified by—the impact of *power relationships in the environment*. The manufacture of television sets in Finland offers an interesting example of changing power relations in the environment providing a driving force.

● In the mid-1960s the industry consisted of barely ten companies, all of which manufactured in small batches for the domestic market. Under the protection of high tariffs that shut the large foreign competitors out, it was possible to sell television sets at prices far higher than those prevailing on the world market. When Finland's association with the EEC led to a revision of the whole question of trade barriers, some of these companies realized that domestic prices would soon drop to the level prevailing on the world market—a level decided by companies whose production was on quite a different scale. The nature of the technology in this industry is such that a certain volume of production is essential to efficiency. It was quite unrealistic to hope for a share of the domestic market large enough to ensure sales on this scale. Today Finland has two relatively efficient, highly export-oriented companies in the television industry.

We have already spoken of Processing Ltd and the Raw Materials Corporation.*

- The Raw Materials Corporation—which also dominated the processing market—accepted and even appreciated Processing Ltd, so long as the latter remained small enough. But when their market share began to creep up over the 25 per cent mark, the smaller company was exposed to a number of small, subtle but effective pinpricks on the part of its larger colleague.

Our studies of the building industry have yielded some clear examples of how power relations can steer a company's development (Normann, 1972; Dahlman and Gärdborn, 1975).

- In the building industry power has been widely dispersed: first, the different 'links' in the building process—planning, projecting, the actual construction, etc.—have come under a large number of different organizations; secondly, various specialities such as painting, electrical installation, etc., have been divided among separate groups dominated by the old guild system. Any knowledge development that has transgressed the boundaries of this well-charted network of power centres has therefore been more or less illegitimate; the power centres have been too weak to effect any genuine change, but strong enough to preserve the *status quo*.

  Any build-up of knowledge around larger units—be it consumer, housing administrator or large individual project—has thus been rendered impossible, or at any rate much more difficult. One sign of this is that the contract system which has been dominant for so long both in Sweden and other countries has put a major obstacle in the way of any improvement in the efficiency of building. However, technological advances, and the substantial increase in the size of projects that has in part been a result of these, have done a certain amount to break down the traditional power barriers affecting the actual building process; this is reflected in particular in the emergence of new types of contract. Some of the most successful building firms in Sweden today are those which have succeeded in combining types of knowhow, so that they command an increasing number of subcomponents and can sell them as a 'total contract'.

  A comparison between Figures 5.1 and 5.2 illustrates some of the

---

*In the following pages we shall sometimes return to companies we have already mentioned, in order to describe them from another angle or to use them to illustrate some fresh argument. We shall sometimes recapitulate certain basic characteristics of the companies; in other cases we shall refer the reader to our earlier description.

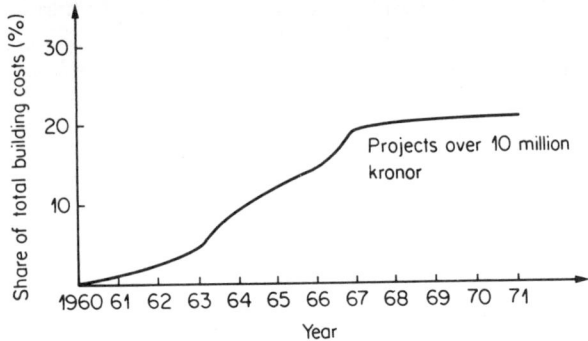

Figure 5.1. How Costs have Developed for Multifamily-house Projects Where Building Costs Exceed 10 Million Swedish Kronor, in Relation to Total Building Costs for Multifamily Houses During the Period 1960–1971

relations between project size and power structure in the building industry. Figure 5.1 shows how the larger projects (over 10 million Swedish kronor) have taken over an increasing proportion of the total construction of multifamily housing during the 1960s. At the same time, according to Figure 5.2, the power relationships have changed; general and total contracts have become more common and subcontracts less so. These two trends are certainly interrelated; more comprehensive contracts allow for larger undertakings, while larger projects in turn call for new forms of contracts.

The power structure, for instance as manifest in the financing system and the Housing Board's norms, has also affected the purely physical shape of the company's development activities. What we might call 'mortgage architecture', for instance, shows us that forms of credit rather than traditional architectural values can sometimes decide the design of a building product.

5.2 Natural driving forces behind new business ideas

We have discussed some of the mechanisms that can lie behind the natural driving forces: restrictions, interdependencies, disturbances and variations, and the power structure in the environment, with which these factors are often connected. In this section we shall try to show how, in different ways, natural driving forces can give rise to feelers or the embryos of new business ideas.

At the beginning of this chapter we defined 'natural driving forces' as driving forces that are more or less 'given'; they occur without any intervention on the part of management and, indeed, without management being able to influence them directly. These natural driving forces may then generate feelers, backed by some kind of support or engagement from members of the company. The amount of active support will vary. Certain inevitable interdependencies

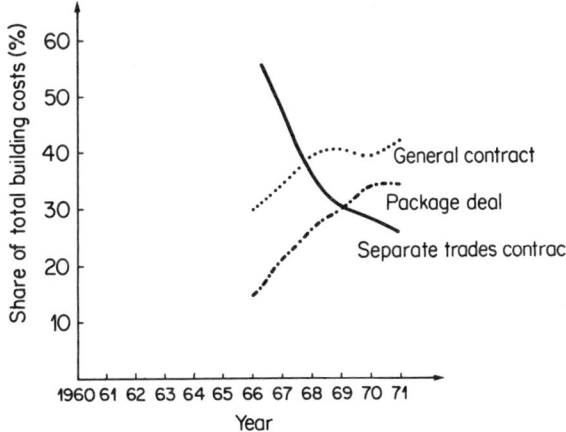

Figure 5.2. Proportion of Total Building Costs for Multi-family Houses During the Period 1966–1971 Assignable to Different Forms of Contract

in the technical production process, for example, may generate byproducts which constitute feelers whose substance and general direction are reasonably clear. On the other hand, a surplus of financial resources admittedly represents a kind of driving force, but neither the content nor the direction of any feelers will reveal themselves without some very active contribution on the part of management or others.

Feelers arising from inevitable technological byproducts are illustrated by alternative (1) in Figure 5.3, while alternative (2) illustrates the kind of feelers which may be generated by such a driving force as a surplus of financial resources. One of the differences between the driving forces we shall be discussing here lies in the different type of input and engagement that they require of the company's actors before any kind of feeler can be generated.

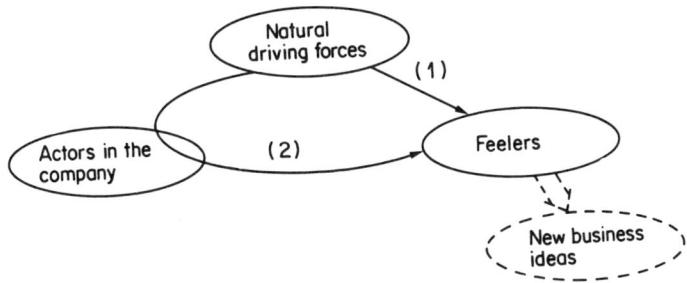

Figure 5.3. Natural Growth Impulses Give Rise More or Less Spontaneously to the Embryos of New Business Ideas

Direct generation of feelers

The further development of certain business ideas—improving their efficiency for example, or introducing product variations—will almost automatically create feelers and the embryos of new business ideas or lines of business. This direct generation of feelers is perhaps particularly common in capital-intensive process industries such as the chemical industry (Rhenman, 1972). There are several reasons for this, one of which is that the actual chemical composition of the raw materials often gives rise to byproducts. We have an illustration of this in Figure 5.4, which has been taken from a brochure published by Perstorp AB. We can see here the logical relation between different chemical products.

But there are also other types of driving forces that may create feelers more or less automatically. An example of this would be a company's attempt—probably with a view to improving production efficiency—to eliminate bottlenecks, excess capacity or any other signs of 'imbalance'. The production-oriented company tries to moderate disturbances and variations, in order to make better use of its capacity. Driving forces may also arise from a variety of subsidiary activities undertaken in support of a company's basic operations. The history of the Sugar Company—a Swedish company now known as the Cardo Group—illustrates all these kinds of driving forces.

● Originally the basis of the Sugar Company's operations was the production of sugar from sugar-beet. For this purpose a number of capital-intensive production plants were built at various places in the country. It was soon discovered, however, that profitability was extremely dependent on such factors as the sugar content of the beets, the yield per acre, and so on. For this reason the company launched into beet cultivation and began to acquire knowledge of various techniques of cultivation to help their contracted farmers to achieve better results. Gradually, as agricultural labour became more scarce and more expensive, the company also began to develop machines for beetlifting and a type of seed that would eliminate the laborious thinning of the beets. Both these operations really started in support of the basic business idea; obviously, though, they also had their own development potential.

At the same time, certain byproducts of the actual production process were also generating another idea embryo. Molasses and beet pulp are two byproducts of the production of sugar. To begin with they were both used as animal fodder by the beet farmers; now, however, the Sugar Company dries them to produce a beet fodder, a feed that is easy to store and handle. Attempts have also been made to utilize the valuable parts of the beet tops, a byproduct of beet cultivation.

At the beginning of the 1940s, in connection with the solution of certain technical problems on the manufacturing side, a method was discovered for producing dextran biotechnologically—a product that is now manu-

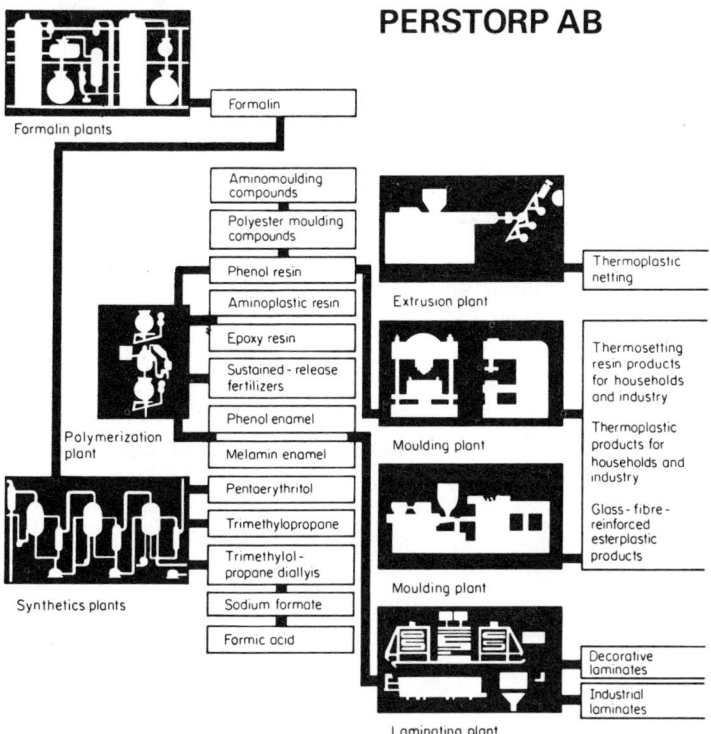

Figure 5.4. Perstorp's Manufacturing Programme with its Multiplicity of Products Spanning a Wide Variety of Areas. This Represents an Example of Logical Technical Relations Between Product Groups in a Chemical Industry, Which are Strongly Influenced by the Company's Historical Growth Pattern. The Figure Presents One Main Group Only (from Perstorp AB, 1974 Calendar)

factured on a large scale and sold to the pharmaceutical industry for processing. Towards the end of the 1950s the Sugar Company decided to cultivate potatoes, encouraged by the agricultural knowledge they had accumulated through the cultivation of beets. The potato-handling side has now been transferred to AB Felix. But the interesting point in this context is that the company's engagement in this field led to a certain amount of microbiological research which resulted in a unique method of transforming starchy waste products into valuable protein. The method can also be used to purify waste water with a high starch content.

As a result of the awkward seasonal variations associated with beet cultivation, the manufacturing plants were at a standstill at off-season times. For this reason the company was constantly on the lookout for something that would utilize at least part of the production resources at these times. Several feelers were generated in this way. For instance, two of the sugar mills are now used from May to September for drying pasture plants and, with an admixture of molasses, producing green fodder briquettes.

The emergence of new business ideas in companies traditionally geared to a single dominating business idea is usually accompanied by certain difficulties. The new feelers were not originally intended to lead to a diversification; they were simply meant to refine and support an established business idea. But such supportive measures are often double-edged: they may well succeed in eliminating problems in traditional operations, but they are also potentially able to grow on their own. It is in this latter role that they may provide the embryo of a new business idea. However, if the feeler does go on to become a new business idea in its own right, it also often loses its ability to solve the problems of the established business idea. We found an interesting example of this—and one which gave rise to major conflict in the company concerned— in the case of the Mining and Processing Company.

- Typical of the company's situation was a combination of frequent, big variations in the nature of the demand on the one hand, and frequent and generally unforeseeable variations in the raw materials acquired from the ore-mining operations on the other. Unexpectedly, there was a drop in the demand for a particular raw-material quality which was being mined in fairly large quantities (although still at an uneven rate). To deal with this change in the structure of the market, it was decided that a department for the processing of this raw material should be established, so as to increase marginal returns.

  For a while everything went well. The processing department took in the raw materials whenever any were available; otherwise its operations came to a standstill. However, this did not happen very often and was anyway not particularly serious, since the fixed costs of the processing were fairly low. The processing department tried to sell what it acquired and what it was able to process. After a while, however, the company manged to work up a customer network and a more stable supply began to be desirable. The manager of the processing department wanted to be allowed to purchase raw materials on the outside market, and in general to be given a chance to develop his department properly.

  But those members of the company who had been responsible for the original, established business idea did not support him; they saw the processing department simply as an appendix to basic operations, existing solely to push up the marginal returns of certain products. Basic operations were the really important feature; the processing department was to stop making a fuss and asking for a more regular supply of raw materials.

Naturally, both parties in the Mining and Processing Company were right, but for different reasons. The processing department could not develop a successful business idea of its own, so long as it had to adapt itself to the conditions of its company's main operations; but if this department's demands were met, the main operations would have to find another solution to the problem of getting reasonable marginal returns on their raw materials.

Generation of feelers as a result of a shift in the focus of attention

In the above examples, the emergence of the embryos of new business ideas was connected with the technology of the production concerned. Driving forces appeared more or less spontaneously and pointed roughly in a particular direction, without management having to do very much about it—at least at first. But there are other ways in which feelers based on established operations can emerge, without having any particular direction. A growing company often comes into contact with new areas where some aspect of its traditional activities just seems to fit and invite exploitation.

The type of technology a company decides to apply to a certain area often turns out to be more broadly relevant. Thus, for example, Avesta Jernverk came into the manufacture of sheet metal largely because it had been making coins at a time when coin had not only a symbolic value but also a certain plate value of its own. In Chapter 4 we described the development of a business idea in Trucks & Machines Ltd. This company provides a typical example of growth through a series of systematic reorientations, one step leading to the next. Swedish Building Materials Ltd—whose operations we have previously described from another point of view—was really geared to mass production, but because of its customer contacts it began to develop another business idea involving products that could more accurately be described as tailor-made.

● Swedish Building Materials Ltd manufactured a number of standardized and mass-produced products, which were sold through the established retail outlets and which kept to specifications generally recognized throughout the building trade.

However, there were inevitably occasional enquiries from architects and builders about the possibility of manufacturing certain items to somewhat different specifications for special purposes—enquiries that were sometimes satisfied, particularly if the company had some excess capacity that it was glad to use. After a while some members of the company became increasingly interested in this side of things; they even began to specialize on orders of this kind. Gradually they built up a new contact network with customers outside the established clientele. They also came in contact with other materials manufacturers, and the first modest product packages emerged in which various products that complemented one another were combined.

To begin with these special orders were tolerated by the production department. Soon, however, it was discovered that they were associated with high installation costs; they were also beginning to require a considerable input of staff resources. But by this time things had gone so far that those in favour of custom-tailoring felt that the company would lose a significant part of its market if this type of production were to be discontinued.

Generation of feelers as a result of an increase in volume

Growth that to all appearances assumes the shape of an increase in volume can in fact land a company in quite new situations, in which the character of its operations changes fundamentally. Sometimes it is only possible for a mature business idea to go on extending if its extension is accompanied by some qualitative development: a mining company gradually consumes its own raw-material resources, a forest company is finally halted by the rate at which forest can reproduce itself, and so on.

Another lesson that many growing companies have to learn is that expanding is quite a different matter in a company that is already large and in one which is still marginal. And that the problems of growing in a stable market are different from the problems of growing in a market that is rapidly expanding. Let us return to the Mining and Processing Company.

● This company did not start as a production company; it used to buy up the surplus on the market and sell it to customers suffering from a temporary shortage. This marginal activity was successful and several regular contacts were gradually established. However, this success provided the basis for a fundamental change in the basic business idea: the company gradually acquired many customers who began to demand a regular supply. To satisfy this demand, the company had to acquire its own production resources.

But to be able to guarantee a basic regular supply some surplus capacity—quite large in relation to the basic supply—is always necessary, if the major disturbances and variations so typical of this industry are not to jeopardize regular supplies. It was therefore necessary to organize the production apparatus so that a series of varying raw-material qualities was available over and above the basic regular supply. Suddenly the company found itself operating two really rather different business ideas: on the one hand it had its market-oriented production (for the regular customers), and on the other it had its production-oriented sales (dealing with the varying surplus of the production side). At this point the processing side also came into the picture and made it even more complicated, demanding ultimately that basic production operations should be made to follow a more stable pattern.

Generation of feelers as a result of surplus financial resources

The successful exploitation of a mature business idea often generates a surplus of financial resources, and this may provide a driving force for new business ideas. However, in this case there is no question of a *specific* driving force such as those we have been discussing above; a surplus of financial means does not itself suggest the direction in which a new initiative should go.

Companies may therefore react very differently to the possession of surplus capital resources. If no other natural driving forces are present and there is neither a strong will nor any entrepreneurial resources, the company will probably stick in its old rut and will end up acting as a bank—it becomes overconsolidated. Sometimes, however—and we have come across many such cases—there is keen competition for the capital resources needed (or wanted) for a variety of growth ideas. In Chapter 7 we shall return to the question of the differences between directed and diffuse driving forces.

5.3 The problem of the redefinition of mature business ideas

A company which has developed a business idea and acquired a territory usually seeks to stabilize the situation and maintain its dominance, partly by elaborating its business idea and influencing power relationships in the environment in the way we have described in Chapter 3. Sometimes, however, these strategies are not enough; structural changes in the environment may remove the very *base for the company's dominance*, i.e. the fundamental resource or competence on which its business idea is based. In such a situation the company will either gradually wither away; or it will reorient itself radically, developing completely new lines of business; or it will have to try to redefine and reformulate the old, mature business idea.

In the previous section we described different ways in which natural driving forces can initiate a *process of reorientation* by creating the embryo of new business ideas. In this section we shall analyse the driving forces behind the *process of redefinition*, i.e. the successive alteration of an established business idea.

First, we need to introduce a few simple notions about the relation between a company's business idea and its environment. The environment in which the company operates constitutes the 'larger system' in which the company has its being as a subsystem. Our basic proposition is that the *successful business idea is based on elements that are crucial or strategic to the larger system.* Crucial factors of this kind may be necessary to some function or functions of the larger system; they may contribute to the efficiency of the larger system; or they may solve fundamental problems for one or more of the major power centres in the larger system. One of the marks of the successful business idea is the consonance that prevails between the base for the company's dominance and these crucial factors. In fact, these two really represent the same phenomenon seen from two different angles: what is a crucial factor from the point of view of the larger system at the same time provides the base for the dominance enjoyed by the individual company. The following are examples of phenomena that can have this dual nature, operating both as a base for dominance and as a crucial factor:

- scarce resources, e.g. shortage of a raw material or a particular type of specially trained personnel
- superior efficiency in production or technology
- institutional affiliation.

The base for a company's dominance can assume all kinds of guises, from a diamond mine surrounded by a double electric fence and guard dogs to a sophisticated type of competence based on a pattern of contacts and problem-solving resources.

If the key factors in the larger system change, then the base for the company's dominance will also be threatened. There will be a lack of consonance or a misfit between the base for dominance and the crucial factors which may call for a redefinition of the business idea. The nature of this misfit may indicate the probable direction of a redefinition of the business idea; the company must move its base for dominance so that it falls into line with the crucial factors again.

Key factors may change for a variety of reasons: perhaps there has been a shift in power relationships, or some advance in technology or knowledge development has gradually (or suddenly) altered the whole system of restrictions and opportunities in an industry. It is therefore extremely important for every company to know what kind of knowledge is being developed in the larger system, and to understand how this might affect the base for its own particular dominance.

Using these various concepts, we can now make a more detailed analysis of some typical growth problems in companies whose business ideas are characterized by different kinds of bases for dominance.

Redefinition patterns in the market-oriented company

The base for the dominance enjoyed by the market-oriented company lies in its knowledge of its customers and its ability to solve the customers' problems. In the environment of this kind of company the knowledge being developed generally has something to do with a greater ability to handle increasingly larger 'wholes' and increasingly complex relationships between the customers and the customers' stakeholders. To prevent a misfit arising between the company and the larger system it is therefore necessary for the company to change the base for dominance by extending it to embrace larger 'wholes'. In other words, the company increases its knowledge of the larger system. The redefinition pattern of the market-oriented company therefore expresses itself as *customer-centred systems development*.

The fundamental natural driving force of this kind consists of dependencies in the environment, particularly in the customer system. The following are some examples:

- When Xerox copying machines were going to be marketed, the company began to realize that what they ought to sell was not the machine but the kind of copying service. Thus Xerox sold to its customers a package consisting of the rental of a machine, the training of operators, regular servicing, the right to replace machines as the customer wished, etc. It is unlikely that the innovation would have spread as rapidly as it did if the system had not been designed in this way. This strategy also meant that the business idea had to be backed up by an elaborate financing system.

● By developing whole systems, tour operators can now supply 'systems of recreation' at prices far lower than was possible before. Tour operators such as Tjäreborg (Denmark) and Vingresor (Sweden) supply their clients with a system including air travel, hotel, restaurants, exercise, anti-smoking campaigns, language teaching, excursions, etc.—often without owning any hotels, restaurants or aeroplanes. Their knowledge has been built up round the 'whole' or the ensemble that the *customer* stands for. They are successful because they have mastered the entire system of components. The customer who wants to buy any components separately has to pay far more than the customer who buys the integrated system.

● Nowadays the more successful of the automobile companies—with Volvo leading the way—tend increasingly to supply their customers with systems rather than with individual products. Volvo, for example, has its own insurance company, its own motor-vehicle insurance, and an extensive service network; at the same time it manages to surround its basic product with an image involving various 'software' components such as safety and quality. (Volvo is not perhaps a markedly market-oriented company; instead it is just taking the first step from production orientation to more genuine market orientation.)

Redefinition patterns in the production-oriented company

A large part of the base for dominance of the production-oriented company usually consists of large, heavy and often capital-intensive production machines, and this makes it possible to manufacture products in long series and with high internal efficiency, i.e. at low cost.

In the production-oriented company a natural driving force is to be found built into the very nature of the business idea. The company is dependent for its efficiency on the high and regular utilization of its capacity. It thus has to try to eliminate any disturbances and variations in the larger system that threaten the stable exploitation of resources.

However, disturbances and variations need not necessarily threaten the production-oriented company's base for dominance. Instead, any problems of redefinition are likely to be connected with structural changes in the particular industry: the crucial factors and the development of knowledge in the larger system are becoming increasingly remote from the company's traditional business idea. As we said when discussing the market-oriented company: in the highly industrialized society and to an even greater extent in the post-industrial society the fundamental development of knowledge tends to take place somewhere in the end-user market and to be concerned with knowledge of ensembles, i.e. it is oriented towards systems rather than components.

There are probably two main alternatives open to the production-oriented company when it comes to dealing with the typical misfit between base for dominance and crucial factors:

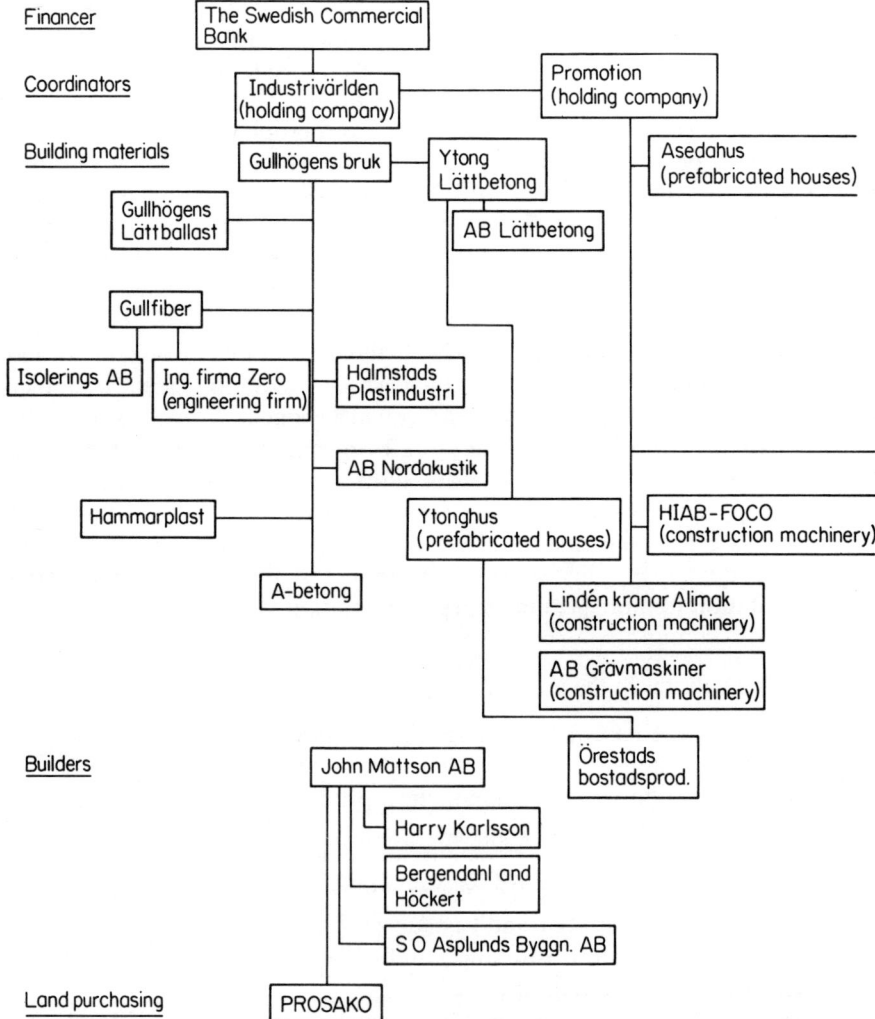

Figure 5.5. The Building Chain has Both a Knowledge-seeking and a Stabilizing Purpose (from *Utblick* No. 17)

1. It can increase its market orientation, to alter or supplement the established base for dominance. The company adapts to the shift that has occurred in the centres for knowledge development in the environment. For example, it may acquire or establish companies that are closer to the centre of knowledge development (integration forwards).

2. It can take action to stabilize the larger system in various ways, and perhaps even to prevent or delay knowledge development. This strategy may consist of exploiting or influencing power relations in the industry with a view to controlling the development of knowledge.

Production-oriented companies often use a combination of these strategies. The cement industry, the pulp industry and other heavy production-oriented industries have tried in different ways to stabilize the larger system *and* to get closer to the centres of knowledge development.

- Integrated Paper Mills Ltd followed this line by selling timber, pulp, bulk paper and special paper internally as well as on the external market. The company also built up a packaging industry and even a contracting company in the building industry, in order to utilize some of the processed raw materials that emerged. As a result of these measures, which were originally intended as a redefinition of the mature business idea, the company gradually assumed an extremely complicated structure with special growth problems.

- The building materials industry is an example of the way companies have tried in various ways to affect the development of knowledge in the industry, attempting to intervene in existing power relationships and at the same time to come closer to the centre where the main development of knowledge is taking place.

Redefinition patterns in the raw-materials-oriented company

The worst thing that can happen to a raw-materials-oriented company is, of course, that its particular raw material is superseded on the market. However, there are also other circumstances which can drastically alter the situation of this kind of company. The base for its dominance is the raw material, and it will therefore be affected by shortages or surplus supplies of this material, and by who controls it (i.e. does the company control it or is there a competing supply?). Thus we can expect the raw-material-based company to employ strategies similar to those of the production-oriented company, namely, stabilization of the external environment, perhaps by agreements or the acquisition of companies with a view to ensuring dominance over the raw material and obtaining control of its further processing.

But like the production-oriented company, the raw-material-oriented company tends to find increasingly that the centres of fundamental knowledge development are becoming remote from the base of the company's dominance.

68

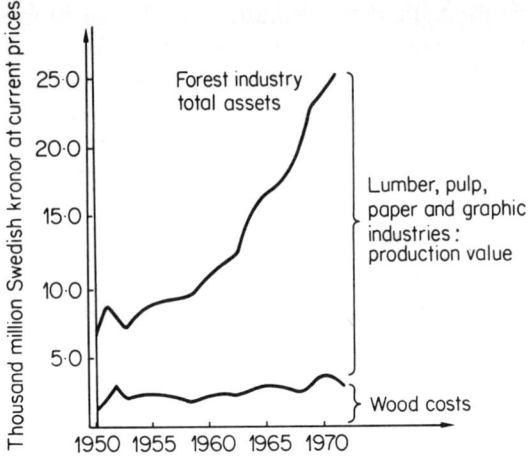

Figure 5.6. Economic Development in Forest Industry
During the Period 1950–1972. Thousand Million
Swedish Kronor at Current Prices. (Source: *Skogs-
statistisk Årsbok*, 1972)

Knowledge development generally takes place further and further away
from the raw material and closer and closer to the end-user markets, as developments in the Swedish forest industry illustrate (Figure 5.6). Since 1950 the
part of total production value that is represented by raw material prices has
fallen steeply.

Growth traps

Although, through dominance, a company can stabilize its environment,
the mature business idea will sooner or later come up against problems.
Generally the company can meet these by redefining its business idea. But
such redefinitions, which may be quite far-reaching, are not always enough;
the business idea behind a particular line of operations may be based on a type
of competence or resource which is doomed to disappear. To take a biological
analogy, we could speak of an 'ecological trap' or a 'growth trap'.

● In biological history the dinosaur is perhaps the most famous example
of a species that found itself in this kind of ecological trap. It was not
really any weakness or failure in the specialization of these animals that
caused them to disappear; it was more that environmental processes
beyond their control caused the niche which they had dominated, and
within which they had learnt to exist, to vanish.

● As a line of defence the Maginot Line was a masterpiece based on experience from the first world war. But as a result of rapid developments

in war strategy and technology, it proved totally out of date as a defence system when Germany invaded France in 1940.

Many similar examples can be found in all parts of the business world— from oceangoing passenger lines to Swedish leather tanneries. Sometimes technological developments or changes in social and institutional conditions have knocked away the basis for a company's operations very suddenly. And there is nothing in the situation itself that might indicate a new path for the company to follow. Naturally there is always the possibility of escaping from a growth trap, but this calls for ability in genuine knowledge development, on a scale that the company has probably rarely had to show before. Life in the old, now vanished niche was too comfortable and there was little chance for such talents to sprout.

5.4 Summary

Our aim in this chapter has been to show that most companies are affected by natural driving forces and by the problems of growth. The driving forces we have discussed have all been built into the very nature of the company or its environment, and have been largely outside management's control. However, the successful management of a growing company often involves commanding a view of these driving forces and knowing how to make the most of them. We have discussed two main types of situation: on the one hand, when growth problems are caused by natural driving forces generating embryos of new business ideas; on the other, when growth problems are connected with the mature business idea (the problem of redefinition). In our examination of the growth problems of the individual mature business idea, we identified some typical growth patterns and redefinition strategies, using a simple model of the relationship between the company's operations and developments in the industry.

One kind of natural driving force is built into the technology or business idea. Another kind is due to various interdependencies in the external environment. In this connection we discussed particularly interdependencies among end-users. A third kind of driving force springs from disturbances and variations in the external environment, which can trigger off growth intended to stabilize the conditions under which the company has to operate. Finally, a fourth kind of driving force is connected with certain aspects of the power system and the value system in the external environment.

Although we have not specifically pointed it out, the reader may have noticed a theme that runs through the whole of this chapter: the natural driving forces can generally be described in terms of imbalance, *tension or misfit*. Thus, in analysing the mature business idea, for example, we started from the identification of misfits between the base for a company's dominance and certain crucial factors in the environment. And even the other driving forces that we identified—barriers to growth, byproducts, surplus resources and excess capacity, the stabilization of disturbances and variations, etc.—all have some kind of tension or imbalance in their make-up.

Could this mean that the handling of growth and growth problems is in fact a question of creating and exploiting imbalance and tension? We shall see later that management can use the creation and exploitation of tension not only to deal with natural driving forces, but also to induce driving forces where there are none.

CHAPTER 6

Learning and the Development of Knowledge

What kinds of knowledge are developed in a company? And how is the process affected by various features in the company's structure? These are some of the questions we shall examine in the following presentation of some of the more fundamental of the prevailing ideas about learning—ideas which we shall be trying to apply later in this study.

We shall tackle this subject from four angles. First, we shall look at the theory of learning and development in social systems which are in the process of emerging. We shall then turn to the case of the individual person and the entrepreneur: how do they learn? In a third section we shall consider the way in which certain features in the company's environment can affect the process of knowledge development. Finally, we shall discuss the relation between organizational structure and learning ability.

6.1 The 'new theory' of learning in social systems*

In recent years innovation and creation have been the subject of intensive speculation and, in some cases, of empirical study among social science researchers. All levels in the hierarchy of social systems have been included: the creativity of the individual, adaptability and innovativeness in business companies and other organizations, economic and technological renewal in industrialized and developing countries, etc. The problems vary according to the particular type of social system in focus; and the conclusions arrived at are far from unanimous. Nevertheless, some basic features in the process of renewal or innovation do appear to have been established. We can now look briefly at some of the interesting results to emerge from this research.

Kuhn's analysis of the development of science

In his book on scientific revolutions (1962), Kuhn has observed a cyclical pattern in the development of various fields of research. It appears that for a certain period every scientific field has been steered and developed on a basis of certain overriding assumptions—what Kuhn calls a 'paradigm'—and most scientific work has then been directed towards the further refinement of areas of knowledge defined by the paradigm. Kuhn calls this process of

*Any reader who finds this section a little too abstract can proceed direct to Section 6.2.

successive refinement 'normal problem-solving' or 'puzzle-solving'.

After a long period of this kind of normal problem-solving within the framework of a paradigm, however, there generally begins to be some indication that the fundamental assumptions no longer hold. Problem solutions based on the overriding paradigm seem to lead into blind alleys. They simply do not accord with the prevailing experience of reality. At first researchers often disregard this kind of deviant observation ('anomalies' in Kuhn's terminology), using more or less far-fetched arguments to explain them away or simply failing to report them because they threaten the fundamental frame of reference.

- By introducing a theory of mobile, transparent spheres to explain the observed movements of the planets, it was possible—at least for the time being—to rescue the theory of the earth as the central point of the universe.

After a while, however, the 'anomalies' will receive a new interpretation and will come to provide the seed of a new kind of 'extraordinary problem-solving'. One paradigm is replaced by another, and this represents a scientific revolution that overthrows the very bases on which established assumptions rest. A revolution of this type is not the result only of an intellectual reinterpretation of data; it has its roots in processes of other kinds as well. Much more than a mere theory is at stake: more or less the whole power structure of the scientific establishment, and the institutions which have been built up on a basis of the fundamental paradigm, are at risk. And even the individual researcher's feeling of identity, his emotional relationship with his work, is deeply affected. Thus Kuhn's observations of regeneration in the sciences clearly have much in common with our observations of what distinguishes reorientations from mere product variations in a business.

Schon on the process of creation

Schon (1963) uses a different approach and other terms; nevertheless he reaches similar conclusions. To him creation ('invention') is the result of a process by which an existing, established theory is used in a new or unknown situation to which it seems only partly applicable. This lack of consonance between the existing supply of knowledge—the established theory—and the new situation seems to be analogous with the anomalies described by Kuhn. Innovation occurs because people try to force some kind of agreement, or because they try to see correspondences in the new situation.

Buckley: the emergence of new social structures

Starting from general systems theory and sociology, Buckley (1967) points out the fundamental difference between 'homeostatic' change and 'morphogenetic' change. He also analyses those attributes of social institutions which provide the conditions for these two kinds of change process.

Homeostatic change is intended to defend and maintain a structure. It is characterized by the principle of negative feedback: the system tries to deal with deviations from the equilibrium or from a desired state by making adjustments in order to restore the balance. Deviation is met by *countermeasures*. Morphogenesis, on the other hand, involves a structural change and is characterized by the principle of positive feedback. Deviations from the equilibrium or from the expected state are interpreted as calling not for adjustments, but for structural change. Deviation is met by reinforcement in the shape of *supportive measures*. These deviations have their analogies in the observations of Kuhn and Schon.

To make this point quite clear, we can also look at a practical example of the difference between negative and positive feedback.

● A retail chain dealing in consumer capital goods has run into serious problems. During the last five years the company has been trying to achieve success using 'modern American advertising techniques'. The advertising budget has been greatly increased and the advertising department has expanded. Just as the company was on the verge of going into liquidation, we witnessed a confrontation between one of the few successful store managers and the advertising manager. According to the latter, the root of all the trouble was insufficient advertising; there had not been enough nor sufficiently sophisticated advertising campaigns. The store manager, on the other hand, was sceptical about the whole advertising argument and felt that other solutions should now be sought. He referred to the increasing variety of customer categories, and pointed out that several new distribution channels for the type of goods his company carried had now appeared. He had even carried out a little experiment: for a time he had sold a rather simple part of the product range at a street stall and this had been very successful. In his opinion this kind of thing should be considered and developed further.

The advertising manager looked at the problem and formulated his countermeasures exclusively within the frame of reference at present prevailing in the company. As far as he could see, the problem had arisen because the frame of reference had not been implemented with sufficient force. This was an example of negative feedback. The store manager had experienced certain things which led him to question the basic ideas behind the company's previous strategy, and he felt that this experience of his should be considered and applied more widely. This was an example of positive feedback. The differences are summarized in Figure 6.1.

Thus the decisive difference between negative and positive feedback lies in whether the problem is interpreted in terms of the *prevailing frame of reference* or *as an indication that this frame of reference needs changing*.

Kuhn, Schon and Buckley have given us several major insights into the actual process of innovation. But in Buckley's work we can also find clues about

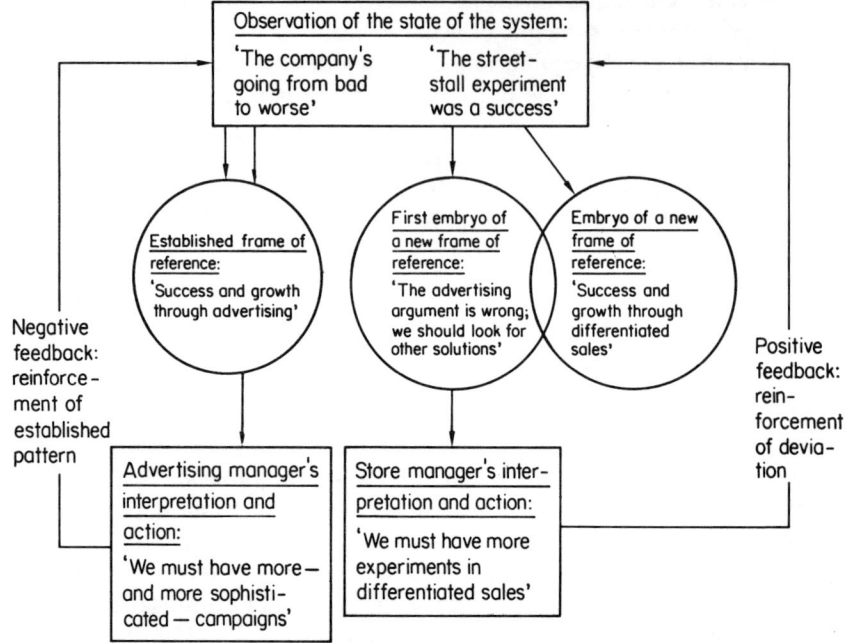

Figure 6.1. Positive and Negative Feedback—an Illustration

the functional and structural characteristics of the type of system that allows innovation to take place, or which even encourages it. According to Buckley, if a social system is to be able to apply the principle of positive feedback and to undergo structural change, the following conditions must be fulfilled:

- some degree of 'plasticity' and 'sensitivity' or *tension vis-à-vis* its environment such that it carries on a constant interchange with environmental events, acting on and reacting to them;
- some source or mechanism providing for *variety*, to act as a potential pool of adaptive variability to meet the problem of new or more detailed variety and constraints in a changeable environment;
- a set of *selective* criteria or mechanisms against which the 'variety pool' may be sifted into those variations in the organization or system that more closely match the environment and those that do not;
- an arrangement for *preserving and/or propagating* these 'successful' mappings.
(Buckley, 1967, p. 63)

Dunn on biological development and social learning

Starting from the biological analogy, Dunn (1971) has made an impressive attempt to summarize and extend the theory of social learning. He looks upon social learning as a process of 'evolutionary experimentation', during which stages of 'adaptive specialization' are replaced by stages of 'adaptive generalization'.

Adaptive specialization implies a refinement and development of the ability to live in and exploit a certain 'niche', while adaptive generalization implies that new 'adaptive zones' are made available to the system. Adaptive specialization involves refinement within given limits, while adaptive generalization changes the actual limits of the system's existence—it opens up an area of new opportunities for the individual or the species that is in the process of changing. Further, adaptive generalization tends to take place in a step-by-step process, beginning with a marginal adjustment or anticipatory adaptation to a new zone outside the original niche. This anticipatory adaptation is then reinforced by positive feedback (although Dunn does not use this particular term). Adaptive specialization and adaptive generalization are obviously analogous to Kuhn's 'normal problem-solving' and 'extraordinary problem-solving', to Buckley's 'homeostasis' and 'morphogenesis', and to our own concepts of 'product variation' and 'reorientation'.

The process of adaptive generalization—the structure-developing process— appears as a complex interaction between internal attributes of the system and events in the environment. The biological individual is characterized by a set of potential responses and action patterns which are determined by genetic characteristics and the individual's personal history. Most of these possible reaction patterns can, at any one moment, be regarded as latent. But in the individual's interaction with his environment, some of these potential characteristics are aroused and reinforced, while others become weaker. Dunn compares the individual and his environment to two sets of conditional probabilities which are interrelated and which provide conditions for each other's existence.

The marginal anticipatory adaptation that sets the structure-developing process in motion can be regarded as a kind of tension or disturbance of the equilibrium between the system and its environment. Thus far Dunn's and Buckley's descriptions agree, but at this stage an interesting difference in emphasis appears. Buckley draws a picture of a system or an organism which is at the mercy of its environment; the structure-developing process becomes essentially a process of adaptation. In Dunn the individual has a more active role.

When we see the effects of the operation of the phylogenetic process ... we can see that most of the factors leading to behavioral transformation are operating endogenous to the system. There is no evidence to support the notion that exogenous or orthogenetic forces are at work to establish a predetermined result for the process at any level. This is clearly not a manifestation of programmed learning. It is a creative learning process. (Dunn, 1971, p. 69)

Here we are obviously approaching a picture of a system or an organization which not only has the ability to change its structure when the environment so demands, but which can also itself take the *initiative* to its own structural change; the change takes on something of the nature of a planning process.

Dunn also tries to identify some of the conditions that are necessary if a system is to be able to undergo adaptive generalization, and he refers in this context to Simpson (1953). From Dunn (1971, p. 148) we can derive the following conditions:

A new adaptive zone outside the established niche must be available.

The system must have access to a kind of variety 'pool'. This pool must not be too narrow or specialized, but should embrace a relatively broad set of potential action alternatives or attributes.

The system should also embody some kind of relatively undifferentiated and unexploited structure which can be used in new functions, i.e. some resources of a general nature.

The last of these points at least—a question to which we shall return— implies something over and above the qualities previously described by Buckley.

When Dunn then looks at the literature of organization theory in order to find organizational structures which appear to agree with these requirements, he can discover very little and has not therefore much more to add. As an organization theorist, one is only too aware of the way this field has been disregarded.

6.2 The individual as bearer of a business idea

One observation we have made about business ideas developing in established companies and about new lines emerging in the shape of fresh companies is that a striking number of such ideas can be linked, at least in their first stages of development, with one particular person. There is therefore good reason to examine a little more closely the way individual people learn and develop business ideas, in order better to understand what kind of structure encourages the emergence of new ideas.

We shall call the person who develops a suggestion into a business idea, or at least into some kind of rudimentary activity, an *entrepreneur*. However, it is not necessary or even common for the entrepreneur himself to be responsible for igniting the first idea that sparks off the new line. In this section we shall discuss two questions that are important to ask about the entrepreneur and entrepreneurial ability: 'What motivates the entrepreneur and what forces drive him on?' and, 'How does the entrepreneur acquire the insight which eventually leads to a business idea?'

Enterprise as a personal strategy: the entrepreneur's motivation

Much research has been done into the background of the entrepreneur, but the many attempts to correlate enterprise with such factors as ethnic background, father's profession or the number of bankruptcies in a family have at best simply led to further questions without providing any insight into the process by which the motivational structure has been built up.

However, some other research leading more directly to such insights (Collins and Moore, 1964) has produced interesting results. Enterprise could be described as a *strategy* employed by an individual to get himself out of an impossible situation.* In the act of creation the entrepreneur tries to escape from conditions established at an earlier stage in his life and generally connected with complex relationships between himself and his parents. Perhaps, too, the businessman who runs a company or develops a business idea with real creative drive is trying to make up for some lack in himself or to find an outlet for some tension in his personality. One interpretation of our own observations, albeit perhaps a bold one, might be that the businessman who is fired by this kind of compensatory drive will often look at his environment in terms of the opportunities for enterprise that it might provide.

Theories of this kind seem able to explain the emergence of the entrepreneur better than those theories which try to establish some kind of link between enterprise and diverse external conditions. On the other hand, there are good grounds for supposing that various external factors are decisive to any understanding of the individual learning process or, in other words, of the way the actual content of the entrepreneurial strategy takes shape.

The slow, laborious learning of a particular business idea

Among the entrepreneurs whom we have come across we shall distinguish here between two types: those who seem to be predestined to learn one particular type of business idea to the exclusion of any other, and those who acquire in a more general way some kind of non-specific talent for enterprise.

The Swedish writer Olivecrona has described the case of Ahl (known familiarly as Kapp-Ahl, or 'Ahl of the coats'), which provides a good example of the slow build-up of a business idea in a series of small, systematic steps:

> ... then it was time for him to do his military service. In the army he made friends with a bookseller, and when the young men had finished their service Kapp-Ahl joined his friend in selling. He had a collection of his own and went off as a door-to-door salesman ... About six months later he got a job as travelling salesman for a furniture manufacturer in his home town ... During this period he came in contact with a furrier and began to sell furs as a sideline. Together with a friend he established the company of Andersson & Karlsson ... His fur sales led to his appointment as travelling salesman for Sommens Mössfabrik, dealing in hats, caps and furs.
> ... while he was with this firm, and with their approval, he started a

*This argument resembles Bateson's description of schizophrenia as a strategy enabling a man to live with an impossible situation (Bateson, 1972).

company of his own ... in Gothenburg, selling coats at the weekends—coats which he bought up cheap from various manufacturers. To begin with he just sold to women he knew, and his prices were well below those in the stores. News of the cheap coats spread, and to stimulate sales even further a kind of commission of 10 kronor was given to any customer who introduced a new customer. In the end the coats occupied most of the space in Ahl's home, and when he and his wife were expecting visitors for Christmas in 1952, they had to do something about finding room for them. Britt-Marie Ahl had seen an advertisement about a basement at Omvägen in Gothenburg which sounded suitable as a warehouse. They rented it and took their stocks over there. People in the neighbouring houses stood watching while piles of coats were carried into the basement, and it was not long before someone knocked on the door to ask whether she could buy a coat. 'Naturally', was the answer, and soon more people arrived.

At that point Ahl happened to have a particularly large stock of coats. He had bought them at bargain prices from some manufacturers who had made a wrong calculation and left themselves with a great many finished coats which they couldn't sell through the usual channels. Ahl exploited this situation and sold the coats at sensationally low prices. Even so, some of the coats had cost him so little that they still gave him a considerable profit margin. News of the cheap coats spread quickly. Ahl even put out a small advertisement, and soon queues began to form outside the basement on Omvägen. The Gothenburg press got to hear of it, and soon he was being called Kapp-Ahl ('Ahl of the coats'). A couple of sales assistants were taken on, but the business was not yet big enough for him to dare to leave his job at the factory. It was about another eighteen months before he took that step. By this time his business had swollen ... Bus-loads of eager buyers began to arrive from all over the west of Sweden ... Kapp-Ahl was content with a lower mark-up per coat, which was possible mainly because his fixed overheads were so low. The rent of the basement was 50 kronor a month, and his stocks were still small enough to be housed there.

But now his competitors began to wake up ... He was regarded as a pirate, ignoring all existing agreements on restrictions of competition ... people wanted to stop him at any price...

Despite the opposition, sales continued to grow. In the end there were sixteen assistants working in the little basement, and annual turnover was up to a couple of million kronor. The difficulties lay chiefly in the limited sales space, and in all the surreptitious manoeuvres necessary to get timid manufacturers to sell to him. The goods had to be fetched in anonymous vehicles, trademarks had to be removed, etc. After three years at Omvägen, it was obvious that further expansion was impossible without new premises. Kapp-Ahl found a suitable place on Allégatan in Gothenburg and the crowds soon flocked there as well.

Encouraged by his success he was soon buying larger and larger consign-

ments. In the end he found himself sitting with stocks that were far too big for the two premises. He had overstocked, and a crisis threatened. Kapp-Ahl solved the problem by starting mobile sales ... Despite everything this was a success, and the economic situation improved enough to allow further expansion of the chain of stores.
(Olivecrona, 1970, pp. 31–35. Our translation)

Thus we have here an original undeveloped idea that was successively added to and perhaps even altered so that the final shape of the business idea was something quite different—or far more—than the entrepreneur could have envisaged from the beginning, although the process was nevertheless characterized by a certain amount of continuity. One ingredient which often recurs in this kind of story is the importance of the organized opposition that meets the new business idea early in its life.

The general entrepreneur

In certain cases, however, the development of the new business idea assumes quite another character and is characterized instead by the individual's sudden discovery of new patterns or new correspondences between a number of disparate elements. Here, too, there is of course some kind of continuous development, but this can only be identified in retrospect; although the subelements of which the new business idea consists can all be traced back and identified in the past, only at a certain point are they combined in a new and unique way.

This is the way a certain aerial photography operation, which gradually evolved to become an international company, originally started.

- In this case the entrepreneur had a pretty varied background, with experience and training from such varied fields as film camera work, flying and navigation. Nor had he ever missed an opportunity to try out his skill as a salesman and negotiator. His first real managerial post was as head of a car sales firm about 100 kilometres from Stockholm. This was the first time he had men under him, the first time he had to provide others with an incentive to work. Just before he took this job as local manager, he had bought himself a secondhand aeroplane, so that he was able to go on living in Stockholm and fly to work every day.

  After a couple of years as a reasonably successful branch manager, an idea suddenly took shape: it should be possible to run a business based on aerial colour photography, although photographic techniques—and particularly all colour photography—were still pretty undeveloped at the time. Our entrepreneur tells of his sudden realization of how different things he had learnt could be combined—'I had learnt all the ingredients, and it was simply a question of putting them together; I knew about flying, I could sell to ordinary people, I knew about photography and had even fiddled around a little with technical developments on that side, and I had learnt how to make people work and how to organize an operation'.

And so he embarked on a period of experimentation, during which certain crucial aspects of the business idea were developed. Approach flying, in particular, proved a difficult problem to solve; but it was also an essential one, since only in this way could the inadequate photographing techniques be compensated for: 'In the end I left my earlier job on favourable terms. I bought six small cars from the firm, I found some people, and we got going ... Gradually I discovered that there were lots of things I had completely forgotten about—first and foremost, the accounting system. In the big company I'd worked for before, all that was dealt with automatically at head office, and it had never even occurred to me that there was such a thing as an accounting system. Now I had to learn about that too...'.

What is the difference between a business idea that develops gradually as a result of a systematic process of learning and experimentation, and one that arises in this comparatively sudden way? The entrepreneurs behind the ideas are not necessarily altogether unlike one another, but in our experience there are nevertheless some differences. The first type of entrepreneur has passed through a learning process, and what is the result? He has learnt *one* business *idea*. And very often a man who has developed a business idea in this way, and who has gained a reputation of being entrepreneurial, will completely fail if he embarks on some other operation.

But in the case of the general entrepreneur this does not happen, and the explanation seems to be that he has undergone a kind of basic schooling in enterprise—an education that precedes the learning of concrete business ideas. If the entrepreneur has already gone through this basic schooling, he will also be able to develop individual business ideas much more quickly.

The basic schooling of the entrepreneur

The life stories of the general entrepreneurs often include episodes like this one, which was told to us by a client.

- My business career really started before I even went to school, when I began to think it was silly to be given money by my parents which I then used for buying them Christmas presents. I went into NK, a large department store in Stockholm, and bought some big packs of Christmas cards. I then went and stood by the exit, selling the cards at a good profit to the passers by.

Olivecrona (1970) tells us how many very successful businessmen started their careers by running some extremely simple operation: buying and selling pencils, caps or other uncomplicated products.

It seems probable that such early commercial activities may reinforce certain characteristics in the individual's make-up, giving him in some respects more confidence in himself. He also learns more about his own ability to negotiate and interact with other people, and about the effect that he has on others.*

To get others to grow—or to eliminate them

An important element in the entrepreneur's schooling is learning how to use other people. In the early stages of a new business idea relations between the entrepreneur and his environment may be marred by several unpleasant features. 'Biting the hand that feeds him' and 'getting rid of partners' are examples of what Collins and Moore (1964) consider to be important elements in the entrepreneur's general education. In fact the very word 'enterprise' is associated in our minds with the idea of exploiting the environment.

At later stages in the development of operations, on the other hand, it is extremely important to get people other than the entrepreneur or leader himself to grow and learn. In fact we believe that this is one of the most important elements in the art of handling growth. Talking to a managing director who had been very much involved in building up his present company, we were told of the following episode.

- At that time our operations were pretty small, perhaps about twenty employees. I remember that we were particularly bothered by problems in the packaging department, which was constantly overloaded with work and where there was a lot of overtime. One day one of the lads there was ill, and for some reason or other I decided to take over myself and see how the whole thing worked. At five o'clock, when the other chap went home, I stayed and went on working. In fact I stayed the whole night.

  In the morning when both members of the packaging department returned, I told one of them he could go home again—one person in the department was enough, and even he would have time for other jobs as well. You see, during the night I experimented and discovered a new way of running the department which made it possible to save labour. So I taught the system to one of the men, and it worked beautifully—it saved lots of money.

The same managing director recounted several other episodes showing the relationship between himself and his immediate bosses and other colleagues in the now quite large company. One particular pattern seems to have recurred continually. He has a way of 'extending his grip' through others, which has always followed the same sequence: first he familiarizes himself thoroughly with a situation and develops a system for dealing with it; then he instructs his colleagues and sees that they follow his system.

Our friend was obviously quite unaware that this was how he worked,

*Or what Collins and Moore (1964) have called 'the transactional mode of interpersonal relations'.

and we were able to examine together with him the consequences of his method. As the company grew it became increasingly difficult for him to work out all solutions himself and issue instructions on all questions. At the same time he had never really learnt to trust his colleagues' ability to work anything out for themselves. In fact unconsciously he had become afraid that his colleagues might initiate activities in the company which would not be known to him in all their detail and over which he would have no control.

Another case provided me with an example of a sudden revolutionary change in an executive's attitude towards his colleagues and their ability to grow.

● This particular business leader was a true entrepreneur who had built up a very successful company. In fact it was now so big that it needed a new strongly decentralized organizational structure, and such a structure was about to be introduced. The first meeting of the new, larger management group was due and the chief executive came to me a day or two before, admitting to a certain anxiety. He was quite sure that his colleagues would want to be told how to act on a number of important matters, and he realized that he did not have answers to all the questions that would come up. At the same time he was eager, as usual, to appear self-assured.

To his way of thinking the suggestion I made was a radical one. I advised him, as an experiment, to lie low, give his lack of confidence a free rein, and see what happened. After great hesitation he decided to follow this strategy, and discovered that the group represented a body of opinion and knowhow on a scale he had never expected. Instead of losing face, as he was afraid he might do, he soon gained a reputation as a man who was able to get the very best out of his team.

6.3 The company's 'choice' of environment as a factor in its learning

In Chapter 5 we discussed some of the natural driving forces which are 'embodied' in the company's environment. Management has not very much control over factors of this kind. It may perhaps be able, with varying degrees of skill, to exploit them and adapt to them; but the factors are still there.

Social psychology has shown us that personality is to a great extent a concomitant of the expectations that are directed towards the particular individual.* Referring above to Dunn and his theory of learning and development, we also suggested that organisms are capable of taking positive action, not simply playing a passive role, in their relations with their environment.

This gives us some of the theoretical background to an observation we have made and which we shall analyse in more detail below, namely, that the company's environment embraces many elements; among these elements the company will 'choose' some to interact with (= to have some sort of relation-

*Cf. Mead (1934).

ship with); *the way it handles this 'choice' has considerable impact on the process of growth and knowledge development in the company and therefore represents a means of exerting control over this process.*

As the company passes through different stages of development, this choice should also be revised. In my opinion the fact that organizations fail to take this into account is often the main reason for the failure to develop satisfactory models for describing the external environment. Thus the stakeholder model (cf. Rhenman, 1968) is well able to mirror the problems and major decisions that are connected with a company's exchange process (i.e. in mature phases of development), but it hardly contains any factors relevant to an understanding of the learning process. A language which could be used to describe the company's environment and which would be suited to this second process needs to consider factors such as the development of knowledge in the environment, misfits in the environment, sources of conflicting demands and values, etc.

According to the learning theory we have presented above, a company's ability to learn should increase to the extent it is able to augment its pool of available variety; in other words, as far as it can increase, for example, the set of impulses, demands and ideas to which it is exposed. At a mature stage of development organizations try to direct their attention towards a segment of the environment that is as homogeneous as possible; in fact in the stabilization phase they even try to make the segment more homogeneous than it already is (cf. Rhenman, 1973; Galbraith, 1967) so that they can exploit their business ideas even more efficiently. On the other hand, it is often useful to look for an environment that is as difficult, demanding and variegated as possible at earlier stages of growth when the learning process dominates.

• At the Centre d'Etudes Industrielles in Switzerland a study has been made of European companies which have tried to establish operations in the USA; the study also follows up what has happened to them. The pharmaceutical industry is one of those that have been examined. Many European companies in this industry have tried to start up in the USA since the war.

Most of the first attempts ended in failure. The companies were not advanced enough for the American market which—for good or bad—was in many respects more developed than the European market: mental illness is considerably more common there, diseases which rarely occur in Europe are widely treated in the USA, and so on. Many of the products supplied by the European pharmaceutical companies were therefore unsuited to the American market—they were just not particularly relevant to the quite different pattern of disease in American society.

In the light of this experience several companies withdrew, others stayed put and made losses, and some have established their own development centres in the USA in order to learn the American market. Among these last are some which have managed to become competitive on the

US market, with the interesting result that after a while they have been able to 're-export' their American knowhow; they are now superior on the European market to the companies which remained behind in Europe.*

The complexity of the market, or the difficulty involved in satisfying a customer, seems to provide an extremely important incentive to growth in a company. In SIAR, for example, we often find we do our best work and produce our most valuable research working for clients of high intelligence who make great demands upon us. A study of the way some large Swedish companies have evolved illustrates this: it shows how decisively a particularly demanding and competent customer (the National Swedish Telecommunication Administration) once affected the development of knowledge in L.M. Ericsson. A great many similar examples could be mentioned, but we will content ourselves with pointing out that contact with the client system or with the market at an early stage in a development process represents an important impulse and a source of indispensable knowledge for any company intending to develop new complex systems.†

It should be pointed out that 'choosing its environment' is a very important matter on which a company's leaders have to make a decision. Any company that hopes to evolve to an advanced level but neglects to seek out difficult and demanding environments has little chance of succeeding in its aim.

- We found that in public and private organizations in the Swedish building sector people often refuse systematically to integrate with individuals or organs regarded as 'difficult'. Although theoretically these organizations have been making great efforts to develop relevant knowledge, in fact they have been getting more and more out of touch. In the end they have lost the ability to innovate altogether.

By involving itself in a diversified, complicated and demanding environment, a company hastens the development of knowledge within itself and increases the likelihood that it will be able to adapt its structure to a variety of situations.

- Universal Wholesalers were presented with a potentially important operation more or less gratis. It would involve a certain amount of systems selling to developing countries and would be financed from UN funds. But operations never really got off the ground; the company just supplied what was ordered but took no steps to learn what the market was really like and who were really the purchasers.

- In the public sector in Sweden the Housing Board provides an example of how certain values that underpinned the design of the original organiza-

*Source: lecture by Lawrence G. Franko, Yxtaholm, Autumn 1972.
†Cf. also Olofsson (1969).

tion later came to dominate learning and the development of knowledge altogether, with the result that these processes lost their way or ground to a halt. In the 1940s the Board was established chiefly as a defence organization to support the consumers against possibly ignorant and badly trained architects, inadequate financing institutes and private speculators. Because, right from the beginning, the organization had defined its enemies so specifically and had 'isolated' them, it failed to see that a very great deal of the knowledge being developed in the external environment came in time to be lodged with the better-educated architects, with certain progressive proprietors and, not least, with a number of clever and innovative building contractors. The Housing Board continued to develop knowledge that ultimately proved irrelevant (new loan regulations, new quality norms, etc.), without realizing that the problems of the Swedish housing sector had been slowly changing, and without using or even noticing the knowledge being developed in other quarters.

6.4 Learning as a function of organizational structure

Learning geared to specialities or wholes

Companies designed around a single business idea are generally organized in functions, as in Figure 6.2, for example. In this kind of structure the top men are specialists, each in his own function: production, marketing, administration, and so on. In a functional organization learning also tends to be specialist-oriented, because the problems that arise are often classified according to the existing functional areas. They are regarded as production problems, sales problems, etc.

But we have already seen that companies can rarely remain in existence for any length of time without natural driving forces in the organization or in its environment making necessary some kind of redefinition of the business idea, or even generating feelers which could be developed into new business ideas. In such cases the functional structure is often an obstacle to the correct interpretation of the new situation or to the development of feelers.

• Provisions Ltd traditionally carried a small number of raw-material-intensive and production-intensive products which provided the base for its operations. And in the company the technologists predominated.

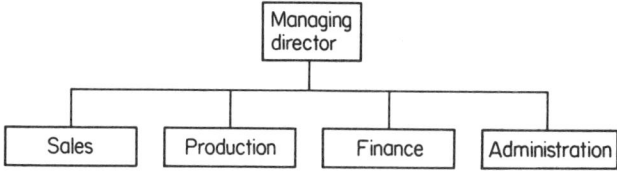

Figure 6.2. Functional Organization Structure

Gradually, as a result of interdependencies on the market and without ever really planning to, the company entered a number of new fields, among others the catering market, the market for frozen products, the market for delicatessen food, and the market for precooked food. The export side was also being built up. The range of products increased enormously, and the company had a great many factories whose production varied, at least in part, although there was also some internal interdependence (i.e. semi-manufactures were bought and sold internally and seasonal variations in capacity utilization were ironed out). On the marketing side the company now had dealings with many different kinds of customer.

This increasingly complex structure within the framework of the functional organization led to a whole series of difficulties in the coordination of activities. We discovered that top management spent 80 per cent of its time discussing questions of coordination and short-run resource priorities. The marketing staff had grown enormously to deal with these problems, and the technical staff even more so. Conflict between the technologists and the salesmen—the former thought the latter were making unreasonable demands and the latter thought the former were being inflexible and ignorant of the real demands—was growing all the time.

Because of the structure of Provisions Ltd, problems and stimuli were interpreted in terms of specialist functions. On the other hand, nobody was really interested in *wholes* (in terms of embryos of new business ideas). Instead of concentrating on ways of growing on the catering market, learning was geared to the solution of planning problems in production and sales.

An increase in the level of conflict in a company is often a sign that the formal structure no longer fits the company's growth situation.

- In Swedish Building Materials Ltd violent conflict was gradually building up between the sales side and the production side as the new tailor-made business idea emerged alongside the old mass-production operations, and the functional organization structure remained unchanged.

- We have already described above how, since the Mining and Processing Company was operating between two systems (one on the supply and one on the selling side) that were subject to violent fluctuations, a crucial feature of the company's business idea was its ability to command knowhow on both the production and the sales sides. But as a result of the company's structure (with its focus on specialized functions), leaders possessing these two kinds of knowhow were not appearing. Thus nobody in the company really commanded a total view of the whole business idea. This situation was further aggravated by the design of the budget system. The main demand which the sales manager had to fulfil was to keep within his sales budget; the production manager came to centre on conflicts connected with the demands they made on each other. The production manager expected things of the sales manager that made it difficult for the latter to keep within his budget, and *vice versa*. Instead of concentrating on the integration of the various types of knowledge required for an efficient exploitation of the business idea, the interaction between the sales manager and the production manager centred on the conflict between them.

The embryos of new business ideas often find it difficult to assume full form in functional organization structures. The embryos are probably seen as a disturbing element, and the division of responsibility obstructs the kind of overall view which is generally necessary if a feeler is to have any chance of going further.

In companies which are nurturing a variety of business ideas, a breakdown of the specialist-oriented structure and the subordination of the organization to a structure geared to a business idea seems appropriate. In this kind of structure, areas of responsibility reflect ensembles in the shape of business ideas or feelers which have been detached from the established operations. The divisionalized organization provides an example of this kind of structure (Figure 6.3).

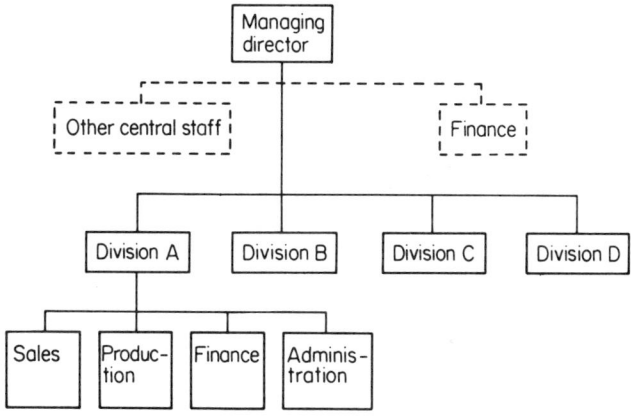

Figure 6.3. Example of a Divisional Organization

However, a divisionalized structure cannot always reflect such things as the complicated interdependencies between different parts of a company's operations. Consumer Services Ltd provides an example of this.

● Consumer Services Ltd had a functionally organized head office, but operated in six very different regions. Because of variations in competition, culture, demographic conditions and climate, the regions really resembled one another very little. Furthermore our analysis showed that the company's products fell into three groups of basically different kinds, which could with justification be described as three different business ideas.

It was obviously necessary for the company to replace its central functionalized structure by a structure geared to the different business ideas. However, the problem was that the company did not simply have three business ideas: it had eighteen, three in each region! How can you design an organization to mirror such complexity? The organizational structure must allow knowledge of regional differences *and* knowledge of the three special ranges to have some influence on the shape of the company's operations.

The solution was a matrix organization as shown in Figure 6.4. The central division of responsibility according to function was broken down and replaced by a structure which included six regional heads responsible for profitability and development and three central sector managers who were responsible for profitability and development within their own range of products throughout the organization. The purchasing department was broken down and placed under the sector managers, and more or less the same was done to the other service organs. The budget system was designed so that sector managers and regional heads *together* were responsible for results and for developments in the respective boxes in the matrix, and the managing director emphasized that he would be expecting results in future from these pairs of decision-makers rather than from each decision-maker separately.

In Consumer Services Ltd learning had to be directed towards each one of the eighteen ensembles. This meant that knowledge about different product ranges and different regions had to be integrated, and the organization was therefore designed to reflect the need for a confrontation between these two types of knowledge. And it was soon apparent that knowledge of the individual regions and the different product ranges was growing, and that the ability to combine these two types of knowledge was increasing satisfactorily.

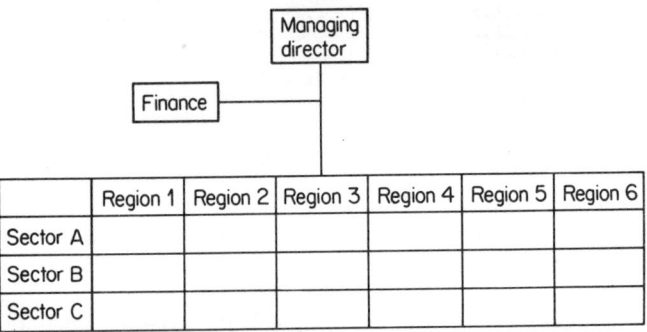

Figure 6.4. The Matrix Organization in Consumer Services Ltd

We shall see later how important it is that a creative management is aware of the kind of knowledge that needs to be developed. It must also have some idea about how to develop this knowledge and how to see that the necessary 'knowledge-development technology' is mapped into the organizational structure.

Structures that impoverish and structures that enrich

There is a strong connection between the organizational structure of a company and its ability to grow. There is also a strong connection between a company's predilection for learning and the individual's opportunities for personal learning and development.

The bureaucratic organizational structure does little to develop the individual; it offers little opportunity for individual initiative and its major requirement is that its members should follow the rules. We have come across organizations—perhaps mostly in the public administration, but also in some large corporations—that almost seem to have been designed intentionally to produce in their members a sort of intellectual—even emotional—impoverishment or apathy. For the individual person this kind of structure provides a thoroughly bad working environment—at least if we give this concept a rather broader interpretation than usual. Some of the mechanisms whereby the centralized and bureaucratic structure generates this kind of impoverishment are illustrated in Figure 6.5, which is taken from a study of public control system in the housing sector (Normann, 1972).

But empirical studies have also been made of structures that do encourage personal initiative and provide people with good opportunities for self-actualization. Such structures have a more organic character, in other words they are less strictly formalized than the bureaucratic or mechanistic* structures, and the demands they make upon the individual are often more general and diffuse. In companies with this type of structure we have often found swarms of new ideas and suggested changes.

Although the organic structure may appear extremely attractive on both ethical and other grounds, we should not simply accept it as the only alternative to the strictly formalized structure. Most companies in fact represent intermediate forms. Too much volition, too little discipline and too little control can often be the reason for the failure of a company at the market-penetration and stabilization stage. And in any case there must be some way of providing the learning and innovativeness of the members with a direction. A feature that distinguished several of the successful companies in our material—and which we sometimes even tried to implant—was an ability to grow between periods of lesser and greater control. One example was provided by Consumer Services Ltd, whose organizational change we have just described.

- Consumer Services Ltd had operated under comparatively strict control and had a rational approach to operations; this had also been very successful. But management was aware that a revision of the business idea—a kind of process of redefinition—would be necessary in the long run.

*The expressions 'organic' and 'mechanistic' structure are taken from Burns and Stalker (1961).

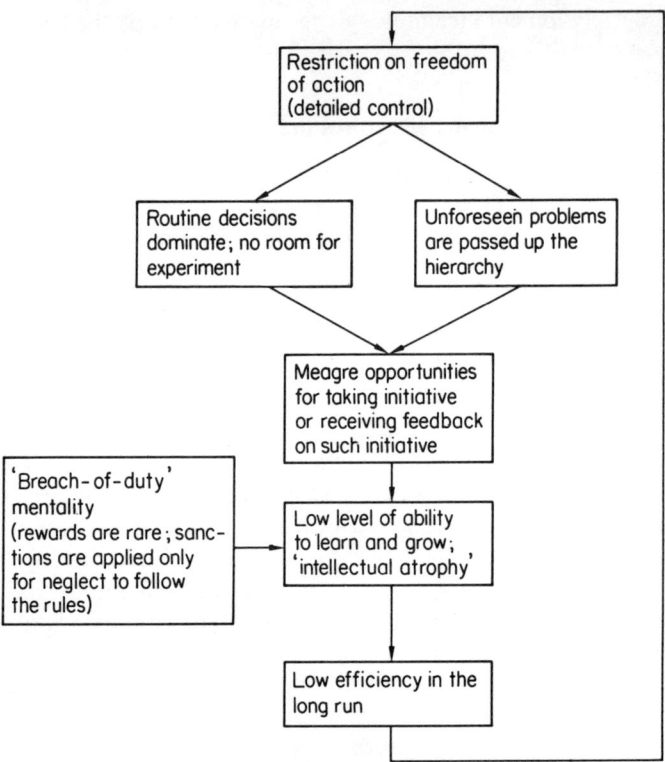

Figure 6.5. Some Mechanisms that Block the Individual's Opportunities to Grow and Which Therefore Gradually Impoverish Him (Normann, 1972, p. 109)

However, when faced with a need to redefine its ideas, the company found that very little in the way of new ideas or suggestions emerged. Management was prepared to support and select among interesting experiments, but no material was provided for them to select from or support. When substantial decentralization was introduced, it was therefore partly to encourage ideas to sprout all over the place, so there would eventually be something to pick from.

And, sure enough, when a meeting was held a year after the reorganization to see what had happened, several seedlings had in fact begun to send out shoots here and there. The new structure had created a pool of variety. The next step was to create mechanisms for handling it.

This way of creating a new variety in an inflexible and homogeneous organizaion has several advocates.

Great disorder in the country leads to great order. And again and again, every seventh or eight year.
(Maotse-Tung)

Control systems that obstruct growth and the penetration of markets

We have mentioned some of the mechanisms by which organizational structures—in particular functional structures—can prevent feelers from being fully developed into new business ideas. Another observation associated with this is that the way the control system of a company is designed will greatly affect the transition of lines of business from one stage of development to another: for example, to move on from the feeler stage and to start the development of a system; or, when a superior system has been developed, to carry it into the stage of market penetration.

In the International Chemical Corporation (ICC) we found an example of the way in which a control system could, by the way it was designed, prevent the extension of business ideas.

- On the domestic market ICC was organized in a number of product companies, each of which had its own organizations for development, production and sales. A couple of these product companies were extremely successful, and had created products which were clearly a hit on the international market. Internationally, ICC consisted of a number of regional multiproduct companies, each of which operated as a profit centre. Relations between the Swedish product companies and the international regional companies were regulated by a system of discount prices. This meant that the product managers of the Swedish companies felt there was little to gain from sales abroad; they became more interested in reinforcing their grip on the Swedish market and in developing new products than in directing their resources towards the penetration of the international market. This stage was therefore hindered and delayed.

In a company with a divisionalized organization it is theoretically possible to differentiate the demands made on the various divisions; in our experience, however, this possibility is surprisingly rarely exploited. All too commonly, the demands are of a very general nature—'a 15 per cent return on invested capital', for example—and no attention is paid to the stage of development which the particular operation has reached. As we have already discussed, it is not until an operation arrives at a mature stage of development that it can be expected to generate more liquid assets than it needs for its own growth. In many cases we have seen how undifferentiated demands for a certain return on capital have effectively aborted various potentially promising lines at the systems-development or market-penetration stages. Since these operations were never really allowed to get off the ground, they were never able to reach the stage where they might have yielded a real return. Investment is rarely wholehearted enough, since the divisional head has to strike a balance between the somewhat unimaginative demands of corporate management and the demands of the actual situation.

Even worse are the cases—which unfortunately are not rare—in which year after year certain fixed returns are formally required, although the various operations show nothing like those results and are not even developing in that direction. Such a discrepancy in a corporation quickly undermines morale and makes it difficult to impose genuine demands. We have found that corporate managements all too seldom employ the other kinds of demand that in fact would be possible: plans to develop resources perhaps, or development results, or market shares during a penetration phase. This generally reflects nothing more than a failure to identify the demands that are relevant to different stages of development, or a certain fear of trying to measure efficiency in terms which are less measurable and which therefore call for an open and more intensive interaction between divisional heads and corporate management.

Another common problem connected with the transition of a business idea from one stage to another is that a company's dominating ideas and values are geared too singlemindedly to rewarding one particular type of behaviour or performance.

● Heavy Conglomerates Ltd worked in an extremely interesting technology with many built-in driving forces that could generate new business ideas. The company was also very successful in creating feelers and advancing them a little along the way. Somebody said, for example, 'We are very good at taking care of an idea and nursing it along to a pilot plant'.

But the many feelers seldom led to anything more than the embryos of new business ideas. There appeared to be three main reasons for this. First, there was a functional organization which did not educate entrepreneurs interested in potentially new ideas and which tried to impose traditional control systms and economic evaluations on the new lines of business. Secondly, the technology-centred parent company had long been committed to technical excellence, upholding norms that directed attention towards scientific merit and elegant theoretical solutions to difficult technological problems rather than towards doing business in the true sense. And, lastly, the demands imposed on the feeler operations by management were often the wrong ones and were usually too weak.

Reward systems and entrepreneurs

It has struck us many times that the difference between companies where the ability to learn and to develop business ideas stands high and others where this ability is low can often be traced back to the design of the reward system.*
One decisive difference appears to be linked to the principle according to which rewards are given. Is it successful interaction with the external environment in the solving of problems arising in the company's relations with this environment? Or is it, essentially, adaptation to rules and

*The concept of the reward system is used here in a wide sense and includes, apart from concrete rewards, also career opportunities, opportunities for group membership, professional recognition, etc.

norms or the acquisition of some unique competence within narrow specialized limits? There seem to be several reasons why this difference in the structure of the reward system is so important.

One is that the first type of reward encourages the emergence of entrepreneurs and businessmen with 'overall views', since in such a system learning is focused on real life, on whole problem areas instead of on more or less artificial disciplines. The universities provide us with examples of the latter type of reward system; their main problem, as is well known, is that the complex problem structure of real life is not matched in the specialized departments of the university.

But the decisive difference is that an 'environment-oriented' reward system tends to make the total supply of rewards dependent on the amount of 'entrepreneurship', since the rewards are generated by the ability to handle the external environment; the supply of rewards in the introverted reward system, on the other hand, is generally relatively finite. In the first case we are dealing with a 'plus sum game', where the total supply of rewards can be increased, and in the other case with a 'zero sum game', where the supply of rewards is finite.

- The difference can be illustrated by a comparison between a successful manufacturing company and a university faculty. In the manufacturing company, the man who works up a new line of business can achieve considerable personal reward, without thus decreasing the supply of rewards available for the other people in the company. Theoretically anyone who has the ability can appoint himself 'professor'. In the university faculty the number of positions is generally finite; nor are the positions geared in the first place to an ability to deal with the external environment. In a reward system with a finite supply of rewards the efforts of the individuals involved, and their relations to each other, can evolve into an internal political struggle rather than a struggle against the environment.

This example illustrates two extremes, but it should be mentioned that we have come across several manufacturing companies that closely resemble the university described above.

A reward system that is linked to the company's ability to interact with its environment directs interest towards external contacts and towards the development of knowledge about the environment. A finite supply of rewards, on the other hand, tends to render the external environment uninteresting in a rewards context. There is no stimulus to learn about the surrounding system. Figure 6.6 illustrates the relation between the principle according to which rewards are given, the supply of rewards, and the company's learning ability.

Organizational structure and learning—a summary

We have been examining different ways in which the company's structure

Principle according to which rewards are given	Finite supply of rewards	Supply of rewards dependent on what you accomplish in the environment
Conformity and ability to follow internal rules and principles	'Zero sum game' Company with little ability to learn about the external environment	
Problem-solving in relation to the external environment		'Plus sum game' Company with a high ability to learn about the external environment

Figure 6.6

can affect learning. We have seen that the design of the organization can direct learning towards specialist skills or knowhow or towards wholes or ensembles; the company must alternate between organic and mechanistic structures at different stages of development; and that control systems—among others the system of rewards—affect the learning in the company.

The effect of the organizational structure on the type and degree of learning appears to operate by means of several intermediate factors or subprocesses which are intimately connected with one another. First, the structure can *focus the attention*; in other words, it defines the problems with which various individuals will be faced and which they will be supposed to be responsible for solving. Secondly, the structure provides the framework within which different kinds of problems and knowledge will come into confrontation with one another; in other words, it defines *the arena in which such confrontations take place, an arena in which knowledge interacts with knowledge*. Thirdly, the structure also supplies a *reward system*; it motivates and directs the individual's efforts to define and solve problems. Figure 6.7 illustrates these relationships.

But at the same time the company's structure is closely linked to the company's dominating ideas which, as we have previously declared, are to a great extent a function of the company's historical and present learning (in a relationship that is also illustrated in Figure 6.7).

Thus the dominating ideas appear to have landed in a circle where they tend to repeat and reproduce themselves. At the same time, however, we know that the system of dominating ideas in the company need not be stable. It can be changed, sometimes quite quickly. Random factors and natural driving forces in the company and in the industry can cause a shift in the dominating ideas and thus also a change in the learning that takes place.

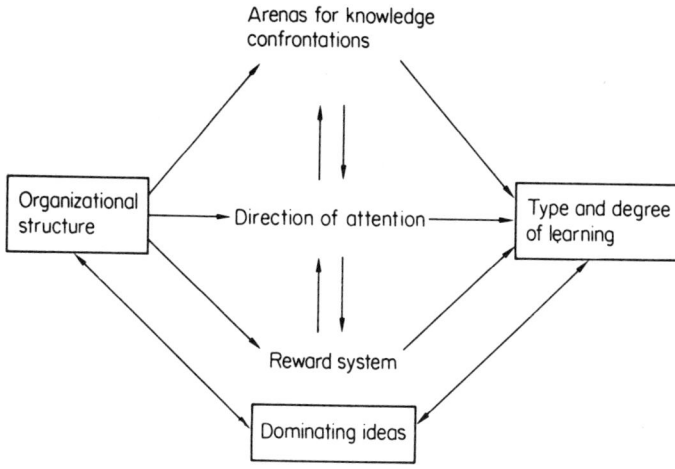

Figure 6.7. Some Factors that Steer Learning in a Company

However, there is another factor which can break the circle and change the learning and the dominating ideas, *namely, the existence of dominating ideas concerned with the 'way of learning' and the 'way of changing'* which are essentially different from dominating ideas concerned with the way of making money, which we have been talking of so far. The management which wants to control the company's growth—rather than simply going along with the natural driving forces—must be able to handle such idea systems and to superimpose them on idea systems geared to the way of making money.

In the following chapters we shall devote most of our attention to ideas systems of this kind and shall try to find out how they can be embodied in the organization.

CHAPTER 7

The Company's Growth Idea

The term *business idea* has been used to designate the system which endows the company with efficiency in its exchange process. The business idea implies harmony and consonance between a number of factors inside and outside the company which constitute a specific and relatively stable structure in support of the exchange process. The business idea also provides the company with an important planning tool, since any action taken should fit the business idea and should be intended to support and develop the idea further.

We would now like to examine another similar concept, providing this time a tool for planning in the development process, i.e. the process which leads to the emergence of the business idea. Just as every effective exchange process is linked to a concrete business idea, so every growth or development process can be translated into a specific *growth idea*. In many ways, however, describing the growth idea seems to be more difficult, since we are now dealing with a process whose outcome—an emergent business idea at different stages of development—is continually changing, whereas the exchange process consists of a series of repeated and essentially similar transactions. The approach to planning and the kind of structure which provides the background for the growth process must therefore differ radically from the planning and structure that are suitable to the exchange process.

In analysing the concept of the growth idea we shall approach the subject from several angles. We shall describe the various ingredients in the process and some of the features that should be present in an environment that favours its success. We shall quote from our personal experience of the way companies do actually grow, and we shall refer to various elements in the theories of learning and development described in earlier chapters.

In Chapter 4 we discussed different planning philosophies and the way in which planning problems change during a growth cycle. We claimed that the 'process view' rather than the 'goal view' should imbue the planning of a growth process. We shall now look a little more closely at what this planning philosophy involves. There is one feature common to every genuine development process which must be taken into account, namely, its *dialectic character*: there must be visions, but there must also be firm roots in concrete, realistic knowledge. This is the aspect of our planning concept which we shall attack first.

When we discussed in Chapter 5 the natural driving forces that lead to growth, we suggested that these forces can often be described in terms of imbalance or tension. From here we can move on to the more general supposition that the growth process needs to take place in an *environment marked by a certain degree of tension and misfits*. This statement will be examined more closely later in the present chapter. In our subsequent analysis we shall break down the individual growth process into a number of major subprocesses, namely:

- the creation of driving forces
- the power system
- the development of knowledge
- the development of resources.

In a successful growth process each of these subprocesses must operate and must contribute to the others. The decisionmaker—management, for example—must understand something of the nature of these processes, not perhaps in order to exert a direct influence on them, but rather in order to create the context within which they are to take place.

7.1 The dialectic nature of growth planning

Visions are different from goals

The business idea assumes shape and is realized in the course of the growth process. Planning for growth cannot therefore be derived logically from a well-defined ultimate goal; it can only proceed step by step. After each step or each measure introduced, the situation must be reconsidered before the next step can be planned or put into effect. Indeed, this kind of planning is characteristic of all learning processes geared to something more than the production of a given final product with the help of some well-known technology, i.e. learning processes aimed at the development of something really new.

But although we accept in this case that we cannot describe the final product or the path by which it will be reached, some kind of general idea about the final product can still be helpful to the planning. Let us call this general idea a *vision*, in order to emphasize its essential difference in relation to goals in the usual sense.

Visions are not goals. They are intuitive ideas of reasonable (although in relation to the present state, sometimes highly deviating) future states of the system, which sometimes only exist as subjective ideas nursed by a few discerning and possibly significant actors in the present system. To have a vision does not mean committing oneself to any special future state, or even to any one of the future states that appear at present to be possible; it means rather that the vision can be used as an aid in choosing the parts of the present system that should be regarded as a source of inspiration and perhaps even as a challenge.
(Normann, 1970, p. 39)

What, then, is the distinguishing mark of a vision and what does it look like? Above all we would like to emphasize the visions's character of being a whole, a system in the shape of a potential business idea. Thus the vision should contain ideas about the niche or the market which is eventually to be dominated, what type of systems or products are to be offered on the market, and what kind òf organization and what resources are to make this dominance possible.

- At Heavy Conglomerates Ltd growth had been based on one major operation which still dominated the company and whose technology had generated a series of feelers. However, the development of these feelers never really seemed to get any further. The company had enjoyed several technological successes and had several pilot plants that were operating satisfactorily. We found that no-one in the company had ever really asked questions such as: 'What larger ensemble or business idea is this feeler eventually to be part of, or to lead to?'. Since no-one had been thinking in these terms, no opportunities had been created for the sort of confrontation between possible alternative visions which might have encouraged the development of a business idea. The absence of such visions, which would have provided a yardstick of the learning that was going on, left everyone in the company feeling pretty satisfied with their technological successes. Thus no growth-inspiring tension had been generated, no niggling contrast between what was being done and what would have to be done to produce a fully developed business idea. As a result, much of the motivation to go on learning disappeared.

Thus the vision is a tool in the learning process, but at the same time it is also subjected to learning; for this reason it will change as learning proceeds. To start with the vision may be rather diffuse, but it will gradually become more specific or even undergo significant changes in its essential nature. The vision is flexible; in fact an inflexible vision is very often a sign of a learning process that is not functioning well. No business leader need therefore feel ashamed of changing his mind about his visions.

Thus the flexible vision plays an important part in the growth process. It *steers learning*; at the same time changes in the vision also constitute a *yardstick of learning*. Moreover, the terms 'vision' and 'visionary' contain an element of progressiveness and invention, which can indirectly provide a driving force by arousing commitment in the company.

But what happens if we bind ourselves to a vision too early, i.e. if we make it a goal instead of an instrument in the learning process? As we have already pointed out, the difficulty of using goals instead of flexible visions in the planning of learning processes is that it is often impossible to understand the whole situation and to know in advance how conditions will change as growth proceeds. It will therefore also be difficult to achieve consonance between the goal and the possibilities of achieving it. Selznick (1957) has discussed this

1. The vision steers the learning, in that the next step in the learning process is derived from it.

2. Changes in the vision are a measure of learning, in that the learning resulting from concrete steps in the process is checked against the original vision which then adapts and changes.

3. The vision makes it easier to generate driving forces in the shape of ambition and commitment in the company.

Figure 7.1. The Role of the Flexible Vision in the Growth Process

problem, and warns of the dangers of formulating goals too soon or of starting a change process without understanding the circumstances.

A wise leader faces up to the character of his organization, although he may do so only as a prelude to designing a strategy that will alter it. (Selznick, 1957, p. 70)

We found an example of goals that were formulated too soon in the pharmaceutical company Europharma.

- It was decided to expand research resources in Europharma rapidly, to start a couple of large new development projects which were to produce original medicines as part of complicated therapies in the psychopharmaceutical field. This was a big step for a company which had previously been devoting itself mainly to relatively simple preparations. However, it was only discovered very much later that certain values in the environment were in the process of undergoing radical changes. These were ultimately embodied in new regulations about the registration requirements for original products. Also, the whole attitude to the treatment of the mentally ill, in which Europharma was involved, was changing in many countries. The whole strategy ought to have been backed up by a supportive system of clinical tests, information, etc.

The very definite formulation of goals in this case accorded ill with certain values that were evolving in the environment at the same time. Because the goal was taken as given, it was difficult to discover the changes in the environment in time.

Visionary planning and earthbound planning

How can a vision *steer* learning, if at the same time it is also a measure of learning? That this is possible depends on the changing perspective, which in the course of a growth process shifts continually between the visionary and the earthbound in what can be described as a dialectic process.

At any one moment the growth idea must embrace a vision of a business idea, but it must also be formulated at any one moment in terms of concrete steps in the process, since there is a continual reciprocal relation between the vision and the next step in the process. The vision is meaningless if it is not combined with concrete and immediate action geared to its realization.

We have often noticed that a long-range plan which does not lead to concrete changes in a company within a few months of its formulation never does have any effect at all. If the long-range plan or the vision does not immediately persuade the leading actors in the company to change their plans about what has to be done next, it might as well simply be regarded as a declaration and nothing more. It is easy—and amusing—to formulate visions, if they do not have to be linked to actual concrete measures.

- In a company in the building materials industry, there had long been disagreement in management and in the board about how to deal with the company's operations, which leaned predominantly towards mass production and which had been showing increasingly poor profits. In the end the chairman of the board managed to push through a plan whereby the company should go in for the 'development of complex structural systems', which involved a basic reorientation of traditional operations.

  However, the managing director was not among those who were happy about this solution. Admittedly the company did manufacture, among other things, structural components, but he felt that there were other at least as satisfactory paths that could be followed, and that it was too early to commit the company to a particular direction. In his view there were several objections to the chosen formulation—'the development of complex structural systems'—one of them being that the company's real knowhow lay in efficient batch production. But above all he was worried that the board—including himself—had not discussed, and seemed to have no idea about, *how to become* 'a developer of complex structural systems'. He felt lost and didn't know where to turn.

In this case a vision had been formulated, but it hadn't been combined with any immediate concrete steps. And the example also highlights another point: that the vision and the steps taken must be related to the company's real situation and its competence.

Anchoring the growth idea

In Chapter 5 we described some fairly common natural driving forces. We also introduced the conept of the 'base of the company's dominance', and said something about the kind of bases that occur. We would now like to suggest that *both visions and the concrete actions immediately following them must be anchored in a thorough understanding of the company's present business idea and the base of its dominance, and of the natural driving forces that are built into this situation.*

There are various ways in which this rule is often broken. The most common is perhaps a thoughtless commitment to development projects which lack any real likelihood of growing into fully realized business ideas. We shall give a few examples of growth ideas which were based on a superficial or even incorrect understanding of the company's situation and of the driving forces at work in the larger system, with the result that the ideas proved abortive.

- The International Home Sales Corporation had gradually managed to acquire a dominating position in three European countries and planned to conquer markets in one or two more countries during the next two years, mainly by reproducing its business idea there. The company also had enough capital to cover the penetration of new markets.

  At this point a man who had been very successful in several companies in other industries joined the corporation's management. As a result, growth ambitions began to flourish even more than before. It was felt that present markets should be exploited much more, and loud voices were also heard in support of quite a new line, involving the sale of products to professional buyers instead of to ordinary consumers.

  Within a very short time several steps were taken to realize the new ambitions. The corporate staff, which until then had been almost non-existent and not very important, grew to include some highly qualified and highly trained product managers with experience from other industries. In order to improve the efficiency of one part of production which had been let out to subcontractors because of heavy investments and quite big seasonal fluctuations, the company acquired two of the subcontractors to complete its production resources. One of the product mangers was also charged with launching operations in the professional sector as soon as possible, using the production resources now available.

  One year later the situation in the company had changed in many ways. The attempt to launch the professional operation had been abandoned after several big setbacks and considerable financial loss. The two production companies that had been acquired proved difficult to handle and, since no way had been found of counterbalancing the seasonal fluctuations, capital was being tied up in unutilized capacity. Conflict between the product managers, the production managers in the new companies and the regional corporate heads had increased enormously. In the end the corporate staff more or less split up, since the product managers resigned on the grounds of 'lack of understanding' on the part of the corporate heads. The latter, on the other hand, felt that their work was being blocked by interference from the product managers. The company was even trying to find some way of getting rid of the production companies, or to find some other radical solution to the problem of how to use them.

The new prescriptions for growth in the International Home Sales Corporation appear to have broken down for the following reasons, among others:

1. The base of the company's dominance lay in its knowledge of the system and in its very efficient sales organization: the ambition to rationalize production did not agree with this base. Flexibility was lost when the company began to tie up its assets in hardware without fully realizing what the consequences of this would be.

2. The new ideas about planning systems and management that were introduced into the company through the corporate staff were in some ways ill-suited to the traditional business idea which, as someone put it, 'needed a bit of the smalltime crook mentality to work properly'. Thus the attempt to introduce new systems and to make the company more respectable collided and even conflicted with the established business idea.

3. The attempt to enter the professional sector was based on an inadequate understanding of the company's present knowledge. Quality norms in the company's production were perfectly adequate, even high, as applied to the traditional operations; but the professional sector required a type of high-quality production which the company simply could not live up to. Moreover, the company tried to conquer the professional sector with people who were used to living with the 'smalltime crook mentality'. In the new operations quite new selling norms and standards of contact were needed. These problems stemmed partly from an unrealistic view of the build-up of resources needed for breaking into the professional sector.

The Swedish-Malaysian Trading Co provides an interesting example of a growth idea which remained abortive and unintegrated, just because opinions differed about the nature of the company's true strength and of its niche in the external environment.

● For a long time this sector had been dominated by two large companies. The founder had originally started operating as a kind of broker between a production surplus and temporary rises in the demand for a particular staple product. He was flexible and he 'picked up the crumbs from the tables of the great'. His contacts were to a great extent personal, and the whole business idea was embodied in one man.

As the company grew and conquered a larger market share, the founder declared that the old structure was to be maintained at the same time as a number of small regional companies for brokerage activities were started. Other voices pointed out, however, that the company had already integrated backwards and created its own production resources—although admittedly on a small scale—and that the important thing now, to secure growth, must be to achieve a better relationship with the political powers in the industry and to give the company a more substantial structure, i.e. to make it less dependent on individual persons. By and large this was the view that won the day, which meant that the company devoted itself to political negotiations in the industry and to the further build-up of production resources, devoting a good deal of effort also to the introduction of a modern organization in which economic and administrative functions, control systems, etc., came to occupy an increasingly important place. But in the opinion of the supporters of the more traditional brokerage line, among whom were most of the executives responsible for sales, the new organization was far too unwieldy and the control systems and innumerable forms and schedules prevented the quick coordination that was necessary if chances were to be grabbed as they came up.

According to our analysis of the problem, both views of the base for dominance and the meaning of an increased market share in a relatively heavily politicized industry were in part correct, but they were also incomplete. The brokerage party clearly had the most realistic notions of the purely commercial conditions for their operations, and their objections to the increasing bulk of administration were in many respects justified. The administrative party, on the other hand, were right in saying that the industrial-cum-political conditions for the company's existence and for its growth had changed, partly because the Swedish-Malaysian Trading Co was no longer a marginal company but had become a power factor in the industry. This party's supporters were also right in saying that the company's size and increasing complexity called for new approaches to organizational and management questions.

Following much thorough analysis of the company's history and of its present way of operating in different situations, a new *common* idea emerged about its true strength and the opportunities inherent in the industry. It then became possible for a growth idea to emerge which was different from either of those that the old parties had been upholding.

We shall have reason to return to the Swedish-Malaysian Trading Co and its growth idea, and shall content ourselves for the present with summarizing in Figure 7.2 some of the common faults we have so far identified in connection with planning for growth.

7.2 The creation and exploitation of tension

Tension in some form or other seems, to a very great extent, to be a necessary

---

1. The vision becomes fixated too soon and becomes a premature goal.

2. There is no vision.

3. There are no immediate concrete measures.

4. The vision and the subsequent concrete measures are not linked to one another.

5. The vision and/or the subsequent concrete measures are not anchored in a thorough understanding of the company's business idea and of the natural driving forces.

Figure 7.2. Examples of Common Failures to Recognize the Dialectic Nature of Growth Planning

condition of growth and innovation. It may take the shape of a deviation from some expected state, of misfits, or of conflicts or crises. Unless some such disharmony is present, the change process is unlikely ever to get started. Tension can fulfil two functions in this context: first, it creates the necessary *motivation* for starting a change and, secondly, in many cases it indicates the necessary *direction of the change.*

It has often struck me that attempts to plan and steer growth are so intimately connected with the whole concept of tension that we could describe 'the art of handling growth' as 'the art of handling tension'. However, during the growth cycle of any one line of business, the handling of tension assumes different expressions at different times. In order to get a growth process started at all, misfits or conflicts are highly desirable, even necessary; at this stage planning must be based on the exploitation or even the creation of tension. In the mature stages of a growth process, on the other hand, when dominance has been achieved and the business idea has begun to be exploited, tension is not theoretically desirable.

Thus the handling of tension is a process that starts with the *production* of tension and proceeds through its *exploitation* to its *reduction.*

Tension is fundamentally diverse in its nature, depending among other things on the way it arises and the role it plays in the growth process. Often tension is the result of some natural driving forces; in other cases there are no such built-in forces and the tension has to be produced by the actors in the company instead. Another major difference, which is closely connected with the way the tension has arisen, is that some types of tension indicate clearly in themselves the way in which they should be resolved (i.e. they suggest the actual shape of the new growth), while other types of tension indicate no such direction.

We shall now study these different types of tension in more detail.

Directed and diffuse tension

In Chapter 5 we discussed different types of natural driving forces and found that driving forces can be described throughout in terms of imbalance or tension. In some cases this naturally generated tension is *directed tension,* i.e. it not only points to the need for growth and motivates changes but it also suggests in rough outline the direction the growth should take. Sometimes,

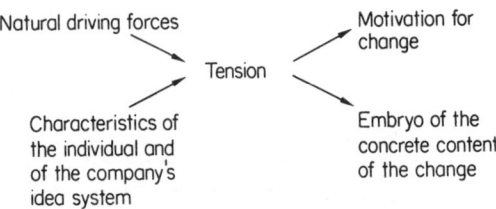

Figure 7.3. The Causes and Functions of Tension

however, there is no clear indication of what the tension involves and how it can be resolved; this type of tension can be called *diffuse tension*.

Directed tension may arise as a result of the nature of the technology or of the particular operations. In the chemical industry, for example, there are often by-products which provide the basis for a growth project in a natural way. Swings and fluctuations also provide examples of directed tension. For a seaside hotel, for example, it seems obvious to try to iron out the imbalance between high and low season, perhaps by taking in conferences during the winter. Most forest companies find it natural to aim at growth through forward integration, to counteract a possible misfit between the knowledge that is being developed on the end-user market and the base for the company's dominance, i.e. the raw material.

Diffuse tension may arise as a result of a surplus of financial resources, i.e. a company generates more resources than it needs for its current operations and growth rate. This can be seen as a misfit between the company's growth resources and the available visions and ideas about how the company wants to grow and the direction the growth should take. As a result of the accumulation of capital, growth ideas and entrepreneurs have become the scarce resources. This is the situation which can easily face the extremely successful company. The Xerox Corporation, entering upon its period of diversification at the end of the 1960s, is an example (Dessauer, 1971). Diffuse tension, just because it indicates no direction for growth, can of course set off tension of another kind. For example, a management may disagree among themselves about the way to tackle a threat to their company; they may even disagree about whether there is a threat or not, in which case there may not seem to be any reason for launching a growth process. But this type of diffuse tension can initiate a struggle between different interpretations of the company's situation, thus creating secondary tension within the system of dominating ideas.

This brings us to another type of tension, to be found chiefly in individuals or groups.

Tension in individuals

In many cases tension represents a misfit between the company's or leader's known performance and the leader's level of ambition (cf. Penrose, 1959). A high level of ambition often appears to be linked to deep-rooted personality traits in the leader, who has a very strong desire to prove himself.

These super-ambitious leaders often find it difficult to get on with their colleagues, who are not as aware of any misfit between ambition and performance and who do not therefore see any strong reason to change. The lack of naturally generated tension makes it difficult for the leader to make his colleagues recognize the necessity to change and grow; it also makes it extremely difficult for him to discover the direction the growth ought to take.

Such situations perhaps call for the greatest skill of all in handling tension and creating growth. It is not enough simply to 'go along with the natural forces'; instead the business leader has to implant new tension and call forth sufficient driving forces within the company to produce the growth he wants.

Tension in the system of dominating ideas

Growth-promoting tension is sometimes to be found in the system of dominating ideas, perhaps as a difference of opinion about what the company's situation requires. There can be many causes of a fundamental tension between different interpretations of the company's problems.

Perhaps among the significant actors are people with different backgrounds and training, people who because of this will put different emphasis on different points. Or there may be people whose levels of ambition are not the same. Or perhaps the conflicting interpretations of the company's situation are simply a means of manipulating the circumstances, of somehow affecting power relationships.

Classical thinkers or philosophers such as Hegel and Pareto, as well as modern researchers such as Schon and Koestler, have all supported the thesis that some form of tension between different sets of concepts (all of which are held by their supporters to be applicable to a particular situation) promotes growth, in fact that it represents the very essence of the innovative process. According to Koestler (1969) innovation takes place as a result of a link-up between several previously independent 'thought matrices'. Schon (1963) claims that innovation (or what we have called knowledge development) occurs when a frame of reference is used in a type of situation to which it has not previously been applied.* But the existence of such tension in a company by no means guarantees that innovation will take place. It may equally well lead to paralysing conflicts.

In the Trading Company, of which we have spoken earlier, we found an example of the successful exploitation of tension in the company's dominating ideas.

- The Trading Company was in a difficult line of business. It was hard pressed between an attempt to integrate on the seller side and an increasing tendency towards direct distribution on the producer side. Added to which, offers to buy the company had been made by competitors, manufacturers and customers. There was continual discussion about these matters in management and among the shareholders. We could see that there was one group who thought the company would find it difficult to manage, in view of the big structural changes in the environment and the incipient problem of financing. However, there were others who felt that everything had been all right so far, that the company had its duty to its employees and to the local community, that they had some very able

*Similar ideas have been put forward by Schutz (1944), Kuhn (1962), Bateson (1972) and Polanyi (1969).

men, and that they had a good reputation among customers and suppliers. This group recommended an aggressive growth policy instead.

The decision was postponed. The deba e continued, but gradually changed as the Trading Company grew stronger within its established line. In fact three new lines were also started, and several feelers sent out as a sort of reserve. Competitors disappeared or were forced into other industries, and the Trading Company eventually achieved total dominance on its market.

How can we explain the connection between the existence of tension in the idea system and the company's growth? It seems that the managing director of the Trading Company played a decisive role here. Part of his strategy seems to have been to exploit the conflict to promote his own learning. As the debate developed and became more sophisticated, the managing director launched the redefinition of the traditional operation, although others actually worked out the final business idea providing the means through which the managing director's growth idea was realized. At the same time the managing director was also nurturing an 'insurance' strategy to spread the risks.

The art of propagating tension and creating driving forces

We have already seen how tension and misfits can have different sources. Tension can be generated somewhere in the environment, for example a company's products may no longer be attractive on the market or important stakeholders become dissatisfied with its performance. Tension may also arise within the company, perhaps because various groups or parties interpret the company's situation in different ways and recommend different strategies. A single person may also represent a source of tension, perhaps someone in management who is dissatisfied with his own or the company's level of performance.

Tension can fulfil different functions. Directed tension can both motivate change and give some indication of its possible direction, while diffuse tension contains nothing to suggest what a coming change might consist of.

The *engendering of driving forces* is one of the most important subprocesses in the growth idea. The generation and exploitation of tension is intimately connected with the problem of creating driving forces, and it is often a question of *spreading or propagating* tension so that it has an impact on the way the company actually develops. Generally, several natural driving forces are in operation at once; a company can often promote growth by exploiting and adapting to these forces. But sometimes the impact of these forces dries up after a certain initial drive. The Mining and Processing Company provides us with an example of this:

- In the course of production a certain mineral became available for sale on the open market. However, in the mid-1960s a substitute was discovered and the price fell considerably. In order to maintain earlier margins, the company therefore invested in a simple processing plant which took care of the surplus. As we described in Chapter 5, in a few years' time, the head of the processing operation succeeded in creating his own brand product and establishing a profile on the market, which meant that he was no longer satisfied with the marginal status of his operations. However, the board of directors could not understand his point of view, since his plant had only been started to solve a problem for the established operations. This problem was now solved to their satisfaction. The idea of continuing to invest in a new operation, and even of buying more of the required mineral from competitors, was utterly alien to the members of the board.

Growth often starts in this way—to solve some problem in the established operations—but it very often ceases when the original problems have been dealt with.* Tension generated by natural driving forces is often effective at an early stage in the growth process, but may cease to work later. It should then be replaced by some other type of driving force; perhaps tension can be transmitted to some of the significant actors.

● One of the most successful growth processes that we witnessed was generated by a seasonal surplus in production capacity—what we have called a natural growth impetus—which happened to coincide with the excessive growth ambitions of one or two top men after a change in the management group.

While some kind of crisis or problem is often necessary to get a growth process going, driving forces of a more constructive kind are needed to develop it further. The natural driving forces 'push from behind'; at later stages driving forces are needed to 'pull' the project through the various obstacles and over the opposition. † The skilful executive succeeds in exploiting the entrepreneurial potential of his colleagues and making a driving force out of their wish to develop as people, out of their creativity, or simply out of their ambition to rise in the hierarchy.

Figure 7.4 illustrates ways in which management can handle tension to create driving forces.

Since the concept of tension is so important to innovation, the following is a crucial question: should it not be possible to build certain types of tension into the structure of a company, to provide a kind of permanent driving force?

*This phenomenon is so common that in Chapter 10 we have christened it the 'appendix syndrome'.

†It is not unusual for the driving forces to change character several times during a growth process from the 'pushing' to the 'pulling' kind, for instance if a growth project has its roots in some external power centre which can change its demands on the company as the project progresses.

> 1. Search for misfits, conflicts and imbalance in the company and in relations between company and environment. This may be combined with:
>
> 2. The creation of tension and misfits.
>
> 3. Tension is transmitted to certain significant actors, or is mapped into the structure in some way so that visions can be born and concrete action taken.
>
> 4. Tension is exploited.

Figure 7.4. The Art of Handling Tension and Translating it into a Driving Force in the Growth Process

We shall return to this question in the final chapters, where we shall also discuss why tension in the system of dominating ideas can lead sometimes to innovation and sometimes to a situation that is clearly negative in its effects.

7.3 Development of knowledge

The most fundamental and perhaps also the most difficult ingredient in any genuinely qualitative growth process is the *process of developing knowledge*. Any successful process of knowledge development must, it seems, possess three main attributes. Together these represent a kind of general principle for the development of knowledge.

1. Knowledge must be developed around an *ensemble*. In other words, it should not be geared only to technological conditions, for example. It is supposed ultimately to lead to a business idea and this must never be forgotten. Knowledge of markets, technology, organization, the build-up of resources, and so on—all this must be integrated. Otherwise the growth idea may never lead to anything—it will be abortive.

2. New knowledge is developed when existing *areas of knowledge rub up against each other and are combined in new ways*. Exactly what the results of such confrontations will be is often impossible to predict. Nevertheless, a crucial ingredient of the successful growth idea seems to be the presence of some kind of idea of the type of knowledge combination which has a chance of yielding interesting results. In many cases such ideas can be gleaned from a specific 'theory' about the way knowledge is developed within a limited system, for example a branch of industry.

3. Ideas about the concrete content of the knowledge-development process and the patterns of confrontation must be embodied or *given concrete form* in a network of social contacts supported by the organizational structure.

Below we give some examples of these theories or mechanisms for developing knowledge.

Development of knowledge in connection with redefinitions

When mature business ideas are in need of redefinition, it is often possible to identify the patterns and mechanisms which have previously led to the development of knowledge by studying the company's history. The actual structure of these mechanisms often remains unchanged, although the concrete content of the knowledge-development process is continually being revised, and this historically established structure is often specific to a particular type of industry or company. The field in which our own research institution operates can provide an example of this.

- We find that certain generalizations can be based on those occasions when fundamentally new knowledge has emerged about the problems of organizations. For instance, we can see that an important feature has been the link-up between different disciplines. 'Organization theory' emerged, for example, when economics, sociology, psychology, systems theory, etc., all came together to focus on a common object of interest to them all. Further, it seems that the most important types of knowledge have emerged in connection with the practical solving of problems, i.e. when organization researchers have been trying to help decision-makers with their concrete problems. Furthermore, we have found that it is not possible to develop real knowledge of conditions at one systems level unless it is combined with knowledge of conditions at another systems level. Thus, for example, none of our theories about the way to organize a research and development department really led to anything until the problem was tackled by researchers who were working on the higher-level problems of overall strategic planning.

- For several decades now the pharmaceutical industry has been following a certain pattern in its knowledge development. From a base in a traditional knowledge of chemicals, etc., it is becoming increasingly involved in clinical–biological knowhow. During the 1950s, for example, pharmacists began to make themselves felt in the structure of the pharmaceutical companies; during the 1960s it was the turn of the pharmacologists; the 1970s looks like being the decade of the clinicians.

- In industries that supply major components and subsystems to other rapidly growing and complex industries, new knowledge often appears to be developed either as a result of a pilot plant in the particular industry which represents the company's market, or as a result of collaboration and joint systems development together with a particularly demanding customer. Thus, for example, Electrolux seems to have acquired a firm of cleaners in order to increase its own knowledge of the expanding cleaning market.

Perhaps these observations of the way knowledge is developed in different branches of industry or in different technologies may give some indication of how to organize a company to ensure an ability to redefine business ideas, regardless of what the actual content of the redefinition may be.

Development of knowledge in connection with reorientations

Naturally it becomes more difficult to formulate theories about the development of knowledge as the changes involved become more radical. A historical study can show something of the way a company can gradually develop knowledge of its industry or its system over the years, but for any more radical innovations—what we have called reorientations—the theories of knowledge development in the specific industry are far too limited.

Layton (1972) shows us different ways of approaching knowledge development in a technologically very complicated industry. He takes as an example some attempts to develop a new type of aircraft with adjustable wings in the French company Dassault and in some large American corporations. He finds many differences in favour of the French company, despite its much lower resource input. Layton suggests that the American companies are wrong in their view of how knowledge develops in this kind of situation and suggests a better way of planning and organizing development work.

In our view when a wholly new technology is being developed there is much to be said for first developing a single prototype, as Dassault did, as a tool for learning. Batch development is suited for aircraft that are within the state of the art, but clear objectives are needed if the aircraft is to be developed successfully.
(Layton, 1972, p. 47)

Behind reorientations, or knowledge development of the more radical kind, there often seems to be a vision which consists of little more than an intuitive understanding that new combinations of different types of knowledge should lead to something new. By embodying this kind of vision in the organizational structure, a new context can be created in which knowledge can more easily be developed: a new flowerbed which directly or indirectly helps to determine which plants will grow. An interesting example of such a 'process hypothesis' is the historical development of polyethylene (Allen, 1967):

- A German university researcher—Mond—believed that it should be possible to solve technological problems in companies more efficiently by applying scientific principles. He also believed that the right problem-solving environment should be close to a market, so that the solution of the technological problems automatically received a use-bound direction. Thus it came about that Mond, together with a commercially minded partner, started the company in England that now constitutes the Mond Division of ICI. A similar 'context creator' is to be found in Mond's successor Freth, who gradually came to realize the importance of combin-

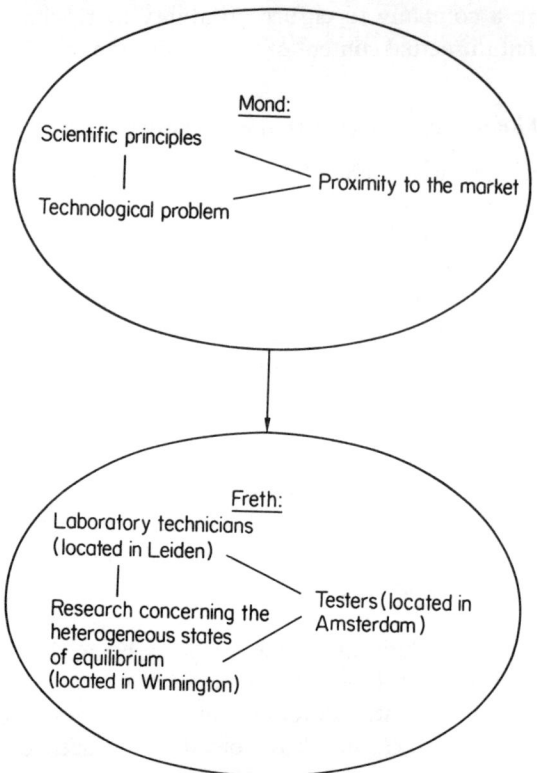

Figure 7.5. Examples of Two Ideas of Knowledge-
development Mechanisms Which Led to the Emergence
of Polyethylene

ing certain special research orientations. He therefore arranged for the
establishment of a stable social network with accompanying interaction
patterns between researchers representing these different fields of knowledge and located at different places within and outside the company.

A similar overlying vision of knowledge development could be seen at the
Swedish pharmaceutical company Astra during the 1930s.

• Through the agency of Jacob Wallenberg, chairman of the board, something very radical for those times occurred at Astra: an economist (Gösta
  Gabrielsson, renowned for his modern views on marketing) was appointed
  as managing director instead of an engineer. This had various secondary
  consequences, with the result that Astra soon became an extremely
  successful company. This development is illustrated in Figure 7.6.

Dare we conclude that in his mind's eye Jacob Wallenberg saw some kind

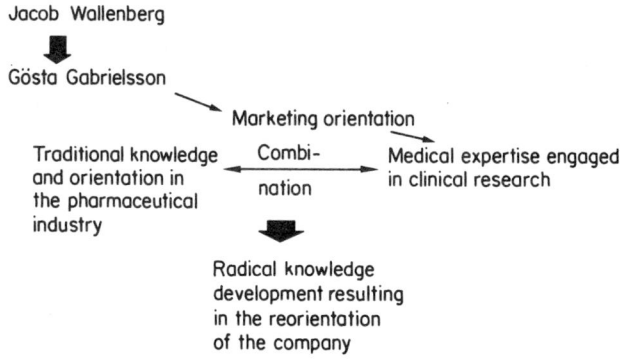

Figure 7.6. The Knowledge-development Process at Astra During the 1930s

of overlying vision of the sort of knowledge development the pharmaceutical industry would need in the future?

7.4 Handling of obstacles in the power system

In the course of discussing the difference between reorientations and product variations in Chapter 4, we mentioned that new qualitative growth outside the company's established operations also presupposes changes in the power system. Obstacles to innovation may be found in the internal power system of the company and in the power system of the environment—oppositional forces which actively or passively try to stop the change. Thus a crucial element in every growth idea is a strategy for effecting the necessary changes in the various power relationships.

When natural driving forces are at work in a company, or when some form of complicated or indefinable problem arises, the result is often a polarization of attitudes in the company, or perhaps the reinforcement of a polarization that already existed: it is generally possible to interpret events conservatively, which means supporting the improvement of efficiency within the framework of existing conditions, or radically, which means that the fundamental principles on which existing conditions rest are called in question. The impetus to change often springs from a radical party of some kind, but a precondition for success in bringing the change to fruition is the possession of a strategy for dealing with the opposition in the conservative party.

But the established balance of power also has its defenders in the environment. These *status-quo* forces enjoy considerable influence whenever the tasks and organizations in an environment are closely interwoven, each one making its own contribution to a complicated ensemble.

● We have already described the Swedish building industry with the great variety of organizations it embraces, each one trying to preserve its own small part of the system. Trade associations and specialist trade unions have often acted as defenders of the established business ideas. In the same way, trade associations in single-line retailing or the convenience goods trade, for example, often find themselves in an impossible situation: they were originally created to support an industrial structure that was threatened and which has subsequently become even more inefficient and out-of-date. Thus trade associations like this often put a brake on the efforts of companies which are trying to create new and more effective business ideas.

Various strategies exist for dealing with this kind of blockage in the internal and external power systems. The following are some of them. Naturally they can all assume a variety of forms according to the circumstances.

- Perhaps the most obvious is the straight *confrontation*, but this only works if the radical party is at least as strong as the conservative.

- Another strategy is *co-optation*, a concept we have borrowed from Selznick (1949), in the sense of buying the support and cooperation of the other party by giving way on certain points.

- *Evasion* is a guerilla tactic which involves trying as far as possible to work unseen at early stages so that a strong position can gradually be built up; it may also mean refusing to admit that anything is going on at all.

- *Dissimulation* means obtaining support by making it look as though a development project has some quite different aim—an aim that is acceptable to the opposition party and even, if possible, that appears to support it. This strategy can also be called the 'cuckoo strategy', a name that the following quotation can well exemplify:
  Then we were going to sell the project to the board; we knew they would never accept it if we told them what we were really thinking of doing in the end. So we made no fuss about that at all; we simply presented the whole thing as an investment calculation which was supposed to increase our use of capacity during the low season. We made it look like a campaign for saving and efficiency improvement; the board was enthusiastic and we got the resources we wanted.

- The *smokescreen* strategy resembles the cuckoo strategy in that some kind of front is put up between the development process and the *status-quo* forces. This protective layer hides the development project, or reveals a suitably foggy version of it. A successful research director who has been involved in initiating and developing several new business ideas put it as follows:
  The main thing is that the people who are getting on with the real work

should be protected from pointless demands and interference. At the same time, though, they should also be exposed to really strict commercial and professional demands from the right sources. But to make this possible, things sometimes have to be done which management might not always approve of, so someone else has to be scapegoat. That is my role; nobody in this company breaks the rules as often as I do.

Many stories of the birth of new business ideas contain examples of this kind of moral immorality.

● Obviously the happiest way of eliminating obstacles is to reverse the situation and *transform the obstacle into a driving force*:

To begin with, package deals were seen as a severe threat to the role and existence of the architects. But one of the most successful companies which has systematically utilized this form of contract has succeeded in using architects from outside in such a way that the architects have acknowledged a marked improvement in their working conditions and have therefore enthusiastically supported the development of the total contract system.

7.5 Development of resources

Growth is intimately related to an increase and possibly a change in resources. The quantitative development of resources is rarely a problem in the very early stages of growth; it is generally in the later phases, when systems are being developed and markets penetrated, that more financial resources are needed than operations can generate. But we are mainly interested here in the kind of growth that is linked more closely to the development of knowledge than to a constant reproduction of what has already been fully developed. For this reason we also look at the development of resources from rather a special angle.*

We have frequently found that in genuine breakthroughs the quantity of the resources concerned plays little part; it is above all their quality that counts. And by 'resources' we mean above all human resources. It is often purely and simply the knowledge and professionalism possessed by certain individuals combined with their qualities of leadership and their ambitions which determine success.

But in the really knowledge-intensive industries, the development of these kind of human resources will be important even in later stages of growth. In several of our cases we found that the ultimate realization and exploitation of a business idea was inhibited, just because there were not enough people with the right kind of knowledge.

---

*In the last section of this chapter, however, we shall see that even in the case of a predominantly quantitative growth, it is still possible to design strategies or growth ideas geared to the development of resources.

†This observation has been confirmed by Price (1965) and others.

- In our own 'industry'—action research and the solving of growth problems in companies—the development of people who combine a thorough basic education, research experience, practical experience, analytical skill and sensitivity to the processes of group dynamics obviously represents a major restriction on both quantitative and qualitative growth.

- A plant-breeding company possessed all the ingredients of a growth idea except a formula for acquiring the necessary number of qualified geneticists.

- A Scandinavian retail company had developed a successful and superior business idea on its local market; but it was not possible to grow without finding some way of getting round the lack of fully qualified opticians.

In many ways there is a close connection between the kind of resource development we are discussing here and what is generally meant by 'management development'. It is a question of getting people to develop so that they can either occupy crucial roles in the growth process themselves, or they can free other resources.

In the last chapter we discussed the connection between organizational structure and the learning processes of individual people. If the human resources of a company are to evolve satisfactorily, then the career opportunities, the demands that will be made and so on, must all be designed so that people are exposed to challenge and stimuli. In this way their situation will inspire them to learn. At one point it was discovered in Ferranti that resource development was a bottleneck inhibiting further growth. However, the company managed to find a strategy for handling the situation.

> Ferranti's expansion into semiconductors was, like TI's, helped by its domestic government market, although to a much smaller extent. In particular, work on a computer used to control guided missiles, helped to apply the technology. Integrated circuits required skill in circuit design. Ferranti found that one of the quickest ways to develop a solid state technologist was to take a systems engineer and attach him to semiconductor technology. The semiconductor development was based in part on Ferranti's main computer centre.
> (Layton, 1972, p. 102)

By taking an existing resource—the specialist—and placing him in a new situation, Ferranti created resources that were qualitatively new.

- The Swedish-Malaysian Trading Company was operating on a very speculative market in several different countries. In the management group, which consisted of two or three people, a vision of the company's future development was firmly rooted. Unfortunately, however, the same men also did almost all the business, since nobody else commanded an overall view of the fluctuations in supplies on the various raw-material markets and the equally marked swings in demand at different times and in different regions. If the company was to be able to go on growing, it would therefore be necessary to create new leadership resources, to generate leaders either to promote and support growth planning or to take over a substantial part of the operational responsibility. The management group chose the latter alternative. A highly decentralized matrix organization was introduced in which the regional directors bore full responsibility; this was combined with a simple but effective new communications system and a system of internal changes which encouraged cooperation in various ways. It was soon clear that the new generation in the company was learning to survey the company's established business idea in its entirety; its members no longer saw themselves as specialists concentrating on production, sales, and so on.

This example also shows that matrix organizations of various kinds can often help to back up the development of resources. They provide many people with stimuli and responsibility; and new channels of communication make it easier for people to combine their own bits of knowledge with those of others.

There is often a direct link between successful resource development and the ability to handle obstacles in the power system. For example, an entrepreneur who appears to be working entirely within the established operations quite often turns out to be building up a resource structure well suited to quite other purposes.

7.6 Growth—the organizational context

We have now analysed the basic conditions of successful growth. These are that growth planning should be steered by both visions and short-term concrete action; and that tension must be created and exploited as a driving force. We have further identified four major subprocesses in the growth process: the creation of driving forces, the development of resources, the development of knowledge and the handling of *status-quo* forces in the power system.

For creating the conditions favourable to growth the main tool available to management is the organizational structure. Some kind of idea about the way in which specific organizational provisions can affect the process of growth is therefore an important part of any growth idea.

As we have already pointed out, the term 'organizational structure' implies something far more than the formal organization chart. It includes a variety of informal relationships, essential aspects of the company's resources, economic control systems, reward systems and career opportunities, the nature of the demands made upon the organization, etc. The organizational structure is really an expression of various relatively stable relationships which affect behaviour in an organization by their impact on such factors as the flow of information, the foci of attention, the problem-solving resources, and the ambitions and ideas of individuals and groups about what constitutes desirable behaviour.

The organizational structure is of fundamental importance to the growth process, which it affects in several ways. Earlier in this chapter we gave examples of ways in which different parts of the development process can be supported by various organizational provisions, and we shall now summarize some general links between organizational structure and growth which can be included in a growth idea.

1. Organizational provisions affect the interaction pattern; they enable knowledge centres inside and outside the company to rub up against each other in new ways. Career opportunities, reward systems and economic control systems can be designed to support new forms of interaction and to reward new types of values and behaviour.

2. New boundaries and borderlines can be drawn, thus identifying and/or protecting particular units or processes, and exposing different units to new differentiated demands.

3. Changes in organizational structure and the opening of new career opportunities can promote the development of leaders and other resources.

Figure 7.7 summarizes the main concepts of a growth idea.

It should be emphasized once more that the various subprocesses, and the nature of the context in which the subprocesses are to operate, cannot be regarded as isolated phenomena; on the contrary, they form an *ensemble*— which is the growth idea.

7.7 Growth ideas and quantitative growth

In this book I have restricted myself chiefly to growth based predominantly on the creation and development of new knowledge, in other words on the

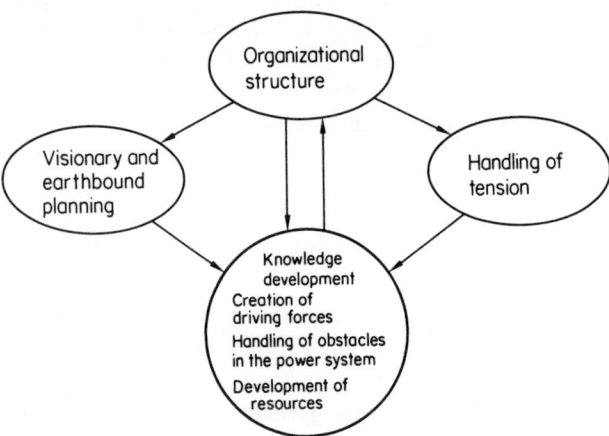

Figure 7.7. Crucial Elements in a Growth Idea

development of a line of business from its first embryo stage to its realization as a mature business idea. However, to complete the picture, I would also like to say something about other types of growth—growth that manifests itself in quantitative rather than qualitative terms. Even here some kind of growth strategy or growth idea can be formulated, although it is likely to be somewhat less complex than those we have been discussing.

Some conglomerate strategies

A form of growth which is common at the present time is that practised by the big conglomerates. Some of their growth strategies can perhaps be described as quantitative rather than qualitative, especially when the companies concerned bypass the fundamental knowledge-development stage and bring mature business ideas in from outside. (Several successful conglomerates have of course grown in other ways, for instance as a result of the intelligent and farsighted restructuring of whole industries.) We can now look at some examples of the different growth strategies used by conglomerates, although the picture we draw will naturally not be exhaustive.

One conglomerate strategy based on quantitative growth is the purely *financial strategy* employed, for example, by investment companies with portfolio investments, by investment funds, or by financial conglomerates who want to achieve financial rather than operational synergy. This kind of strategy may be geared in the first place and in the short run to increasing profit in relation to share capital by acquiring companies that appear to be undervalued in relation to their profit or which are available on favourable financial terms. Companies may also be acquired for purely fiscal reasons.

Another conglomerate strategy is more sophisticated and often involves growth that is obviously more oriented towards quality or knowledge development. In this case a company acquires other businesses which have relatively complex and preferably diversified structures, valuable tangible assets, and low profitability. These businesses are then parcelled out, some bits being retained and others resold. The art lies in *carving up* a company in such a way that the various bits form a natural complement to its own and other people's established business ideas in the industry, so that the sum of the parts will represent more value than the company did before. In such cases, if all goes well, conglomerates can act effectively to rationalize the entire structure of an industry. Cavenham provides an example of a carve-up strategy which developed into an industrial-restructuring strategy.

- Cavenham bought two companies in two industries, one a food-manufacturing company, the other a retail firm. Both companies have been carved up and reorganized; parts which did not seem to fit have been sold; some retail chains have been merged so as to get rid of one or two unsuccessful units.

Electrolux and Svenska Tändsticksaktiebolaget are two Swedish companies among others which have used this kind of strategy.

A third growth strategy that is used by conglomerates very much resembles a *strategy of systems-building*, except that the system concerned emerges chiefly as a result of takeovers; in other words, growth is quantitative, even if the actual systems-building is closely linked to the development of knowledge and an increase in overall quality. Volvo provides an example of this. By acquiring other companies, Volvo has gone a long way towards merging the production side with sales operations, servicing and insurance activities.

Penetration strategies

What we could call *penetration strategies* represent growth strategies of another kind. Admittedly in such cases growth is mainly quantitative and multiplicative, but it differs from the growth of the conglomerates in that it is generated internally within the growing company.

It is a question here of extending an established system or a business idea that is already mature. The quantitative penetration of a business idea is not the same as the penetration which we have already described as a stage in the emergence of a new business idea, which calls for qualitative as well as purely financial resources. Penetration in the shape of quantitative growth can occur if three conditions are fulfilled:

1. If the business idea is so *superior* that it can be used as it stands without local adjustments, or if it needs only minor modifications before penetrating other markets. This is naturally easier if
2. the penetrated system is *homogeneous*, and if
3. the company has sufficient *resources*.

● Coca-cola is often taken as an example of this kind of extension. A uniform strategy that worked well has been reapplied over and over again. In our terms, we could say that growth involved the application of a single business idea to one market after another.

● Danielsson (1974) has described how AGA, after building up its lighthouse operations particularly in South America, started around 1914 to extend a new business idea—gas operations. Its strategy was based essentially on the following simple formula:
1. Start from the regions where gas stations for lighthouse operations have already been built.
2. Establish a new juridical unit (a subsidiary) there, for gas operations.
3. Appoint a young, ambitious and clever engineer; make him head of the subsidiary and send him there to develop its operations.

A familiar version of the extension strategy, although it has only become popular recently, is the *franchizing* operation. Franchizing facilitates the extension of a fully realized and tested business idea by eliminating certain kinds of obstacle. This does not require much in the way of financial resources, and exploits the higher motivation that is generally more easily generated in the small company.

Other growth strategies using mature business ideas may be geared towards counteracting the various institutional barriers that can block traditional forms of extension.

- In the pharmaceutical industry companies often find it difficult to penetrate overseas markets, because of differences in local medical 'culture' and tradition, because of the different needs imposed by the local pattern of disease, and because of local regulations and so on. It is therefore often easier to penetrate these markets by collaborating with local companies. Thus the industry has developed a complicated pattern of international licensing agreements. Similar tendencies can also be discerned in the building industry.

The 'institutional growth idea' can often be decisive to a company's chances of expansion. Because of its association with the dominating political party, the Swedish Consumers' Co-operative (KF) has always found it easier than other companies to obtain permission from the local authorities to establish new hypermarkets, or generally to acquire favourable business locations.

CHAPTER 8

The Company's Core Group

We have now identified and described some of the main characteristics of the company's exchange and growth processes, and introduced the concepts of business idea and growth idea as tools to analyse the conditions on which efficiency in the two processes depends.

Starting from our analytical model of the company's growth, we have also identified a number of typical growth situations. The most important of these are summarized in Figure 8.1.

It should be emphasized that these situations are oversimplified to represent pure or ideal examples of their kind. For this reason we have not tried to make any exact description of reality here; our rough typology simply provides a general point of reference from which an analysis of specific realities could start.

Underlying our description of these growth situations are various propositions regarding the relations between situation, organizational structure and type of dominating ideas. Perhaps this is the moment to recall the basic organizational model we presented in Chapter 2. There we introduced the ideas now shown in Figure 8.2 to provide a frame of reference for probing the growth problems of business companies.

Single lines of business or single business company:

- can be found in different stages of growth (the feeler stage, the development stage, the penetration stage, or the stabilization stage)

- can be found in the process of transition from one growth stage to another

- can be redefined when the base for dominance is threatened

- may fall into a growth trap.

Multiple lines of business or multibusiness company:

- can result from feelers generated by natural driving forces

- can arise through the creation of tension and 'induced growth'

- may embrace essentially different business ideas that may have arrived at different stages of growth in the same company.

Figure 8.1. Some of the Most Important Types of Growth Situation

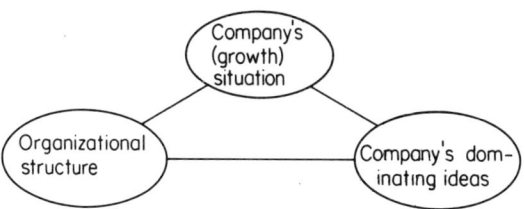

Figure 8.2. Basic Organizational Model

In Chapter 2 we also suggested that the fundamental cause of growth problems is generally a lack of consonance between the company's growth situation and its dominating ideas. A change in organizational structure may help a company to adapt to the new situation, but very often some change in the system of ideas—in the values, beliefs and philosophy embodied in its management group—is needed as well.

In the last part of this book we shall discuss the process by which the dominating ideas in a company can be changed and adjusted to the current situation. First, however, we shall describe some cases in which consonance prevails between our ideal types of growth situation, the company's dominating ideas, and the company's organizational structure.

We shall not spend too much time describing the structure of the company in any great detail. It is difficult to give any general rules about the exact nature of a structure which will be efficient in one situation rather than another. We shall concentrate on structure at top-management level, i.e. on the main functions that must be fulfilled and how these should be mapped into the company's group of significant actors. It is after all these significant actors who are in a position to influence the company's dominating ideas. Thus, in this chapter we shall really be describing some examples of consonance between type of growth situation and type of significant actors, where the latter reflect the management structure as well as representing the dominating ideas.

8.1 The significant actors: the company's core group

In an efficient company the dominating ideas are continually being adapted to the requirements of the current situation; they are also given adequate concrete form in the structure of the company. The dominating ideas are more influential than the other parts of the company's system of ideas; they also have the support of its power structure. In all companies these dominating ideas seem to be embodied in a small group of actors. Typically the members of this group occupy the highest positions of real power in the company. (Usually, though not always, these will be the highest positions of formal power as well.) We shall call this little group of significant actors *the company's core group*.

The core group certainly reflects the dominating ideas; it need not, however, necessarily have created them. Very often these ideas are only partly a product of the company's *present* core group. Moreover, the composition of the core group is to some extent an expression of the power system and the dominating ideas that steer recruitment into the group. People who leave the core group are replaced by others who more or less fulfil the same functions. The expectations of the roles the new entrants will play are fairly specific, and this in turn will affect the way they behave.

A good deal can be understood about a company's ability (or even inability) to grow and learn by analysing its core group. However, the idea of the paramount importance of a small group of people at the top of the company is not new in organizational literature. Two writers who have particularly emphasized this point recently are Thompson (1967) and Stymne (1970). Thompson discusses what he calls the 'dominating coalition', while Stymne speaks of 'sway groups', by which he means more or less the same as the 'elite'.

However, there is one interesting and rather fundamental difference in the way these two authors approach the problem. Thompson, who follows Crozier (1964), sees the dominating coalition as a result in the first place of processes in the environment and in the technology of the company that generate uncertainty. According to Thompson, the dominating coalition will consist of the people who are able to handle and reduce this troublesome uncertainty. Stymne, on the contrary, mainly follows Selznick (1957) and gives his sway groups a more active role. The ideas and values prevailing in a sway group are reproduced at all levels in the company, and decide both its strategy and its structure. Thus Thompson sees the nature of the leading group as a function of other processes in the company, while Stymne reverses the order of things and sees other processes as a function of the nature of the sway group.

We have no need here to decide whether one of these approaches is more or less correct than the other. Instead we will regard them as ideal types, both of which in certain cases may resemble real life, but neither of which will be found in their pure form. It is a dialectical process with reciprocal causal relationships that decides whether the decision-makers will be mainly victims of the power of circumstances or whether they will themselves create the circumstances. As the same time, however, there are obviously situations in which one or the other relationship is the stronger. A reasonable hypothesis would be that the Selznick–Stymne model often approaches the conditions that prevail in early stages of a company's growth, while the Crozier–Thompson model is applicable to more mature stages of development.

To describe the company's core group we shall use the concept of the role constellation, thus following Hodgson et al. (1965), a study of the top executives in a mental hospital.

- In the mental hospital the three top executives have come to occupy very different roles. The hospital superintendent is described as the man who devotes himself to building the future conditions of his organization and his profession. The clinical director aims to build the young therapists, making them into skilful professional men with the knowledge, insights, attitudes and motivational patterns required for their difficult work. The assistant superintendent, on the other hand, takes care of research and knowledge development, trying in particular to foster creative people and ideas.

One of the three top executives also assumes the role of the relatively tough leader. He sees that even unpopular decisions are carried out. Another executive plays a more submissive part—he is unwilling to assume power; on the other hand he is someone whom subordinates can easily confide in, and so on.

The main proposition of the above study is that members of a management group tend to evolve roles for themselves and for each other as they interact with one another in the organization. This process gradually leads to a pattern of differentiated but complementary roles.

Since my interest in organization and management does not always focus on the aspects that chiefly concern these authors, I find that I am interested in other aspects of these roles. But the basic idea of differentiated and complementary roles in a management group does appear to lend itself to inclusion in our present frame of reference. It seems possible, in fact, that many of the failures and successes we have witnessed in 'our' companies could be usefully explained in terms of consonance between the role constellation of the core group and the company's actual situation.

Our theory about the conditions that promote growth and about the nature of the growth idea should lead us to expect to find certain qualities in the core group of a successfully growing company. We would expect to discover various kinds of tension and mechanisms for regulating tension, for example.

8.2 The core group as an embodiment of the company's business idea

Some examples

In a mature stage of development—when a territory has been defined and perhaps already conquered, when resources have been built up and the organization adequately structured—the dominating ideas should then reflect the fully realized business idea. In Chapter 3 we described a hypermarket company which perhaps represented our most successful example of this kind of consonance.

- The typical business idea in this industry embraces various ingredients such as the design of the actual buildings, the goods-flow system, the control system, personnel policy, and the introduction of professionalism on the floor. For a very long time the loyalty to all parts of this business idea was almost total in the company, and the creed and principles prevailing had also been very clearly formulated so that they could be followed by practically all employees. A few rebels who had asserted other values and tried to develop ideas conflicting with the basic business idea soon felt out of place and resigned. Even people who sometimes thought a bit differently were basically extremely loyal to the hypermarket idea. In fact the managing director was the only one who sometimes seemed to feel the need for a little opposition to relieve the almost total harmony that surrounded him.

At first we found it quite surprising that this and one or two of the other companies we studied were so successful although they showed few signs of conflict and tension—two features which in many other contexts we had come to regard as indications of good health. But the simple and instructive explanation was that the hypermarket company had already evolved a business idea that was sufficiently superior to those of its competitors. An organizational structure had then been designed to protect the business idea and promote its full exploitation. In view of the stage of development of the industry as a whole, this was exactly what was needed. The company had also introduced several improvements within the framework of its business idea, and had frequently revised and improved the way it worked.

But what was the company's core group like?

- In the Hypermarket Company the core group consisted of two persons only—the managing director and the purchasing director. The managing director, supported chiefly by this same purchasing director, had also been the key figure when the present business idea first began to evolve about fifteen years ago. Thus both men knew in great detail almost all aspects of the company's way of working, and they used to discuss things together and make decisions on various questions that arose in the course of operations. Each one of them represented to a very high degree the company's business idea *as a whole*. No aspect of it was unfamiliar to them. Under the two directors were a number of functional heads, that is to say *specialists*. These men did not command at all the same overall view of the business idea as the two members of the core group.

  Within this basic framework, however, the two top men had gradually come to play rather different roles, depending partly on their different interests. Thus the managing director was more concerned with resource development and in designing a strategy for the extension of the business idea. He was particularly interested in nurturing relations with power centres in the industry and with political power centres in the regions where the company was planning to establish operations. The purchasing director devoted more attention to the design of the internal organization, to control systems, and to the various improvements that were introduced within the current framework.

  However, there were other respects too in which the managing director and the purchasing director gradually came to differentiate their roles. On any question of a change in internal operations the purchasing director often functioned as a kind of *variety-generator*, presenting various suggestions and ideas. The managing director on the other hand acted as *selector*—he was able to make the often very difficult decisions; in fact he was known generally for his remarkable decisiveness in critical situations. This informal differentiation between the roles of idea-generator and decision-maker sprang partly from the two men's natural dispositions and personalities, but it had also taken shape and been continually reinforced in the course of their long interaction with one another. Also both they and their subordinates had begun to have pretty clear expectations of the roles they should play, and this served to underline the differences even more strongly.

This pattern of a variety-generator and a selector as two important complementary roles in a core group will later be clearly illustrated in some examples from our cases.

HIRMC (the Heavy Industrial Raw Materials Corporation) was another company in which the core group largely reflected the company's business idea.

● HIRMC was one of a small number of companies on the world market manufacturing from a vegetable raw material a type of material that was subsequently sold to a relatively small group of buyers. HIRMC and its competitors had joined in an informal but solid cartel. Together these companies had managed to acquire almost total dominance over the relevant raw material, which could only be obtained from one or two clearly defined subtropical regions.

Another ingredient was also required for the manufacture of HIRMC's product. This material was generally available on the world market. Technically the two ingredients were to some extent interchangeable, a fact which the company tried to exploit economically, taking into account the annual variations in the quality of the vegetable raw material and the highly fluctuating world-market prices for the other ingredient.

The manufacture of this product required large capital-intensive plants; sales on the other hand did not require much effort, since everything was decided in agreements within the cartel. These agreements were reviewed at regular intervals, when the various cartel members played a subtle double game with one another.

HIRMC was one of the most successful companies in the industry, apparently because it had clearly understood the various ingredients in the business idea and how they were related to one another. The formal management group consisted of six persons, but among these there were three who were obviously the most influential: the managing director, the technical director and the director of finance and administration. It was also these three who were apparently responsible for the major ingredients in the company's business idea.

Naturally, the technical director made himself responsible in various ways for the smooth flow of production, and saw to it that capacity was fully and evenly exploited as was required. He also spent much time on research on the cultivation side so that he could have some influence over the quality of the vegetable raw material. Some of the clauses in the cartel agreements were also interpreted rather freely, so the company was gradually able to ingratiate itself with some of the producers, thus being able to influence the quality and regular supply of the raw material. The financial director had gradually taken over responsibility for another of the factors which were central to the earning of money in the industry— the striking of an economic balance between the two main raw materials. He was in constant contact with the London stock exchange, with the shippers and with various industries around the world, and devoted himself among other things to speculating in the purchase of surplus stocks.

These two also supported the managing director in his main task, which consisted of continually preparing and conducting negotiations within the cartel in order to obtain better conditions in subsequent agreements by pointing to the poor results engendered by the present unfavourable agreement. To succeed in this crucial aspect of the company's business idea—the game against the cartel—the managing director also had to find ways of making good results look poor. One of his methods was to seek for profitable investment projects so that certain investments could be written off as costs.

Role constellations in the examples

These two examples have been chosen to illustrate that widely varying role constellations may still fulfil the criterion of reflecting a business.

- In the Hypermarket Company the two top men resembled each other very much in their mastery of the different components and the *ensemble* of their company's business idea. Naturally, in their everyday work they carried out at least in part quite different tasks, but even here they could easily have changed roles or allowed a subordinate to take over without any very obvious difference appearing in the short run. Both emotionally and cognitively the differentiation in their roles lay elsewhere: in the difference between 'the small agressive man with the non-stop flow of ideas' and 'the thoughtful judge and strongminded decision-maker'.

Moreover, the Hypermarket Company would probably have operated perfectly satisfactorily for quite a long time even if the core group had completely disappeared. But there would then have been no group or person representing the *whole* business idea. This kind of situation can have unfortunate results, as we shall see later.

• The core group in HIRMC looked quite different. In this case the three role-occupants had divided the main ingredients of the business idea among themselves—'the game against the cartel', 'the game for world-market prices' and 'the game for raw-material quality'—and none of them understood very much about what the others were doing. The only common interest which really brought them together now and again was their joint discussion of 'the game against the cartel'. Since the managing director had taken on this particular task, he was also the core-group member who had learnt most about the business idea as a whole. In HIRMC's core group we thus have a clear differentiation of roles at a functional level. Each role-occupant is really a kind of specialist in his own particular area, and the ensemble is reflected in the sum of these specialists' knowledge.

Our experience has taught us how important it is *that the business idea as a whole—its integrated systems character—is mapped in the core group.* This can be achieved by the presence in the core group either of *specialists* together representing all aspects of the business idea, or of *carriers*, i.e. some person or persons representing the business idea as a whole. In the hypermarket company the core group consisted of two such carriers, since both men spanned all aspects of the business idea. HIRMC's core group on the other hand consisted of three specialists who together covered the essential ingredients of the business idea.

Theoretically it may not appear to matter very much whether the overall idea is represented by specialists or carriers. However, we have often seen how difficult it is to support and maintain the extraordinarily delicate and complex systems character of the business idea unless at least one person represents a truly overall view, i.e. acts as carrier of the idea. This is particularly important when some change in the business idea is in the air—a redefinition perhaps, or a product variation, or some improvement in the efficiency of a specialized function. In such cases a man 'with the business idea in his bones' will have a vital role to play as defender of the integrity of the business idea. He checks that no change is introduced which is not founded on a full understanding of the base for the company's dominance.

8.3 The core group as an embodiment of the company's growth idea

Let us briefly recapitulate what we have identified as the main characteristics of a growth idea:

1. There are four important growth subprocesses, all of which must be embraced by the growth idea:

• the development of knowledge
• the creation of driving forces

- the handling of obstacles in the power system
- the development of resources.

2. Growth planning proceeds in stages in which visions and the immediate concrete measures taken stand in a dialectic relation to one another.

3. The art of handling growth is based to a great extent on the art of creating and exploiting different types of tension in the company and its environment.

4. The special conditions necessary to a growth process must be embodied in the organizational structure.

If the company's dominating ideas are supposed to represent the business idea at a mature stage in the development of a line of business, at earlier stages of growth they obviously ought to represent the growth idea. We shall now describe some cases in which varying degrees of consonance prevailed between situations of early growth and the dominating ideas of the companies concerned as reflected in various core-group constellations. These examples also show, however, that it is more difficult to stipulate suitable role constellations in core groups reflecting growth ideas than it is in core groups reflecting business ideas. This is hardly surprising, since growth ideas develop and change continually throughout the learning process, while the mature business idea is distinguished by its harmony and stability.

Some examples

In the last chapter we described how a new structure gradually evolved in the Trading Company under the impact of tension between two basically different interpretations of the company's situation and opportunities. While the company's established business idea was being redefined, several quite new lines of business were also getting under way.

- All members of management were fairly knowledgeable about all aspects of the established business idea. However, the real carrier of the business idea was the sales manager. He had been involved over a long period in the development of the company and had perhaps provided the major driving force about 25 years earlier in steering the company towards what became its main line of business, although the line had started as something rather different. The sales manager was generally acclaimed— as far as we could see with full justification—as the ablest man in the country in his field. He not only mastered all the necessary details; he also had a thorough understanding of the function and opportunities of the industry as a whole. To a great extent the managing director also represented the business idea as a whole, although his main role was now to handle the often very complex relations in the industry's power system.

The purchasing manager was fairly new to his post, relatively young, more of a theorist; without doubt he was full of interesting ideas about the industry. However, he lacked the sales manager's long and intimate contact with the industry and was therefore unable to 'think, live and dream' in terms of the industry when it was necessary to do so.

As time went by these three people assumed roles that differed in more than simple job content. The purchasing manager—mainly perhaps because of his theoretical training, his relative youth and his high ambitions—came to function as the aggressive generator of ideas. He called in question the company's whole established way of operating and made lots of suggestions about changing both overall strategy and various details regarding product range and organization. The sales manager, with his unique knowledge of the industry and the base of the company's dominance, fulfilled the role of judge: he examined all these suggestions critically and decided whether they would conflict with the industry's way of working.

Gradually, however, relations between the purchasing manager and the sales manager became more complicated. Their different roles on the problem-solving plane extended to the emotional plane as well, and a certain amount of tension grew up between them. The purchasing manager tended to look upon the sales manager as a diehard who was blocking the company's development, while the sales manager thought the purchasing manager was disturbing the smooth running of the day-to-day jobs. Looking at what was happening in our terms, we would go one step further and claim that the beginnings of tension on the emotional plane actually reinforced the differentiation in roles that already existed on the cognitive plane. The purchasing manager found himself making even bolder suggestions than he perhaps really believed in, while the sales manager was made to look even more reactionary than he really was.

The managing director was careful to strike a balance between these opposing forces. Two things appeared to help him: one was his skilful handling of interpersonal relations and the other his knowledge of all aspects of the business idea. The result was a whole series of actions which skilfully but quite clearly redefined the company's business idea. Major ingredients in this redefinition were the development of a new system of customer relations, the incorporation of new customer groups, and a completely new way of selling some parts of the product range.

We can now examine a little more closely the situation in the International Home Sales Corporation, whose unsuccessful redefinition process we have already described.

• A sharp schism in the company led to a change in the managing directorship and the retirement of the founder from the company. The new managing director had also grown up with the business idea and had been involved in its original development. He was what we have been calling a carrier of the business idea. However, there was a feeling among members of the board that the company's general competence needed reinforcement, and an experienced industrialist from outside the company was therefore given a management post. The new manager soon began suggesting changes in established operations and recommending new lines of business. Two production companies were acquired and the company no longer had to hire production resources or put out work on contract; a corporate staff was established and new men brought in who knew about marketing; a new management system was introduced and an operation resembling the established line but directed towards the professional sector was launched.

The result of all this was a series of failures and problems. In our earlier analysis we suggested that the trouble lay in a partial failure to recognize the base for the company's dominance. We shall now try to interpret this case on other grounds. First, however, we can look at one more example.

● Foodco, which started in the 1940s as a small company dealing in preserves and pickles, was founded and managed by a man who combined ability in salesmanship with knowledge of just this kind of product.

The chairman of the board was an experienced lawyer and businessman, who identified himself with the company partly because he regarded it as an important institution in the life of the locality. A few years later a young and ambitious engineer was appointed as technical director—the founder had been impressed by the fertility of his ideas and suggestions. These three men—the founder, the chairman and the young engineer—were the significant actors in the company throughout the 1950s. Figure 8.3 illustrates some of the characteristic features of this core group.

For this company the 1950s was a period of tremendous growth. Various changes in the environment such as an increase in living standards, shifts in the structure of distribution, technical developments and so on were all part of the reason for this, but these trends alone could not explain the company's enormous expansion. And certainly another explanation has to be sought for the whole series of experiments that took place, most of them stemming from the young engineer. One of the first things the young engineer did after joining the company was to go to England to study. When he came home, he announced that he had bought a disused military factory on the company's behalf for the production of potato chips. And that was how things went on: collaborative agreements with foreign companies, internationalization of production, penetration of several foreign markets, considerable expansion on the production side

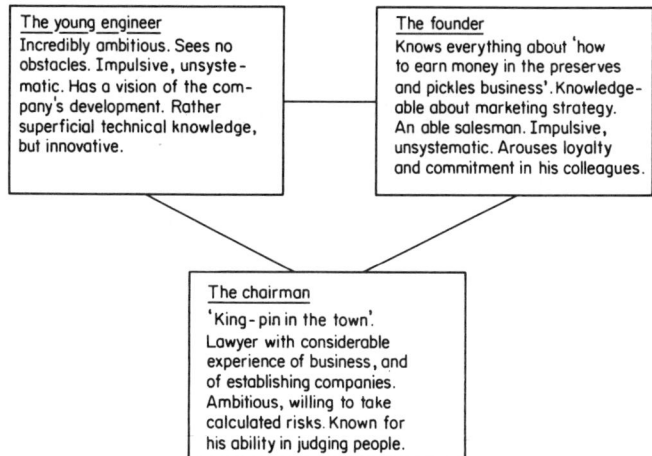

Figure 8.3. The Core Group in Foodco During the 1950s

and in the range of products, launching of ready-cooked foods, investment in catering and frozen foods, etc.

Not all these experiments succeeded. But the founder readily accepted experiments so long as they didn't affect the original pickles and preserves operation, which apart from a huge increase in volume was still operating as it always had done. Otherwise the only person who could influence the irreverent young engineer was the chairman, with his authority and his sound business commonsense.

Thus the 1950s was a very successful period, apart from a few ripples on the surface. Figure 8.4 illustrates, in a way that is partly theoretical and partly intuitive, the mechanisms that achieved this result.

In early 1960 the chairman suddenly became seriously ill and died. Nevertheless, several decisions on important new steps were still being taken in the spirit of the 1950s. The most important of these appear in the following list, which also shows the consequences of the various steps. All these measures were decided and put into effect after the death of the chairman.

1. Purchase of a fishing fleet and associated canning factory on the coast of Portugal. Unfortunately that particular part of the coast turns out to be exhausted and the capacity cannot be used. Big losses.

2. A new production method for pickling introduced. A castastrophic drop in quality and the loss of half the market share.

3. Purchase of a fleet of refrigerator trucks in West Germany, where a subsidiary is founded and the previous agreement with the agent terminated. However, there is no further penetration of the West German market, and the costly transport fleet is only used at a fraction of full capacity.

134

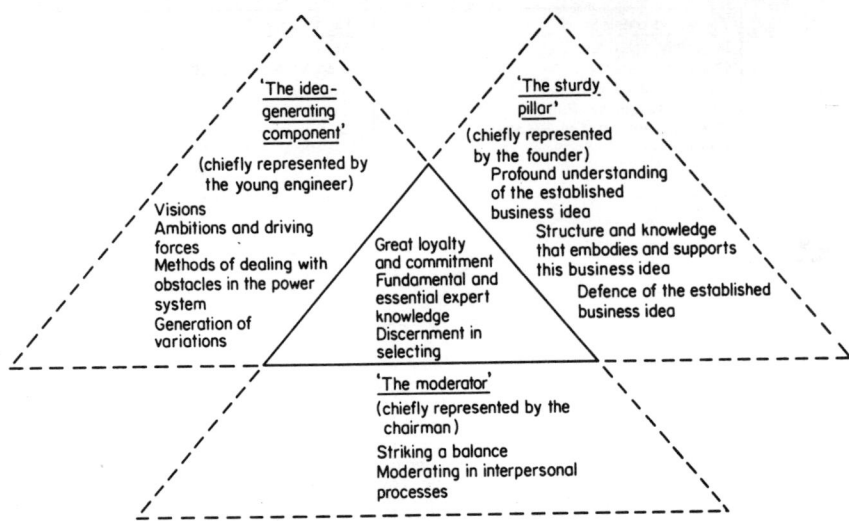

Figure 8.4. Basic Features in Foodco's Dominating Ideas During the 1950s

4. A new plant built in Switzerland. Unfortunately it turns out to have been built in an unsuitable region and the newly appointed general manager proves incompetent and has to be fired.

In one year Foodco managed to get itself into a financial crisis that led to a change in ownership and a new management. Obviously the excellent mechanism described in Figure 8.4 was no longer working as it should.

Interpretation of the role constellations in the examples

How far is it possible to identify some pattern in the different core-group constellations?

An integrated pair of complementary roles that occurs regularly is the one we have already mentioned: the *variety-generator* together with the *selector*. The purchasing director in the Trading Company and the young engineer in Foodco are both variety-generators, while the managing director and the chairman in the same two companies clearly fulfil important roles as selectors.

But we have also seen other supplementary selector roles. The sales manager in the Trading Company and the founder in Foodco occupied such roles. As carriers they frequently rose in defence of the crucial ingredient in their company's established operation, the ingredient that gave the business idea its special identity. These cases show that the carrier role frequently coincides with the role of 'defensive' selector when a mature business idea is being redefined, i.e. when a business idea and a growth idea are superimposed on one another.

In the International Home Sales Corporation, however, we found a core-group constellation—consisting of a variety-generator in the person of the new member of management and a carrier (of the business idea) in the person of the new managing director—which was not working satisfactorily. Obviously in this case the managing director was not fulfilling his selector role; new ideas were being taken up indiscriminately, with the result that the company's business idea was blown to bits.

If we compare the International Home Sales Corporation with the other two companies we can perhaps find an explanation for this breakdown. Both the Trading Company and Foodco were clearly subject to considerable tension which constantly threatened relations between the variety-generator and the selector; but the core groups of these two companies included other members who were able to combine the role of selector with the additional role of *inter-personal process moderator*. This role seems to call for skill in personal relationships and a talent for mediating between different opinion groups, and for a reasonably good overall view and understanding of the problems that arise. The case of Foodco illustrates dramatically how the tension between a variety-generator and a selector/carrier could be fruitfully exploited, so long as the process moderator (in this case the chairman) was a member of the core group. After his sudden death, the balancing mechanism broke down and the tension could no longer be controlled.

We have also learnt that the full realization of a growth idea seems to require a structure that is relatively free and undifferentiated, within which learning about the ensemble can be successively incorporated.* It is just this condition that often seems to be absent in companies that fail to grow. Such companies presumably imagine that learning can take place in various specific parts of the structure. But since these parts are already fully occupied with other tasks, or have little motivation, or are very specialized, it is not possible for any overall picture to emerge. Allowance is often made for this in the role of the *potential carrier*.

Yet another important role involved in giving concrete form to the growth idea is that of the *visionary*. The young engineer in Foodco, for example, was a visionary. In the next section we shall see how the importance of this role varies in different situations.

The last of the various roles we have identified is that of the *politician* or *shield-maker*. The politician is the man who deals with obstacles in the internal and external power system—he makes shields to protect the growth process and ensure the availability of resources. Much of the success of the Trading Company can be explained by the fact that its managing director was so skilled in handling the complicated power system in the industry. We have also seen an example of a research manager who was prepared to be known as 'the man who broke the rules', providing in this way a shield for the growth process.

8.4 The core group and its roles in some complex situations

The company's situation is seldom such that the dominating ideas in the core

---

*This proposition also has strong roots in the theory of learning in social systems. Dunn, for example, has given as a condition for learning 'some undifferentiated tissues capable of being employed in the evolution of new structures' (Dunn, 1971).

group can reflect pure examples of either business ideas or growth ideas. On the contrary, they generally have to embrace business ideas and growth ideas at different stages in their development. The following are some typical situations in which business ideas and growth ideas have to exist side by side in the company's idea system:

● when a mature business idea is in the process of being redefined
● when there are opportunities for the further extension of a mature business idea
● when natural driving forces have generated feelers which exist alongside established operations.

When there is a case for redefinition, for example due to a misfit arising between key factors in the environment and the company's base for dominance, the established business idea and the new growth idea which exist side by side have somehow to be combined, while tension must still be maintained. This 'double culture' often expresses itself in the existence of two parties, one radical and one conservative, as we described in the previous chapter.

● The Forestry Company provides an example of this. On the one hand it was necessary for the idea system to reflect the present business idea more satisfactorily; there was still too much of the rather bureaucratic and administrative tradition and too little of the business tradition. At the same time it was necessary to add something to the dominating ideas to make sure that the business idea could be redefined. It was obvious that the really big profits were beginning to appear at later stages in the chain of customer companies although the companies at those levels— sawmills, among others—had done practically nothing about their own market orientation.

There is another situation when the core group has to embody something over and above the business idea, namely, when the mature business idea is ready for exploitation and there are also opportunities for further expansion over a wider and more or less homogeneous market segment. In this sort of situation, during a process of internationalization for instance, the company may need both a business idea and an extension strategy of the kind we discussed at the end of the previous chapter.

Our earlier descriptions of core groups and role constellations were based on ideal types of consonance between the growth situation and the dominating ideas of a company. In fact, of course, the character and significance of the roles vary with the contents of the business idea and growth idea to be reflected in the composition of the core group.

The role constellation depends among other things on whether the company is embarking on a process of redefinition, or whether completely new lines of business are going to be developed. The functions of the core group will also be different—and easier—if natural driving forces are present and growth does not have to be induced. Below are some examples.

- In a redefinition process, when a business idea and a growth idea are being maintained simultaneously, several roles often coincide. Thus, for example, the carrier (of the business idea) may not only act as selector; he may also provide one of the potential carriers of the redefined operation—always provided he possesses enough underexploited capacity, is prepared to learn, and feels motivated.

- During redefinition the carrier fulfils in the ideal case an important part of the selector's function. In reorientations, on the other hand, the selector has to be found somewhere else. The visionary, for example, can perhaps take over much of the selector's function since his role is more important when growth is highly innovative (as it is in the case of reorientations).

- The presence, or absence, of natural driving forces perhaps mainly affects the function of the variety-generator. Natural driving forces can to some extent indicate the direction or content of the growth. If there are no such natural driving forces, variety must be furnished in some other way;

Relation to previous operations \ Driving forces	Natural driving forces start growth off and give it a content— natural growth	Ambitions and expressions of will are the main driving forces inducing growth
Mature operations redefined	Variety-generator and visionary exploit the driving forces as a motivation for their own ideas Carrier as selector	More difficult to find variety-generators and visionaries—they have to create ideas themselves and justify their own position Carrier as selector
Completely new operation or radical reorientation	Natural generation of variety, but this natural driving force must be gradually replaced by new driving forces that have no relation to established operations Visionary, rather than carrier, makes the best selector	Growth 'is all in the air' Strong visions and entrepreneurial resources needed to initiate growth and carry it through

Figure 8.5. Different Growth Situations Make Different Demands on the Core Group

the visionary—or the vision itself—may conjure up some other driving forces, thus becoming a kind of driving force itself.

- The importance of the interpersonal process moderator seems to depend on the degree of differentiation of the other roles in the core group. Thus a moderator may not be very necessary—perhaps even quite unnecessary—in core groups embodying a business idea in the exploitation stage. But as the roles become less involved in traditional tasks and more concerned with complicated growth mechanisms, some kind of process moderation in the core group becomes increasingly necessary, because tension and friction on the intellectual plane tend to reproduce themselves on the emotional plane as well.

Some of the qualities that distinguish different growth situations are shown in Figure 8.5, together with their implications for the constellation of roles in the core group.

8.5 Dominating ideas and corresponding role constellations in the core group—a summary

We have seen how the members of a company's core group—the significant actors—tend to assume different but complementary roles. We have identified some of these roles and shown how the core group can embody either pure business ideas, or growth ideas, or both kinds of 'ideas' together.

Our discussion of roles brought us to the question of the different functions which have to be filled. A single set of functions or roles can assume quite different guises in different core groups; for example, one person may play several roles, or the roles may be divided differently among the members.

The roles which we have identified in a core group that reflects the fundamental characteristics of a *business idea* are: the *carrier* and the *specialist*. The idea-carrier answers for making the business idea an *ensemble*, while the specialists answer for the different functions in the exchange process.

When we turn to *growth ideas*, we find that the roles fall into a different pattern, since the core group in this case has to reflect a complex learning process. Important roles here are the *variety-generator*, the *selector*, the *interpersonal process moderator*, the *potential carrier*, the *visionary* and the *politician* or *shield-maker*.

PART IV

The Company's Growth Culture

The art of the creative leader is the art of institution building, the reworking of human and technological materials to fashion an organism that embodies new and enduring values. The opportunity to do this depends on a considerable sensitivity to the politics of internal change. This is more than a struggle for power among contending groups and leaders. It is equally a matter of avoiding recalcitrance and releasing energies.
(Selznick, 1957, pp. 152–153)

We have now examined the implications of the exchange process and the growth process for a company's different lines of business. We have also seen how the business idea provides management with a tool for its handling of the exchange process, while the growth idea fills the same role in relation to the growth process. Further, we have noted that the different stages of development must be mapped in the company's dominating ideas and in the constellation of roles in the core group.

One question remains, and it is pivotal. How is transition from one state to another brought about? This brings us to the question of changes in the dominating ideas: how do they occur and what problems accompany them?

We shall call the process by which changes are made in a company's dominating ideas the process of *interpreting and adapting ideas*. We shall identify a number of characteristics of the company which affect this process and which together make up what we shall call the company's *growth culture*. The growth culture includes features that explain the company's growth pattern and its way of handling growth problems over a fairly long period, as well as its way of acting in new growth situations.

In examining the company's growth culture and the interpretation and regulation of its dominating ideas, we find several parallels with psychoanalytical theory, particularly in trying to understand the blockages that so often appear to inhibit the adaptation of the dominating ideas to a changing situation. We shall find, in fact, that the regulation of this 'ecology of the dominating ideas' calls for a special type of leadership that differs essentially from the leadership bearing immediate responsibility for individual lines of development. In the last chapter of the book we therefore discuss the business manager in the special role of 'statesman'.

CHAPTER 9

Some Examples of the Functions of the Growth Culture

9.1 The ecology of the dominating ideas

Up to now we have been dealing with the individual growth process, i.e. the process from budding embryo to mature operation and territorial dominance. We have tried to show how the problems that arise are quite different at different stages of this process; it is therefore vital that organization, planning, leadership style, etc., should also be able to change. Our major conclusions are summarized in Figure 9.1.

We have said that an inability to solve growth problems often springs from a lack of consonance between the demands of the situation and the company's dominating ideas. It is not unhealthy to have growth problems—on the contrary, nothing is more natural; but it is unhealthy for the company's dominating ideas actually to obstruct a solution of the growth problems.

The conclusion to be drawn from our argument is that a successful company ought to be able to alternate between different philosophies and structures as its growth problems change. The following are some examples of what is required.

- When a line of business has completed a learning stage and is ready for the penetration stage, the organizational structure and the dominating ideas will have to start expressing a business idea rather than a growth idea; mechanisms will be needed to effect the changeover.

- When a mature business idea is in need of redefinition, mechanisms are required to effect the superimposition of two systems of dominating ideas, one representing the business idea and the other the growth idea.

- When a company with more than one business idea—perhaps a divisionalized company or a conglomerate—runs several lines of business all at different stages of development, a great variety of idea systems will have to exist in the company alongside one another.

Thus, it would be desirable for companies to be able to adapt their dominating ideas to the demands of new situations, and to change their structure

	Early stage of develop-ment	Mature stage of develop-ment
Planning philosophy	Process view	Goal view
Conceptual planning tool	Growth idea	Business idea
Most important subprocesses	Knowledge development	The exchange process
	Creation of driving forces	Maintenance —product variation
	Handling of obstacles	—institutional maintenance
	Development of resources	
Typical roles in a core group	Variety-generator	Carriers
—	Selector	Specialists
	Process moderator	
	Potential carrier	
	Visionary	
	Politician	
Attitudes to tension and misfits	Desirable; they are interpreted, reinforced and exploited	Undesirable; eliminated
Organization	Tool for conducting and mapping the various subprocesses in the growth process	Clearly defined and structured to reflect the exchange process
Efficiency criterion	Learning	'Return on invested capital'
	Changes in the vision	

Figure 9.1. Summary of Major Differences Between Early and Mature Stages of Development

accordingly. But can we really expect management to be able to handle this ecology of the dominating ideas in practice? Or must we resign ourselves to an almost defeatist attitude, as Argyris does? Intrinsically Argyris accepts Burns and Stalker's propositon that a 'mechanistic' and in some ways bureau-cratic structure will work efficiently in a company in a stable environment, while a changeable environment requires a freer and more 'organic' structure (Burns and Stalker, 1961). But Argyris continues:

> We conclude that all organizations are continually subject to developing entropy and dry-rot, that the best known antidote may be an organic system... Thus even if one could prove that the external environment

of an organization would tend to remain benign, one has to face the fact that mechanistic systems generate internal conditions that lead to an internal environment that makes it increasingly difficult for the organization to remain in valid contact with its external environment and with its internal resources.

Moreover, if this were not the case, mechanistic organizations would find it extremely difficult to become organic when the environment becomes turbulent. Thus recommendations such as Likert's (1967) that the System IV* environments and technology may be worth serious attention. (Argyris, 1972, p. 33)

We shall try here to go a little further than this.

9.2 The function of the growth culture in some typical situations

The function of a company's *growth culture* is to regulate the dominating ideas and adapt them to changes in the company's situation. Later we shall examine the various constituents of the growth culture in greater detail. The most important of these ingredients are *certain features of the company's power and idea systems* (in particular any tension in these systems), and the *company's mechanisms for handling tension and conflict*. Thus we find ourselves returning once more to the importance of tension in connection with growth.

We shall now provide some examples of growth cultures and how they work in some typical growth situations. We shall also illustrate from our case material the importance of a certain balance in the growth culture.

The company with one business idea

At a time when conglomerates and other multioperational companies are in the fashion, it is perhaps surprising to find how many of the really large corporations are in fact based on a single business idea.

Industries and market segments tend to grow relatively quickly at first, after which they slow down and ultimately begin to contract. The average rate of growth for all industries is no higher than the rate of increase in the gross national product. But these cycles sometimes last a long time, and it is therefore possible even for expanding businesses to grow by concentrating mainly on a single type of operation. Sometimes—as in the case of General Motors for example—a combination of social and economic factors may have made it possible for a company to grow very big while sticking to a single line of business. At other times—as in the case of L.M. Ericsson or IBM for example—certain operations may become increasingly indispensable to a growing number of social functions as a result of various technological developments.

* = 'Organic-type system'.

If the business idea of a company is such that the base for dominance lies in a single expanding niche, then it will be possible for growth ambitions to find an outlet without any diversification into other kinds of operations becoming necessary. In a company like this the dominating ideas and the organizational structure should, in the main, embody the business idea. On this point, however, a few reservations have to be made. There may be times when the business idea has to have some kind of growth idea superimposed upon it because of a radical change in the industry itself. When IBM changed over from punched-card machines to electronic computers, it was not so much a complete change of direction as of assimilating a new expanding technology in its established operations. But the new technology revolutionized the company in many ways, and generated a growth rate which brought quite new problems in its wake. Danielsson (1974) has described how L.M. Ericsson also lived through two crucial technological revolutions in its field. Many companies are unable to cope with changes on this scale and break down under the strain; others manage time after time to overcome any tendency towards inertia, redefining their business ideas, or major parts of them, as circumstances require. And here we have one of the chief functions of the growth culture: to overcome inertia of this kind.

But companies also have to handle the transition from one stage in the development of a line of business to another, i.e. from systems development to market penetration, from market penetration to exploitation, and so on. To recognize that one stage of development has finished and needs replacing by the next, and to adapt the company's idea system and structure accordingly, is another of the functions of the growth culture. But how are these transitions and adjustments effected? Sometimes they are consciously steered, sometimes they appear to come about more haphazardly as the result of a power struggle.

• A good example of consciously steered transitions from one stage of development to another in a single-business company is once again provided by L.M. Ericsson (see Danielsson, 1974). There were changes in leadership each time the company moved on from one stage of development to another. The various leaders represented ideas which suited the particular stage: technological systems development, collaboration with the National Telecommunications Administration on the domestic market during the war, international market penetration, and so on. In this case the regulatory mechanism seems to have been lodged in the company's board of directors: according to Danielsson mainly in the person of Marcus Wallenberg. Wallenberg was obviously able to make a sort of all-embracing diagnosis of the company's growth problems, after which he would manipulate the management structure in accordance with his own interpretation of the needs of the situation.

Often, however, changes in a company are the result of an internal political process, sometimes expressing itself as a struggle for power. In fact such struggles seldom occur quite by chance, although they may seem to. The rise of a radical party, which gradually increases its power and eventually provokes far-reaching changes in the company's dominating ideas and organizational structure, is often an indication that there are problems and that these problems have been interpreted on different grounds by different parties.* The internal political processes feed off the knotty problems of life and may, if they are not put out of action, provide a kind of general mechanism for the replacement of one generation of dominating ideas by another.

- Sloan (1963) tells us how, around 1920 and in dramatic circumstances, the 'Sloan administration' took over from Durant, founder of General Motors. We can better understand the tremendous inner strain in the company if we take a look at what was going on outside. Durant built up his own empire himself, and he continued to rule in a style well suited to empire-building. In the meantime, however, the industry had changed, and the lack of consonance between the way the company was being run by Durant and the new situation outside led to very obvious trouble. Without this trouble to nourish them, the new generation would have had nothing to feed on and would never have been able to assume power and take over the responsibility for the company.

The company with a business idea that is past maturity

One day a company may discover that its business idea has become overripe, i.e. the industry and its own territory within the industry are beginning to contract, and its growth rate has therefore slowed down or even gone into reverse. We have already seen that the chances of coping with this sort of situation depend very much on what natural driving forces are present and what the company is able to achieve in the way of a major redefinition or reorientation.

But companies which have been successfully operating for any length of time in a stable and mature line do tend to get slack. They don't bother to nurse the ability to generate innovation or exploit natural driving forces. The financial planning gap in such companies is often positive, which means that financial resources are more than adequate to cover growth plans. When it comes to problem-solving ability, ideas, enterprise and leadership resources, however, the planning gap is negative. And, of course, expansion calls for much more in the way of creative leadership than a relatively stable situation does.

It may sometimes be possible to extract a new vision and a new centre of

---

*In Chapter 7 we described how the existence in a company of problems that are difficult to pin down exactly may reinforce any existing polarization, setting off a struggle for power between the established conservative party and a new radical party.

power from this kind of situation. In the absence of any internal tension or requisite variety, however, it is almost always necessary to get an 'ideological' battle going in the company first. Substantial decentralization may often be a step towards a growing variety of ideas. In the long run the decentralized structure can provide an arena where natural driving forces can be 'caught' as they appear and where internal, innovative confrontations can take place. This kind of structure, after all, leaves more room for individual enterprise and provides opportunities for exploiting local differences between markets.

Centrifugal diversification from an established operation

In most companies, natural driving forces can generate feelers and the embryos of new kinds of activity. A great many multioperational or diversified companies have emerged in just this way, as the result of a centrifugal diversification from an established business idea.

If a single-business company is really going to diversify, sooner or later there will have to be a change in its dominating ideas. It is no longer enough for the core group simply to carry the one established business idea; it must now reflect the diversity of the company's business—each line requires its own core group. And the company's growth culture must be able to handle the variety of growth problems that will arise.

The pull between a radical and a conservative interpretation of the company's situation often marks the growth culture of the single-business company. In the multibusiness company the growth culture has another function. Some kind of knowledge of 'cultivating' business is required. What is important now is that subcore groups emerge, adapted to the various situations; that the natural driving forces are nursed by entrepreneurs; that each line of business is exposed to demands that suit its own particular stage of development; that the organization and the control system can cope with new business perhaps associated with a different industry; and so on.

In other words, in a situation like this, the growth culture is going to have to cope with a variety of new demands. Thus the situation will naturally include many kinds of growth problem. In the next chapter we shall be discussing this side of things in more detail. For the time being we shall simply mention some of the more important of the possible maladies of growth.

- The established operation is allowed to run down; the original territory is inadequately exploited because too much interest and too many resources are being diverted to new lines of business or new feelers.

- The new lines find it difficult to advance beyond the feeler stage.

- The new operations don't exactly stop growing, but development is too narrow to allow for the 'wholeness' that characterizes the successful business idea. In this way growth can become distorted and budding business ideas may never fully flower.

The established multibusiness company

By an established multibusiness company we mean a company running several business ideas at once, all of which are treated in theory at least as equally important; total commitment to one central idea is a thing of the past. This state may be arrived at after an intermediate stage of centrifugal diversification from a parent operation; or the company may have planned it from the start.

If there has been any special idea or intention behind the emergence of the multibusiness companies (most of these companies have in fact developed as a result of natural growth forces), it is generally the idea that the combination of several independent lines of business 'under one roof' does have certain advantages. As we have already seen, the idea that a conglomerate structure allows for a superior financial strategy has been much in vogue lately. It makes it possible, for instance, to strike a balance between new lines (which require learning and 'building' resources) and more mature lines (which have achieved dominance and are therefore generating resources). The two types of business thus complement one another, creating balance in the cash flow. On the one hand the learning and building phases need resources; on the other, resources are generated by the business which has achieved dominance and is now at the exploitation stage (Moose and Zakon, 1971).

Incentive, the investment and development company of the Wallenberg Group, appears to be using a version of this financial strategy. It combines in its conglomerate structure several stable trading companies and a few technology-intensive companies which are still developing.

> Thus, from the start, it has been the company's intended policy to embrace both trading companies and technologically oriented manufacturing companies. The trading companies are more adaptable in the face of rapid, unforeseen changes in business activity and market conditions. At the same time these companies, with their high profits and relatively small investment requirements, provide the opportunity for the big and often risky investments needed by the technologically oriented companies. (Incentive's Annual Report, 1970, p. 5. Our translation)

We can also discern here a desire to strike a reasonable balance between established business on the one hand and operations in new, rapidly growing lines involving greater risks on the other.

Another common justification for the multibusiness company concerns the advantages the conglomerates are said to enjoy on the management side. Certain sophisticated management methods, it is claimed, can be applied to several lines of business or several companies at once. If by 'management' is meant strict systems of control and planning, then we are doubtful—even sceptical—about this. If on the other hand it is the possibility of developing a real understanding of the way business activities can be created and developed through different stages that is meant, then we can agree. But this second strategy requires a highly sensitive growth culture; it makes demands that have little in common with traditional ideas about business management, demands which seem in fact to conflict with these ideas.

9.3 The balanced growth culture—learning values and exploitation values

In many successful companies we have found it possible to identify, at the highest level, power centres that represent ideas and values suitable to the different stages in the development of a line of business. One group of actors commonly upholds values concerned with learning, while another upholds values concerned with stability or exploitation. This dual culture is expressed in feelers and development work supported by the learning values, and in the exploitation of business ideas backed up by the exploitation values.

There is an interesting illustration of the tension between learning and exploitation value groups in Danielsson (1974), a study of the rise of some large Swedish companies operating on the international market. One of the companies studied is AGA.

- From its start and until about 1920, AGA was notably innovative and expansive. A great many unique ideas blossomed and grew into a variety of operations all over the world. This was particularly true on the light-house side, but ultimately it applied to the gas operations as well. After 1920 experiments continued and new ideas were generated as often as before. But now no new lines of business emerged which could penetrate new markets, and there was nothing which could produce much in the way of earnings. All that was left, in fact, was really just an extremely fascinating laboratory which was being financed by several very successful established operations.

    This change in the company's way of working coincided with a change among the significant actors. The company had been started by a man named Nordvall, a skilful organizer, financier and businessman. On several occasions Nordvall had tried—and in the end had succeeded—to bring in a second top man. This man, Dalén, has often been described as a technological genius. He was the one with the ability to organize research and development work so that new and interesting products emerged. These two men, representing completely different sets of ideas and values, became the dominating personalities in AGA, and their fruitful interaction lasted until 1920, when Nordvall left the company. After this, the tension between the two semi-conflicting idea systems seems to have disappeared. Dalén's ideas prevailed unchallenged, and the company lost its earlier dual skill in developing and exploiting products.

What was the mechanism that held the balance between the different values? In this particular case the answer probably lies in the characters of the two people concerned and their relationship with one another, but our observations of other cases suggest that the usual pattern is a combination of balance and oscillation between the two subcultures. Swings from one to the other may occur as power alternates between them, or as individual lines come under the protection first of one power centre and then of the other, depending on their stage of development.

The historical development of Trucks and Machines Ltd has been described in Normann (1971). We see that the company grew in a series of growth processes. In our terms, it underwent a number of systematic reorientations.

- Trucks and Machines Ltd was a very successful company. It had a reputation for unusual success in the commercial exploitation of a variety of innovations. During the 1950s, starting from a basic electric motor operation and applying its considerable general engineering knowhow, the company entered the market for mining machinery. After a while, however, it was realized that electric motors were not really very suitable on this market and that quite a different kind of motor would have been better. It was therefore hardly a coincidence that when the technical director came across an undeveloped suggestion for such a motor in the course of his external contacts, he snapped up the idea. And so a new type of hydraulic motor evolved.

   The next step was the realization that this motor, which had new and unique attributes, could probably also be used in other fields. And at this point the company's deck cranes came into the picture.

In Chapter 4 we mentioned briefly how the deck cranes in Trucks and Machines Ltd came to be developed (to illustrate the different stages in a growth cycle). Now we can let the chief construction engineer, who was in charge of the construction of the cranes in the early stages, tell us a little more:

- In 1958 we had two technical directors. One of them—Mr Bill Peterson—was the assistant managing director. He was always the one who promoted new products. He was responsible for production and for part of the technical side. In 1958 his brother—Mr Fred Peterson—was managing director. The two brothers always worked well together. The managing director acted as a sort of brake, which prevented the company from expanding too rapidly. He looked after the company's finances. As well as acting as managing director, he was also really 'financial director', although someone else actually bore the formal title. This was because the managing director had been involved in the establishment of the company, and was unwilling to let that side of things slip out of his hands.

   Under Bill Peterson was a technical director and head of the engineering departments ... In 1958, when I joined the company, I was given a department of my own for the development of the hydraulic motor, and I was directly subordinate to Bill ... Then I began on the construction of the crane. Management controlled the whole thing, in that Bill came down here, talking, sitting and drawing with us often till late in the evenings. He was very interested in this project. As far as I could see, management was unanimous in wanting to see the hydraulic motor and crane project come off. But they may have disagreed about how quickly it should be pushed through, since the managing director acted as a brake and Bill was all for pushing on. The managing director was an economist and wanted to have value for money.

If there was any other soft-pedalling, it must have been because of other product lines. There has always been a lot of competition between different products in this company—the production managers and sales managers were always doing battle for their own particular products. When I joined the company, you could see they were competing for space in the engineering workshops. We managed to get a foot in just because Bill was determined we should do the job here. I don't think the selling side was particularly interested in this project; they had other products to sell and other suggestions on the go.

Priority has always been given to products that have been ordered. Bill had not been able to alter that. On the other hand, when it comes to prototypes, he has a good deal of influence. For instance he can see they get workshop capacity, even when there isn't really much to spare because of orders. In a case like that, it is really important to have a man who can put the pressure on and make it quite clear to the engineering people that the prototypes are to be produced as quickly as possible.

Bill Peterson was thus an able production man. He also seems to have been able to discover new ideas everywhere, and people knew he was always travelling all over the world. His particular skill in exploiting good ideas to the full seems to have been combined with an ability to spot how the opportunities he saw on the market tied up with the kind of knowledge he knew existed in the company. The production manager can tell us more about the development of the deck cranes.

- Mr Smith, the marketing director, was the one who forced the pace— because of him the company really invested a lot in the sales of the cranes, and he saw to it that a separate sales department was established for this product. But that was just before the first wave of cranes arrived . . .
  It was director Smith who said we'd greatly underestimated the problem of selling the cranes—remember that it was a big new product directed towards markets that were completely new to us. So thanks to Smith we began to work on the sales problem, and, as I said, we established a separate sales department and sales organization for the product. . .
  We also established servicing units at various places round the world. . .

At this point Bill Peterson more or less withdrew from the project, while the managing director became increasingly interested in it. This was no coincidence; it fitted what was a recurring pattern, apparently based on a kind of informal agreement between the two dominating personalities in the company.

● Bill used to devote himself to new ideas until they had more or less reached the finished-product stage. From then on it was the managing director—with his interest in economics and his demand for a good return on investment—who looked after things.

   The brothers had evolved a sort of code; they discussed things together and had ideas about each other's 'territory', but they had quite clearly divided the actual right of decision. In fact, some of Bill's decisions during the learning stage in the development of the deck cranes—for example regarding the build-up of resources—did not meet with the approval of the managing director at all. But it never went further than silent disapproval, and it did not affect the actual decision. All this was in accordance with their code.

Thus Trucks and Machines provides us with another example of a kind of balancing mechanism between two members of a core group, one of whom represents over a considerable period of time the learning or development values, while the other represents during the same period the exploitation values. In this particular case the balancing mechanism can perhaps be described as a combination of mutual respect, a certain amount of joint problem-solving, and a clear division in the right to make decisions. Naturally the two men also shared certain ideas, for instance about the relation between the company's product and market strategies on the one hand and its financial situation on the other, and this helped to keep a successful balance. A comment from Bill Peterson is illuminating.

● But if you've already made some money, you've got to put it somewhere. If we hadn't used the money we'd earned during the 1950s to develop our present products, we wouldn't still exist today.

In the next chapter we shall see that if a core group lacks either of these ingredients—learning values or exploitation values—the company's dominating ideas may become distorted.

CHAPTER 10

Synergy or Schizophrenia? The Problem of Handling Tension

One of the functions of the growth culture is to seize upon tension, to relay it and resolve it. Tension may be generated by natural driving forces or it may be the product of various manoeuvres on the part of the actors. It is reproduced in different parts of the company; at the same time, it can assume different shapes and give rise to a battle of ideas. Thus the ability to handle tension is closely linked to the presence of an effective *process for adjusting and adapting the dominating ideas* as the situation requires.

In the last chapter we described some of the functions of the growth culture and examined the way it ought to operate in various kinds of growth situation. In this chapter we shall approach the growth culture from another point of view. We shall look at some examples of failure to create and resolve tension successfully, and we shall see how difficult it is to change the dominating ideas of a company in such situations. We shall therefore also examine some of the mechanisms we have found blocking the process of interpreting and adapting the dominating ideas.

A growth culture is expressed in the pattern of growth ideas and business ideas in a company, and in the way these ideas have developed. From another angle, the manifestation of the growth culture is also an expression of a 'pathology of growth'. It may therefore also be fruitful to investigate the growth culture by looking at problems, especially in the shape of systematically repeated failures and inability to handle certain types of growth situations. If, for instance, a company repeatedly fails to exploit new lines of business, if it generally succeeds in launching new production-oriented operations but fails in similar ventures on the marketing side, if it usually succeeds in the spontaneous generation of idea embryos but fails to develop embryos into feelers, then there is reason to believe that the pattern of success and failure must tie up with some identifiable property of the company's growth culture. And in fact it is difficult to identify the growth culture other than by studying the history—in particular any really critical events in the history—of the company.

The reader will find that in this chapter we keep returning to stories of individual people. This is no coincidence. We have found that it is very often the personal strategy chosen by a few significant actors—possibly even by one—and the ability of these actors to cope on the personal level with living in a field of tension that moulds the company's capacity to grow and renew itself.

10.1 Different outcomes of tension

Good and bad conflict

We have frequently claimed in these pages that some kinds of tension are beneficial—even necessary—to companies in certain growth situations. Obviously, though, this tension can lead to really sharp conflict between people or groups in the company. Can this sort of personal conflict, for example, always be beneficial?

Organization research has wavered in its attitude towards tension. In most cases it has been taken for granted that conflict is a bad thing, and few people would presumably question that the kind of deep and lasting conflicts which can seriously disturb an organization's social climate are unlikely to be fruitful. Nevertheless, some researchers—Burns and Stalker (1961), for example— claim that a certain level of conflict may indicate that a company is functioning satisfactorily.

We can add a few brief comments to this debate, without making any claim to have found a final answer. According to our growth theory, we expect the level of tension and conflict to be higher in situations where growth and renewal are the predominating elements—that is, in the learning stage rather than in the exploitation stage of a growth cycle.

If we are to judge the value of a conflict, it is very important to understand where its roots lie. In our material we have found that the most common type of conflict arises when a company's organizational structure fails to match its business idea and therefore also fails to provide the right background for an efficient exchange process. Conflicts of this kind are rarely beneficial— except as material for the consultant, who sees them as symptoms of a misfit which may be jeopardizing the company's efficiency. The potentially beneficial conflict, on the other hand, consists of *tension between diverging interpretations of the company's situation*.

In the last chapter we described the well-balanced growth culture in Trucks and Machines Ltd, where the existence of two sets of values—learning values and exploitation values—and the balance between them went a long way towards explaining the company's frequent success in developing new lines of business. In this case, however, the tension did not consist of any fundamental difference between interpretations of the company's situation; it was rather a case of distinct but complementary components in a growth process. In this multibusiness company it was a question of *balancing* and *maintaining* tension; both the idea systems were necessary to support different phases in the development of the different lines.

The types of tension which we shall be discussing here, on the other hand, do involve a definite conflict between diverging views of the company's strategic situation, with different parties supporting different strategies for its behaviour as a result. Sooner or later this type of tension must somehow be eliminated; the best outcome is, of course, for it to be *resolved* and *exploited* so as to induce growth and generate new growth ideas.

But we have also seen more than once that tension alone is not enough to guarantee that new feelers will materialize and develop. If outbursts of tension are to be fruitful, various conditions must be fulfilled: there must be people who can moderate or regulate the tension, there must be arenas where representatives of the different viewpoints can confront one another, and so on. But companies often fail to create and, more significantly, to exploit tension, as we shall be illustrating in some examples below. As far as we can see, these failures often depend on the leader's inability to handle a tense and perhaps very conflict-ridden situation. In the next section we will therefore examine some personal strategies which we have seen being used by business leaders to master situations of this kind.

Let us now assume a field of tension in which two or more sets of ideas oppose one another. We can call these sets of ideas and values *poles of tension*. We discuss below five ways of dealing with tension, namely:

- expulsion
- overlegitimation
- compromise
- incongruence
  synergy

Expulsion

One way of dealing with a field of tension, of course, is simply to do away with one of the poles of tension. It can be expelled from the company, declared illegitimate, or suppressed in some other way. The remaining pole of tension then exerts undisputed influence on the dominating ideas.

The power situation is one factor which decides whether a state of tension is resolved in this way, but the power situation in turn is affected by what is happening in the external environment and by the general state of the company's operations. This is one reason why changes are easier to introduce into a company at times of crisis. In the midst of problems or crises it becomes obvious that new and radical action must be taken; it no longer seems so necessary to get rid of people with unconventional views.

Overlegitimation

We have seen some cases in which a budding threat to the dominating ideas or an incipient opposition is apparently accepted with open arms—possibly after a certain initial resistance—and allowed to acquire considerable influence. But it often turns out to be nothing more than a bit of pretty decoration, co-existing with the traditional values but quite unintegrated with them.

- The Forestry Company provides an example of this. At one point the company was involved in a major conflict between representatives of the old forester approach to running the company and a new administrative school. The new school wanted to modernize the company, by introducing an advanced system of long-range planning, for example, so that new strategies could be plotted for the future. After a certain amount of struggle, the new school appeared to have won total dominance in the organization. A large staff of planners was created, long-range planning was launched and new projects set in motion. People felt that the company had been given a real shaking-up; they now had a modern design.

The reality was in fact quite different. Operations were run in the same way as before by the old school, while the new school spent its time planning. The most obvious result of their efforts was a certain amount of grumbling from people who had to fill in lots of forms. In fact the company was divided into two separate cultures, which had nothing to do with one another and which therefore had no effect on one another either.

- The Chemicals Company, like most companies in the industry concerned, had generated a number of feelers over the years and these had given rise to a very complicated and variegated product–market structure. The company was becoming increasingly tension-ridden, partly because its structure suited some of the various products better than others and this was beginning to be noticed. The old culture of the small manufacturing company still persisted, but several voices could also be heard calling with growing vehemence for innovation, modern management, research, and product development. These voices also pointed out that although things had been going well up to now, a couple of the company's main products were getting old and needed replacing.

This company, too, was given a facelift: a highly qualified research department, development departments, long-range planning departments, and so on, were introduced. But these departments were only accepted by the traditional party so long as they kept to themselves and did not interfere with operations. Thus while the company continued along much the same tracks as before, it enjoyed a reputation in the world outside for being ultra-modern, innovative and progressive. The outward appearance did not correspont to the inner reality; it was simply a decor. In the end, two cultures or idea systems were living alongside one another in the company: on the one hand was the old small-manufacturer spirit, and on the other hand the elegant decor of what looked like growth. But the tension between them was resolved in such a way that the demands of both sides were met, without either having to give way. The development work was radically reorganized several times, but each time it simply meant that resources became more specialized; nothing really interfered with current operations.

What distinguishes situations like these seems to be that the established power centres are too weak to expel the new ideas without risking their own position. There may be several reasons for this. One might be that the new pole of tension represents ideas which are anyway in the air, perhaps in the particular industry or in industrial society as a whole. If lots of other companies are introducing long-range planning, it is difficult for the established power centre to oppose the idea altogether. It seems better to accept long-range planning formally, while making sure it is designed so that it can do no harm. But there remains a risk that this kind of overlegitimation may give rise to lasting tension. After all, the company is establishing two cultures which, although isolated from one another, are going to have to live side by side.

As a way of resolving tension, overlegitimation is really a more subtle version of expulsion, in that it achieves the same result while appearing to do exactly the opposite. This strategy has been described by researchers in several disciplines. The philosopher Marcuse (1969), for example, speaks of 'repressive tolerance' to describe the process by which oppositional groups are wholly accepted on the pretext that 'opposition is always healthy'. In fact, all that happens is that the opposition is so thoroughly absorbed into the established system that it loses all its sting. In organization theory Selznick (1949) has minted the expression '*coöptation*' to describe the mechanism by which an organization tries to eliminate certain external groups which it sees as obstacles to its own goals by absorbing them into itself.

Sometimes, too, this kind of strategy may reflect a fundamental split in the personality of a leader. Overlegitimation is not only an expression of fear and defensiveness; it may also be the expression of a secretly nurtured hope, or of some ideal picture that the leader has of himself and of which he may barely be consciously aware.

Compromise

The compromise may often appear as a kind of integration of two poles of tension. However, it is typical of the compromise that any integration is purely superficial. The outcome of the compromise—whether it be a new strategy, a new growth idea or a new structure—is not usually particularly good or particularly bad, and it contains a mixture of elements from the two poles. These can coexist and to some extent even support one another, but they do not create a really new whole or ensemble.

Compromises are often a sign of goodwill; at the same time they show that the people concerned have been unable to live long enough with tension to allow it to find a genuine resolution. In the short run at least, a compromise may provide a better alternative than many other ways of resolving conflict. Unfortunately, though, apart from any other disadvantage it may have, it also tends to smother the potential energy in the field of tension. If some other solution is found, this energy may be able to survive—although possibly only as an underground movement.

Commodities Ltd designed a structure which is typical of this kind of compromise.

- In the mid-1960s the company found that conditions regarding markets and competition, together with the spontaneous generation of new lines which had been taking place, had resulted in a new pole of tension that was growing increasingly strong. It consisted of a market pull—a counterweight to the company's traditional, production-oriented values.

In the smoothly running and effective management group it was not difficult to agree in time that the new ideas must be taken into account. More resources were directed towards the marketing side: a marketing department was established, product managers were appointed, market analysts carried out studies, and so on. However, all this left the old production-oriented structure practically untouched. In the end this began to make it difficult to coordinate the technical and the marketing sides, particularly on questions of product development. Attempts were made to solve these problems by establishing various committees and appointing special coordinators.

This structure functioned reasonably well. It was realized that the different poles of tension in the company had to be coordinated and integrated somehow, but the measures imposed were not original or radical enough. People were still either 'technicians' or 'marketing people', they didn't see themselves as belonging to an ensemble or all-round knowledge team—and the return on invested capital fell progressively.

A compromise is naturally only possible between ideas and values within the same frame of reference (or logic); you can give and take only so long as this remains the same. The parties involved will experience this as a 'zero-sum tension'.

Incongruence

In any particular situation it is often very difficult to know whether we are facing a conflict between frames of reference (or logics) or simply between 'variations on the same theme'. But if we try to reach a compromise across the borders of two frames of reference (for example, two business ideas), the outcome is most likely to become *incongruent*—a misfit-ridden aggregate of elements belonging to essentially different systems. This is an outcome that is qualitatively different from the original poles of tension, and to all the parties involved, an inferior one. We could perhaps call this a 'negative-sum tension'.

An example of an incongruent outcome is to be found in Medical Products Ltd, whose abortive business idea we described briefly in Chapter 3. When we first came into the picture, two poles of tension had become crystalized in the company: one firmly upholding the traditional policy and one recommending products and markets of a less sophisticated character (Normann, 1971).

● Medical Products Ltd had always manufactured high-quality products. The company was not particularly anxious to change in this respect, but an external professional consultant had persuaded them to start manufacturing a comparatively simple skinfood series. A special subsidiary was established to take care of the new products, but right from the beginning there was a dualism in its structure so that it was never quite clear what the company was supposed to be aiming at: the managing director of Medical Products was also head of the new subsidiary; all staff were recruited from the parent company and they even continued to work in their old offices, and so on. The lack of consonance (incongruence) which arose in the new operation is illustrated in Figure 10.1.

Properties of the product	Ideas about the product		Final product
	According to traditional company policy	According to the suggested new policy	
Direct advertising to the general public		x	
Described as a cosmetic		x	
Cosmetic image		x	
Prescription not necessary		x	x
Distribution through stores and department stores		x	
Advertising in the professional medical press	x		x
Medical name	x		x
Medical image	x		
Registered as a medical product	x		
Distribution through chemists' shops	x		x
Medical cleansing lotion as a complementary product			x
Image of a cosmetic with marked medical advantages	x		x

Figure 10.1. An Example of Incongruence as the Outcome of Tension (Adopted from Normann, 1971, p. 13)

The first column in the table reflects the traditional view of the company's products, while the second column shows how representatives of the new values regarded the new skinfood. The third column shows what the product is really like. Here we see that the absence of prescriptions and the product's nature as a cosmetic are obviously features that are inconsistent with its more medical attributes. Admittedly the company eventually began to sell the product through stores and department stores, but that meant that the new distribution channel in turn conflicted with several of the other attributes of the product.

In this case actions taken conflicted with several of the criteria of a good growth idea. In the end both the new subsidiary and the product that was being manufactured there were suffering from a fundamental dualism and lack of integration. Although we have not had the opportunity of analysing this company's growth culture in any great detail, we nevertheless felt that the dualism stemmed from the top of the company, where there seemed to have been considerable doubt about whether the new step should be taken or not. And when it was finally taken, the new subsidiary was subjected to such strict control that it was very difficult for it to develop on its own.

- We have already described the awkward situation of the International Home Sales Corporation. The pole of tension represented by the external consultant associated with the management group acquired too much influence over the redefinition of the company's business idea. The result was that within a year the company's organizational structure and its system of ideas were riddled with conflict and inconsistencies. Various ingredients in the new system of ideas had caught on in some parts of the company, but they didn't agree at all with the old business idea, which had actually been a very happy one. In our view, however, the company had become so complex that many of the values embraced by the new pole of tension would have been fruitful, if they could have been integrated into the established culture. As it was, the new ideas which did catch on simply gave rise to incongruence.

Synergy

In a compromise, some elements of the two polarized idea systems are combined into an ensemble which, to some extent at least, manages to function. In the case of expulsion one of the systems survives, while in the case of overlegitimation both systems survive more or less unchanged. In the incongruent outcome, elements from both the idea systems are combined in such a way that the new entity is misfit-ridden and inconsistent.

Synergy differs from these outcomes in being neither a reflection of one of the poles of tension nor a mixture of them both. Instead it represents something quite new in relation to either of the two poles of tension. And once synergy is achieved, all the parties involved are proved right—and wrong! What has actually happened is that an overarching frame of reference has been created, in which both of the original sets of ideas can be interpreted in a new and broader setting. The outcome forms an ensemble with a new consistent logic of its own.

- At our first contact with the Swedish-Malaysian Trading Company, we were aware of a tension in the air and a sense of conflict perhaps stronger than any we had met elsewhere. One group, consisting mainly of people who had been with the company from the beginning when it occupied a very marginal position on the market, believed firmly in the importance of having a 'business nose' and of being able to make 'snap decisions'. Another group, which had become increasingly vociferous as they saw how the company was growing, pointed out that the organization was now very big and blessed with a corps of regular customers who demanded stable quality and regular deliveries. They also pointed out that the industry as a whole really represented a kind of oligopolitical cartel, where skill in the power game was more important to success than a 'business nose'. The company ought therefore to seek to stabilize its structure, buy its own transport vessels, and even perhaps make itself less dependent on the raw material by starting a research department to investigate the possibilities of doing its own processing.

  We also found considerable tension between the sales managers in the different countries, and between these managers and head office. The regional heads had little influence over the destination of the cargoes, and objected that they were held responsible for a result over which they had little control. In addition to which, they all felt they were being treated unfairly in comparison with the other sales managers.

Obviously, in this case, the business idea suitable to a large company in this industry was different from the business idea suitable to a marginal company. Now that the company was so large, it needed to stabilize its environment by eliminating various types of disturbance *and* maintain its 'business nose' for use in individual situations. It also needed to make the most of its regional connections *and* of the advantage of sitting 'like a spider in its web, directing and redirecting boats as the raw-material market in London swings this way and that', as the sales director used to put it.

In Chapter 7, when we were analysing the situation of the Swedish-Malaysian Trading Company partly from another point of view, we suggested that the two opposing views were based on incomplete knowledge of the company's and the industry's way of working. Gradually, however, a new common view of the company's situation emerged which, together with a new structure in the shape of a decentralized matrix organization, made it possible for many more people to grow and learn, and to develop the business ideas as an ensemble.

In the next chapter we shall analyse in greater detail the process by which management was able to uncover and interpret the tensions, which could then be resolved as synergy was achieved.

10.2 Changing the dominating ideas

Interpreting and regulating ideas—the leading process

The dominating ideas represent the established interpretation of a company's situation and of what the situation demands. As a company passes through different stages of development in a structurally changeable environment, continual reinterpretations of its situation will be necessary. In other words, there must be a process by which the dominating ideas are adjusted to the needs of the current situation. Naturally this does not mean that previous experience, or the existing definition of the situation, is worthless. On the contrary, the most satisfactory way of changing the dominating ideas is in conjunction with a continuous *interpretation of current events* inside and outside the company as a way of testing the existing frame of reference, and with a continuous *reinterpretation* of earlier events in order to fit them into new patterns.

The interpretation of ongoing and historical events and the associated adjustment or regulation of the dominating ideas is probably the most crucial of the processes occurring in the company. If the interpretation process breaks down, other processes will often fail as well. Among the various subprocesses, this process is therefore a kind of leader. We have already diagnosed what we believe to be the basic cause of growth problems in companies, and have suggested among other things that misfits between the company's organizational structure and its actual situation in a deeper sense are merely a symptom of a malfunctioning interpretation process bringing about a misfit between the dominating ideas and the prevailing situation. *The only way to bring about lasting change and to foster an ability to deal with new situations is by influencing the conditions that determine the interpretation of situations and the regulation of ideas.*

In this section we shall describe some of the typical obstacles or blockages that can obstruct this important process. But first we must take a closer look at two features of the dominating ideas, both of which will affect the way the ideas are regulated: first, the historical roots of the dominating ideas, and secondly, the important connection between the personal situation of the significant actors and the dominating ideas.

The dominating ideas as an historical product

In depth psychology it is felt that in order to understand, and therefore to deal with, the individual's conceptual world it is necessary to go far back into his history. In the same way, the clinical organization researcher must go back into the history of the individual company in order to reach a real understanding of its system of dominating ideas. The real shape of this system cannot be discovered just by asking questions. Far too many of the ideas concerned are subconscious, latent, or even (with or without the awareness of those concerned) hidden behind some kind of decor or front. Only by reconstructing the genesis of the ideas is it possible for the clinical researcher to discover what they are and, together with the client, to set about changing them.

Naturally, the ideas and values which come to dominate in a company are in part the result of a gradual development. Even so, a very great many of them are obviously connected with critical events in the company's past. The situations which generally lead to changes in the dominating ideas are those for which nobody in the company seems to have any established prescriptions. It is in this kind of situation that the established ideas prove inadequate for the interpretation and handling of events, and a feeling of crisis—sometimes obvious, sometimes less so—arises.

To illustrate this we can quote a well-known description of a crucial event of this kind, namely, the crisis at General Motors at the beginning of the 1920s when work was being done on a new and revolutionary 'copper-cooled' (air-cooled) engine. Sloan (1963) was very much aware of the importance of this critical event.

> This chapter is a painful one in the General Motors story, but I see no way to avoid it if I am to account for General Motor's progress. For, as often happens, the lessons of such experience are the best learned lessons. The years 1921 and 1922 fortunately offered time to spare for a schooling that was to have a considerable part in shaping the future of the corporation.
>
> The problem was one of conflict between the research organization and the producing divisions, and a parallel conflict between the top management of the corporation and the divisional management. The subject of the conflict was a revolutionary car with an air-cooled engine of Mr Kettering's design, which Pierre S. du Pont proposed as a replacement for the corporation's conventional cars with water-cooled engines.
> (Sloan, 1963, p. 71)

- The problem at General Motors at this time was to improve some of the decentralized divisions, especially Chevrolet, which were struggling on the low-price market. Particularly on the technical side GM was much inferior to its greatest competitor, Ford. The top man on the central technical staff had begun to work on an idea for a revolutionary new engine, and he managed to sell it to the most powerful faction in the management. This group decided that there should be no further development work on the existing water-cooled engines in the Chevrolet division; instead the division should start collaborating with the central technical staff on the air-cooled engine.

  In the course of the development work, however, all sorts of problems cropped up. People in the Chevrolet division were thoroughly put out and didn't like having their other development plans shelved in this way; central staff and the division found it difficult to collaborate; other divisions showed more interest in the innovation; there was irritation in several quarters about what was felt to be corporate management's unrealistic line of development. Several years later failure had to be admitted, and the first cars on the market with the new engines had to be quickly withdrawn. Altogether it was felt that General Motors had lost a couple of years in its struggle with Ford on account of the adventure with the copper-cooled engine.

However, people realized that this kind of situation could well recur, and a real attempt was made to learn from these critical events.

The significant influence of the copper-cooled engine was in what it taught us about the value of organized co-operation and co-ordination in engineering and other matters. It showed the need to make an effective distinction between divisional and corporate functions in engineering, and also between advanced product engineering and long-range research. The copper-cooled-engine episode proved emphatically that management needed to subscribe to, and live with, just the kind of firm policies of organization and business that we had been working on. Altogether the experience was to have important consequences in the future organization of the corporation.
(Sloan, 1963, p. 94)

We could say that a new set of dominating ideas, deeply rooted in an episode that had been unpleasant for everyone, emerged as a result of management's efforts to interpret and learn from these events. Often, however, the upshot of crucial events like this is that new values and ideas are forced on a company from outside. In such cases we can say that the changes are more a result of invasion than of any process originating inside the company.

This kind of invasion is often the result of a recruitment decision and the subsequent appointment of new and important members who represent different values and ideas. However, it is often necessary first that some marginal change should have occurred in the system of dominating ideas, thus creating the conditions necessary for action such as the recruitment of new personnel. This action will then reinforce the first marginal change.

- Traditionally Europharma had always been dominated by technicians, in particular by chemists. In the mid-1950s there was much discussion in the industry about the significance of certain new orientations—one of them was the importance of applying pharmacological knowledge to the manufacture of medical products. The managing director felt that this new turbulence in the environment should be taken into account, and he therefore appointed the company's first pharmacologist.

This man turned out to have a very strong personality. He was able to push his own ideas through, and he soon got the ear of the managing director. Only a few years later most of the strategic posts in the company were occupied by newly recruited men with backgrounds in pharmacology. At headquarters the view was dominated by a vast new building that housed the pharmacological laboratory, while the chemists were tucked away obscurely somewhere in the basement.

But new recruits are not the only source of invasion. If two companies merge or one company acquires another, two basically different sets of dominating ideas may come into confrontation. The way they subsequently blend will greatly affect later events. In the previous section we discussed some of the ways in which tension between two conflicting sets of ideas can be resolved with varying degrees of success.

The personal situation of the significant actors

When a man joins a company he brings with him not only his professional experience and skills, but also various personal traits. This has been well expressed by Levinson:

1. A man brings attitudes, expectations, and modes of behaving to his work which have evolved from his life experience.
2. A man brings his continuing efforts to maintain his personality equilibrium to his work ...
(Levinson, 1968, p. 16)

The first of these propositions relates to what we have already mentioned, namely, that earlier experiences and crucial events provide people with norms and ideas about reality. It may be a question of purely professional values, for example: 'In this industry success comes mostly through aggressive advertising'. Or there may be values of a more general type such as: 'Saving is a virtue'. In our material we were often struck by the fact that some problem or mode of behaviour in a particular company seemed inexplicable until we discovered its deep roots in a simple prescription or assumption of this kind that formed part of the inner reality of one of the significant actors, often the chief executive.

A more subtle form of interaction between personality and work situation is suggested by the second of Levinson's propositions.* Every individual creates an inner reality, consisting of ideas, assumptions and illusions about his own identity. Consciously or unconsciously the individual sets up ideal images of his own ego and judges himself in various ways against this yardstick. People are subject to various forms of imbalance or internal misfits. These tend to generate special needs or driving forces, and strategies have

*Cf. also Zaleznik (1966).

to be developed to handle both the driving forces and the misfits. Everyone's needs and impulses are different: they also change in the course of a person's life.

Inevitably the internal struggle with his own misfits continues while a man is at work. Clearly, therefore, the personal needs and driving forces and other individual attributes in a group of significant actors will have a profound influence on the company's dominating ideas.

Before looking at some concrete illustrations of this situation, I would like to make two comments. First, it does not seem to me that current classifications of needs and driving forces—the need for self-actualization, the need for power, the need to achieve and the fear of failure and so on—are by any means always adequate. It is much more important to try to understand individual situations and the special pattern distinguishing every individual case.

Secondly, there seems to be an interesting link between the growth situation of a company as a whole and the personal growth situation of its significant actors. Sometimes, for example, a company may need leaders who nurse a strong personal ambition to achieve great things; at other times a leader whose predominant need is for security or safety may be just what is wanted. Thus, in many cases, the degree of consonance between the company's growth situation and the leader's growth situation may be of crucial importance to an understanding of the company's growth problems.

Obstacles in the cognitive system

The knowledge and skills of the significant actors have a very great impact on the dominating ideas. Factors such as educational background and earlier career partly determine how management will act; these factors help to decide which problems are perceived, what solutions are recommended, and the way the problems are handled.

Among reasons why a company's dominating ideas may be slow to change and adjust to the real demands of the current situation, obstacles connected with knowledge (or lack of knowledge) are perhaps those that come first to mind: the mechanisms for sensing what is really going on in the company or in its industry are not adequate; problem-solving resources are inadequate; certain causes and effects are insufficiently understood; and so on. When blockages are of a purely intellectual nature like this, we can say that there are *obstacles in the company's cognitive system*.

In the course of our work with various companies we have frequently come across a number of widely-held ideas which seem to stem from a sort of general *management culture*. They can be found in management literature, they are taught at universities and in the business schools and so on. Together these ideas represent what we shall call the *rationality myth*, which is based on the idea that innovative development processes and structural changes can be tackled with the help of planning methods like the means–end model or the goal view that we have discussed above. The rationality myth may lead, for example, to the introduction of a continuous automated system of long-range planning. This may work perfectly well as a way of controlling the exchange process, but it will almost certainly serve to obstruct any real change in structure. Or it can lead to the introduction of sophisticated instruments for controlling product development. These may work quite satisfactorily in the case of product variations (a new label on a package perhaps), but they put a barrier of bureaucracy in the way of any really exciting systems development.

A special variation of the rationality myth is the *sequence myth*. This really means: 'First research, then marketing'. For instance, first we have basic research in a research laboratory; then the results are taken over by an engineering department whose task is to develop a prototype for ultimate transfer to an exploiting company. But if a development process is broken down artificially into phases or parts like this, for subsequent introduction into different sections of the company, the results may easily be incongruent. Admittedly, it is often easier to deal with complex systems by breaking them down into parts, but there has to be some mechanism continually at work to check that the different parts are being developed in a way that will result in an ensemble.

It is easy to misinterpret the causes of earlier successes or failures, and this gives management false premises on which to base its future action. One kind of misinterpretation stems from *self-deception*: management, misled by the results of natural driving forces, becomes overconfident in its own innovative ability. We found several companies which believed themselves to be extremely innovative and whose managements were convinced of their own special skill, while really it was a few natural driving forces that had generated a series of feelers. If a company misinterprets its own ability, it will probably ignore or underestimate the difficulty of replacing the natural driving forces by other driving forces when the time comes. In fact a very noticeable feature of a successful growth culture is a perceptive and realistic understanding of the driving forces.

Let us take Robert Heller's satirical comments to illustrate the argument that things can go very wrong if management ascribes its successes to the wrong causes, and then acts in accordance with its belief.

When Texas Instruments, rushing away on a micro-circuit whirlwind, decorates itself with alphabetical programmes like TTE (Total Technical Effort), OST (Objectives, Strategies, Tactics), and TAP (Tactical Action Programme), all applied to the personnel with TLC (Tender Loving Care), business-school admirers flock round. They only pay attention, however, because the alphabet soup is so rich with growth and earnings. If both are watered down, as happened to TI when micro-circuit prices fell apart, the chain of cause and effects collapses. The earnings and the growth didn't follow from the management experiments, theories and practices: on the

contrary, the management gimmickry followed from the wealth, for management innovation is an expensive pastime.
(Heller, 1974, p. 13)

Cognitive obstacles to the continual readjustment of the dominating ideas are in turn a function of conditions in the company's power system and in other parts of the organizational structure. Since every organizational structure serves to *focus attention* in a certain direction, a single event in the environment can be interpreted quite differently by different companies. In a predominantly production-oriented company, it may suggest that production methods should be streamlined, while in another company the same event may suggest that the company's advertising or marketing methods need looking into. A costly failure, perhaps to do with a new product, could be taken to mean that people haven't enough freedom of action and it has not been possible to develop managers of sufficient skill and responsibility, or it could mean that control needs tightening up—depending on what the prevailing assumptions are about cause and effect.

There are several ways of changing the cognitive system. By analysing the business idea and the growth idea in depth, management may reach a better understanding of the real base for its company's dominance. An historical analysis can reveal the driving forces behind the company's development, and show how events have been interpreted in the company on earlier occasions. Sometimes additional problem-solving resources—perhaps a new kind of specialist—may be all that is needed. Any really lasting changes in a company's cognitive system will also presuppose other supportive changes affecting the organizational structure as a whole.

Obstacles and weaknesses in the company's power and value system

The adjective 'dominating' in our expression 'the dominating ideas' suggests that when several interpretations of a single event exist alongside one another, differences in knowledge and skill cannot provide the whole explanation. On the contrary, *power* is the chief factor that decides which interpretation will become the dominant one. Even within the group of significant actors, some people will be more dominant than others.

The cognitive system and the power system are highly dependent on one another. If the dominating interpretation of a company's problem, for example, is 'We have marketing problems', then the marketing people will enjoy high status and great power, which will in turn make it easier for them to underpin this interpretation. But power can also be used to influence people's ideas about what the company needs in a particular situation. Crozier (1964) tells us that he found people manipulating information in order to increase other people's uncertainty. In this way they were able to make themselves appear important and useful. I have also seen how people can join a company and then exploit the special knowledge and skills which they command to sap the confidence of the chief executive or other top men. This has sometimes led to major shifts in the balance of power and to radical reorientations in the companies concerned.

It is not always easy to tell whether the power centre of a company is strong or weak. Sometimes, for instance, power is heavily concentrated but is used mainly to break up other groups and kill off any opposition. This kind of power centre is strong in the sense that it alone wields power in the company; on the other hand it is also weak, since its policy is destructive and it serves as an obstacle to change. The total supply of power is small. A company in this situation will either find itself unable to act at all, or it will be subject to hasty ill-founded decisions on a shallow understanding of its own real identity or the base for its dominance.

Another common weakness in company power systems is a bias in one direction, a lack of polarization. After all, in the tension between two opposing interpretations of a problem lies the source of renewal. Sometimes, however, companies are almost entirely free of any kind of tension at all. Perhaps they are just too good at crushing opposition parties and guerilla movements; or perhaps the company is simply unable to live with tension.

We have already seen that a well-balanced growth culture in which learning values and exploitation values complement one another provides the right soil where feelers can grow into fully realized business ideas. If either set of values is missing, the dominating ideas go awry.

- The Quality Manufacturing Company was full of interesting technical ideas, and several small operations had been built up around a few original products. However, these all seemed to suffer from permanent birth-pangs and it was touch-and-go whether they would survive or not. In fact the company enjoyed a world wide reputation for the originality of their products, but somehow there was no real growth. On the other hand, it wasn't easy to get rid of the various feelers. For instance, twice the Board decided to discontinue one of its lines, but the people involved literally hid themselves away in a corner of the company and went on working. Another line did actually manage to penetrate a small segment of the world market and was very profitable, mainly because its divisional manager was a very able businessman.

This company obviously nurtured a healthy set of growth values, and it was unusually easy for new ideas to sprout all over the place. Unfortunately, though, there was no back-up from any set of penetration and exploitation values. There was simply a kind of general value recommending caution; there was a fear of taking risks and perhaps of losing. Because of this consistent lack of courage at the moment of truth, support for a new line always began to waver or even to cease altogether at the very moment when decisive resource allocations should have been forthcoming.

This is not an unusual situation: a company regularly puts out feelers;

it lets them reach a fairly advanced stage, but fails consistently to carry them any further. It often turns out in such cases that there is an element missing in the power system, something which would have been able to support the new lines through this critical stage. This situation can arise even when learning values and exploitation values are both included in a company's growth culture; in this case the missing link is a mechanism for transferring the project from the protection of one value system and power centre to another.

Note on the appendix syndrome

To start with, the management of a single-business company rarely has any major problem in handling feelers that give direct support to the established operation. We have seen that natural driving forces may generate a new line for this very reason—perhaps to counteract overcapacity or undercapacity in the main operation for instance. To begin with, the new line is not really thought of as a line at all; it is simply part of an attempt to solve a problem in the established business. So long as these feelers operate purely in support of the traditional business idea, they are generally given all the back-up they need.

But once the new line starts to get up speed on its own and to develop without the support of the established operation, then management starts to have more trouble. Feelings about new activities are divided from the start, because of their ambiguous identity. Also it is obviously much more difficult to judge things and make decisions as a new feeler moves further away from the basic operation. As this base is left further behind, there is more uncertainty about how to interpret situations and how to evaluate feelers.

We can call the cluster of problems that arises in cases like this the *appendix syndrome*. Obviously it is difficult, purely technically, to go on developing operations which have fulfilled the particular job for which they were started, i.e. to act as an appendix of the basic operation for the purpose of solving a specific problem; moreover, the new line easily loses its original legitimacy and may even be feared as a threat to the established operation and the accepted identity of the company. Thus any independent development beyond the appendix stage is likely to lose the support of the company's power system. This may put the new operation in fear of sanctions and jeopardize its access to the resources necessary for growth. Result: growth comes to a stop.

Obstacles in leadership style and norms for interpersonal relations

The idea of the 'lonely leader' is so widespread that it is difficult to say where it originated. The theoretical background has been described in great detail by several writers. Zaleznik (1966), for example, points out that every promotion to a top position has a positive and a negative aspect. It brings more power, certainly, but it also to some extent reduces a man's opportunities for social contact and normal relations with his former equals. The man who occupies a powerful position does not always hear honest reactions to what he does; his subordinates, after all, are more or less dependent on him.

It has sometimes seemed to us that what distinguishes one business leader from another most noticeably may be the way he is able to handle the loneliness of his position. Some leaders manage to establish relationships of great frankness, in which the problems we have mentioned may be eliminated altogether. But these successful people are not the ones we shall be discussing here. Instead we shall examine some of the strategies employed on occasion by people in leading posts who want to avoid taking up a definite stand in awkward situations and to be spared a possibly unfavourable feedback.

One such strategy consists of *establishing myths* intended to conceal the true circumstances. Here are some examples.

- In Universal House Appliances there was a firmly established norm according to which everyone was to be friendly and open in their relations with everyone else. People making short visits to the company did in fact get the impression that here was a really warm and friendly atmosphere. But we gradually realized that despite the friendliness norm there was quite a lot of conflict and aggression. One member of top management confided: 'This idea that we should all love one another is certainly important in the company, but it loses strength the further you are from the President's room'.

  In the end we realized that personal relationships in the management group, and between this group and the next level in the company, had been very complicated for a long time. The managers were all playing a kind of game, and the love-one-another norm was little more than a myth. It was a long time since any attempt had been made to tackle serious personal or interpersonal problems: in some of its lines the company was therefore getting into difficulties on the business side.

- In one of the companies we studied, it was almost impossible to discuss any kind of problem with top management, because whenever we approached any really serious development problems the managing director started preaching about the importance of the company being 'one big happy family' and telling us how successful they had been in achieving this state. Everyone would then sit silently looking at the table for a few seconds, obviously wondering whether to give up or whether to have another shot at it.

  In fact, the leading actors in this company spent their time backbiting one another in a way that we rarely witnessed anywhere else. Our diagnosis was that because of the design of the organizational structure, and the budget system in particular, the various managers were almost bound to try to score off one another instead of being able to cooperate; at the same time any attempts to make a serious examination of the causes of the problems or to tackle the organizational issues were illegitimate from the start because of the prevailing myth.

● In the Mining and Processing Company the managing director used to speak of his immediate colleagues as 'a winning team'. But it soon became clear to us that the winning team consisted of an assortment of players, some extremely able and some rather less so, but that as a team it was certainly not in particularly good trim. In fact the managing director was really aware of this and wanted to change the situation, but he didn't quite know how to go about it.

What is the function of myths like these? Presumably, in the first place, they help the chief executive or the management group to avoid dealing with matters that are beyond their powers or which, for some reason, they don't want to tackle. This may mean that the really difficult problems never even get discussed, because more digestible interpretations of the situation are provided by the myths.

In this way the leader is spared confrontation with difficult problems, and a vicious circle is set in motion: neglected problems grow worse and the idea of dealing with them becomes even more menacing, until the situation is serious enough for a revolution. Often, though, the myth-makers are aware at heart that the myths do not reflect the true situation, and they may even be deeply concerned about it. It is just that the lack of any suitable medicine inhibits the making of a probably unpleasant diagnosis.

Another way of avoiding confrontation with awkward problems involves exactly the opposite approach. Whatever is felt to be dangerous, awkward and difficult to handle is given an aura of legitimacy. (We have already described a similar strategy of overlegitimation in connection with the resolution of tension.) This method is wholly or partly unconscious and is often employed with the best of intentions.

● We have already written about the Chemicals Company in another context. We could now say that the company's big investment in development projects represented to a great extent a way of dealing with an active opposition. Neither the managing director nor the board really understood the demands of the opposition. In fact, intuitively, they disapproved of them. Since nobody quite knew how to handle the situation, the opposition was neutralized through overlegitimation and an elegant decor was erected.

We have found that this kind of decor-building is often the result of a particular leadership strategy—a strategy which more than any we have discussed is based on the defence of an established position of power. It is neatly expressed in the slogan *divide and rule*. The outward signs of this leadership style are not difficult to spot: members of the management group only get together for formal meetings and even then do very little in the way of problem-solving; otherwise it is rare for more than two of them to meet at a time. Their interaction pattern consists almost entirely of a series of pair relationships in which the chief executive is always one of the pair.*

Because of his divide-and-rule strategy, the chief executive is in the end the only person able to integrate the various kinds of knowledge embodied in the company, and this dramatically reinforces his position of power. He is the spider at the centre of the web. Other parts of the company gradually become increasingly specialized and increasingly unsatisfactory as decision-makers, since they have no chance of subordinating their particular functions to any kind of overall view of operations. Thus the leader who uses the divide-and-rule strategy buys his position of power at a price: the company is unable to embody a business idea or to learn and develop growth ideas effectively. The concentration of power increases, but the supply of power diminishes.

Sometimes a business leader may be guilty of making too many concessions to different groups in the company, and possibly to others outside as well. He then finds himself in a dilemma, because if he keeps his promises in one quarter he can't make them good in another. One way of dealing with this kind of overcommitment would be to allow the different groups to confront one another, but a leader who has already let himself in for so many inflated undertakings is probably unlikely to choose such a brave way out. Instead he will cultivate more of those pair relationships with the different groups which are so characteristic of a divide-and-rule strategy.

An inclination to promise too much to too many may indicate a failure on the part of the business leader to understand fully his company's identity. In other words he knows too little about the base for dominance, about the growth opportunities that resources allow, or about the natural driving forces that the situation contains. Because of this lack of insight, the leader will be left without any means of choosing among all the suggestions that are put to him, with the result that he makes promises all round.

There are of course other types of personal strategies, apart from those we have mentioned here, by which business leaders hope to escape from awkward situations but which in fact will only damage the company in the end. However, the myth-making strategy and the divide-and-rule strategy were the two that we came across most often. Applied by a business leader at the personal level, they often lead to incongruence, expulsion or overlegitimation at the structural level—in other words to some of the less happy ways of resolving tension that we have described above. Compromises, too, may be employed by leaders of this kind, but it is difficult to imagine that this sort of situation could ever lead to synergy unless the real leadership is taken over by some other person.

It would be wrong to suppose that the problems of leadership which we have been discussing here arise because people in leading positions belong to a special class of men. Rather, many business leaders obviously find themselves

*Cf. Burns and Stalker (1961).

in somewhat similar situations which contain the seed of special kinds of strategies. Most people feel a need to eliminate tension, to reduce uncertainty, to reinforce their positions and their power, to neutralize threats, etc.; these needs are expressed as the individual's situation allows. The head of a company is particularly exposed to conflicting demands; his chances of obtaining reliable feedback, however, are rather limited, although nobody is in greater need of it than he. The strategies we have described above should be seen as his way of dealing with demands which are so incompatible and so complex that he cannot find any other way of doing it. The demands on him may come from many quarters, even from himself.

● The Diversified Manufacturing Company, like the Quality Manufacturing Company, was reasonably good at generating growth ideas and new lines of business, but it never managed to push them through or exploit them. This success and this failure seemed to be matched by two strong but conflicting sets of norms, both of which had a strong grip on the company's top executive. One was a good old-fashioned creed stemming from the company's original head, under whose tutelage the present man had learnt the business. It included such virtues as an extreme reverence for thrift, the effect of which seemed to be that just as a new venture reached the resource-consuming stage the company always drew back or was so half-hearted in its efforts that it failed to penetrate the new market or only managed to achieve a marginal position there.

   The other set of norms stood in direct opposition to this: it implied a reaction against the old man and everything he stood for. Under the influence of this view the present head of the company saw himself as a modern and creative innovator. He was constantly trying to live up to this image, which perhaps explained his enthusiasm for supporting new ideas and projects.

We came across several cases like this, where the 'ego' and a kind of 'alter ego' appeared to conflict. But here too, as so many times before, it was generally possible to trace the problem—the coexistence of conflicting norms—to factors in the external environment.*

---

*Cf. Bateson (1972) and Laing (1961).

CHAPTER 11

The Business Leader as Statesman

11.1 Leadership at the level of the growth culture—statesmanship

The management of the individual branch of operations is directly engaged in administering the exchange process or some kind of re-definition or innovation process. Ideally, the dominating ideas of the management group will reflect either a business idea or a growth idea, depending on the stage of development which the particular operation has reached.

But now that we are going to examine more closely the process by which the dominating ideas are adjusted and adapted as changing situations require, we find that the kind of leadership required at this level is essentially different: a leadership with the function to regulate the company's system of ideas. We call this kind of overarching leadership *statesmanship*, and those who are exercising it—the statesmen—are members of a *meta-management*.* †

Meta-management does not embody, in the first instance, any of the company's business ideas or growth ideas; instead its task is to balance the total set of the company's lines of business. Typically, we can expect to find a meta-management in companies in the process of diversifying, or in mature multibusiness companies where every branch of operations has its own core group and meta-management operates on a higher level.

Thus, since meta-management is not directly responsible for the individual lines of business, its way of ruling neither can nor should be the same as the idea-carrier's, for example. The statesman does not step in and start deciding about prices or improvements in production efficiency. His task is to see that each branch of operations has a management and a structure such that it can cope with these and other problems itself.

We often came across top executives who were typical idea-carriers in

---

*This view of the leader as a kind of politician is far from new in organization research. Cf. for example Selznick (1957).

†The use of the expression 'statesmanship', borrowed from political science, is intended to arouse certain associations in the reader's mind with the way political systems function. On the other hand, I would like to emphasize very strongly that I have not taken over all the connotations that are sometimes attached to this concept–politicizing, manipulating, lobbying, and so on– which generally have a negative ring. In my conceptual world the statesman stands above all low political manoeuvring. What I have tried to suggest by using this metaphor is that the statesman and the meta-management observe and act, to a great extent, *via* the internal power system of the company; they often function as a kind of coupling device, constructing social and other networks (on this point see also Friend and Jessop, 1969, and Schon, 1971).

companies where new operations were growing up alongside the established business ideas. When such companies have to be reorganized to reflect a new multibusiness structure, the top executive also has to change his role; instead of an idea-carrier, he now has to be a statesman. A common problem as a company diversifies is connected with this transition: how can people who have been functioning up to now as idea-carriers or specialists be made to start acting as members of a meta-management?

This transition can be an extremely complex experience for a man who suddenly finds that the knowledge and skills which have helped him to achieve success in his career so far are no longer as valuable as before. He may have only the vaguest idea of how to act in the new situation; at heart he is often uncertain whether he can cope with its demands. The most difficult problem for the idea-carrier who must start playing the statesman is often that he has been alone is mastering most aspects of the company and has therefore exerted some direct control over all activities; now he must exert control essentially by getting other people to grow and develop.*

Idea systems at such a supreme level call for greater skill in handling situations and problems with a marked psychological and emotional content. The statesman, who is going to live at the centre of a field of tension and who will be helping other leaders to develop, will need a high degree of skill in these respects. Unfortunately the necessary skill is often inhibited by a malady which specialists and idea-carriers rather often seem to suffer from and which we could call 'superrationality'. The man afflicted by this disease has somehow come to believe that he is truly in command of things if he is always—or if he appears to be—the one who knows best or is cleverest. This feeling is in fact fairly natural to the specialist or idea-carrier within the field of his particular competence, but to assume sole responsibility for all problem-solving is hardly going to help the statesman in his main task, namely, to get other people to learn and to see that learning proceeds freely in various parts of the organization.

What, then, does statesmanship involve, and how does it differ from the other types of leadership which we have been discussing? In this chapter we shall try to answer questions such as:

- When does meta-management intervene?
- How does it get information?
- What means are available to meta-management—how does it control things?

It should be noted that the meta-management acts and reacts on essentially different types of stimuli and information than the management of a single line of business does. But still this information somehow has to reflect what is happening in the various lines of business. At some point everything that

---

*Cf. also the observations of Buchele (1967) and Greiner (1972) on the problems of entrepreneurs and company founders when their organizations begin to grow.

is going on has to be *translated* into a language suited to a 'meta-diagnosis' of the situation and adapted to the kind of measures meta-management has at its disposal.

11.2 The political system as a translation mechanism

We have found—and it has been a pivotal feature of our whole presentation— that some degree of competition between different interpretations of the current situation are likely to be part of a company's make-up, and this competitive spirit will also be reflected in the internal power system: individual people and groups will line up behind the interpretation they favour and in doing so will come into conflict with one another. We have called the system of ideas and values that emerges as the outcome of this process the company's *dominating ideas*. We shall now examine more closely some of the conditions of this struggle. What interests us in particular is the relation between the operations' stages of development and the internal political processes. We have already seen that political processes—the redistribution of power, status and resources—are a necessary condition for accomplishing change in a company facing structural changes in its environment. But the process also works in the opposite direction: external circumstances, i.e. changes of the company's actual situation, tend to resolve into internal political processes such as struggles for power, competition for resources, attempts to assert new views of the real conditions, etc. No organization researcher has pointed this out more consistently than Burns:

> Political action, even on the scale with which we are concerned, often does seem predetermined by more extended, external sequences of events, of which the actors seem to be unaware, at least as having a direct bearing on their actions.
> (Burns, 1961/62, p. 265)

And Burns goes on:

> Each actual change of this kind in individual concerns may be carried through without conscious reference to the changed context which appears to the outsider not only to have made the internal change possible, but even to have prompted it. But there is more involved than a difference of inter- pretation resulting from the difference in perspective of actor or observer. Political action is the necessary instrument for the accomplishment of internal change of this kind, which, to an outside observer, is the inevit- able consequence of a new situation. Looked at another way, that is, the new situation may be seen as a favourable set of opportunities, a releasing mechanism, which allows people to implement political action already being fruitlessly undertaken or being held in abeyance for the opportune occasion.
> (Ibid., p. 266)

This process, of which we shall be giving some examples, opens up interesting possibilities. Could the internal political system be the translation mechanism that we are looking for? Could it operate as a system of signals, providing meta-management with the information necessary for interpreting the company's situation—the base for planning and action?

We shall suggest below that the political system is important as a basis for the exercise of statesmanship. But if the system is to operate satisfactorily as a translation mechanism, it will have to be functioning adequately as a whole. It thus follows that *meta-management's possibly most fundamental task is to see that the company has a satisfactorily functioning internal political system.*

The political system does not only reflect external events. Excessive ambition or surplus managerial resources in the company, for example, can also result in internal tension. And even the *absence* of political processes may be an important signal. Thus meta-management also has to be able to interpret the cause of political processes, to know something about the kind of situation in which they are significant, and to recognize when they should be present.

Some examples of the translation mechanism at work

A most illuminating example of the relation between external events and political processes in a company is provided by Burns' study of the British electronics industry and its readjustment to postwar conditions (Burns and Stalker, 1961).

- In the companies studied there was much tension between the research departments, the marketing departments and the production departments. This was the result of big structural changes in the environment, where traditional (mainly military) markets were being replaced by markets of quite new kinds. For the companies this meant demands for a radical change in the composition of specialized knowledge. The power structure in the companies thus shifted in favour of the marketing departments, and it became very important to find new mechanisms for integrating different kinds of knowledge.

Internal tension is often the first sign that a company's operations have been becoming successively more complex and that the company, perhaps as a result of natural driving forces, is in the process of becoming a multi-business organization whose established structure is no longer adequate to present needs. Swedish Building Materials Ltd and Provisions Ltd are two examples of this state of affairs.

- In both these companies we witnessed a continual escalation of conflict between the marketing side and the production side. The marketing people claimed that production was not sufficiently flexible and did not comply with the necessary requirements. The conflict found expression, among other things, in quarrels about the design of the budgeting system and the establishment of project groups to improve the production-planning system and sales forecasts.

In both cases these problems came to be regarded by the actors concerned as mainly a question of coordination, but in fact this interpretation was far too narrow. As more information was collected about the companies' historical growth patterns and about the changes taking place on the market, the fundamental problem gradually became clear to the two meta-managements: the companies had evolved a business mix in which all the different lines were characterized by their own special way of making money and of growing.

- As a result of this realization, the action taken (the restructuring) was not the same as the companies had originally been considering. Swedish Building Materials Ltd was divided into two separate companies, each with its own business idea and with separate structures and control systems, while Provisions Ltd changed from a functional to a divisionalized organization.

- In Heavy Conglomerates Ltd, a company which had been basing its operations for many years on a standardized mass-produced product, a vigorous debate was now taking place. Some people claimed that the company's wage policy, its personnel policy, its routines for investment decisions and its budgeting system were all completely unsuitable—a criticism which many people including the technical director and the financial director failed to understand.

   However, a closer examination of these complaints and of the tension they were generating between the establishment and the revolutionaries showed what the trouble was: because of its particular technology the company had been putting out a number of feelers into new lines of business over the years, but present control systems were not geared to operations in the early stages of growth, and the company was not able to cope with the special requirements of the new lines. One or two top men were beginning to realize that a streamlining of present control systems was no longer enough; a fundamental change in the structure of the company was going to be necessary. In our terminology, this indicated that a meta-management was beginning to emerge.

In other cases, the political processes may be evidence that a company is in the process of passing from one stage of development to another.

- Project Administration Ltd was established in the mid-1960s by a visionary who recognized the inadequacy of established methods for the administration of building operations. The overriding value that emerged found expression in the declaration that: 'We are to stand for radically new

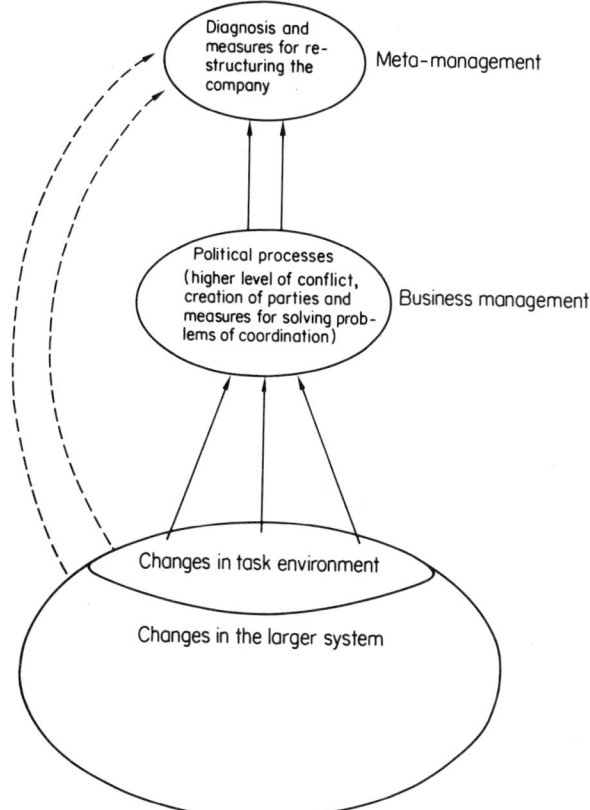

Figure 11.1. Process of Translation in Swedish Building
Materials Ltd and Provisions Ltd

systems and the highest professional quality'. For the first few years
the comapny could boast of an impressive amount of development activities; it also acquired a good reputation on the market but without showing
much increase in volume.

However, after the first five years signs of tension and controversy began
to appear. Most members of management felt that the systems so far
developed still fell short of the original vision; in their view the company
should continue to concentrate on development work. One or two minor
factions wanted to take up a few of the products that had been developed,
and even to establish special subsidiaries to exploit them.

Gradually the realization dawned—particularly on the founder—that
the company had moved into a penetration stage and what it needed now
was a new structure and a different leadership style. In this case, too, it
was the identification and interpretation of the tension in the company
that produced the diagnosis.

- In the last chapter we described the marked state of tension that we found in the Swedish-Malaysian Trading Company, where opposing parties were supporting very different strategies for future action. At the same time this company enjoyed a very open climate, so that the internal political debate was able to function very satisfactorily. By reading the internal tension correctly and interpreting the pattern that emerged, the managing director gradually acquired a basis on which to build a new structure better adapted to the company's new business idea.

The Industrial Gas Company provided one more case in which escalating internal tension showed that a company had entered a new phase in its growth.

- The company sold gas and various kinds of equipment. Its marketing side had always been divided into an industrial sector and a medical sector. The latter sold direct to the hospitals, while the former sold to industry and to local distributors. In 1972 a violent conflict flared up between the two sectors, in which both parties accused the other of poaching on their markets. Tension was also increasing within the medical sector, between top management and some of the younger members of the business. These young men pointed out that profitability was falling off and the rate of growth was too slow.

  A closer examination of the situation revealed that big structural changes were taking place on the market. Municipalities and county councils were increasing their efforts to coordinate their purchases for various public undertakings, and were creating municipal and regional purchasing departments to this end. This meant that purchasing decisions no longer fell into the same patterns as before, and some of the company's customers in the industrial sector were being considered as suppliers (particularly of gas) by the municipalities and county councils.

  As management gradually learnt to interpret this tension correctly, the old strategy of trying to improve the system of internal charging was abandoned. Instead the whole question of whether the company's structure and development resources accorded satisfactorily with the major trends on the market came up for a more critical examination.

Consumer Services Ltd provides us with an example of a meta-management which reacted to the *absence* of political activity.

- The managing director realized that the company was passing the peak of maturity, and that it would now benefit from having a large pool of internal variety and some opposition to the old-established ideas. As we described in Chapter 6, part of the solution in this case was to create a new and considerably more decentralized organization. Built into this structure were also a number of institutionalized arenas for confrontations between managers in a variety of positions who were able to see the problems from different points of view.

11.3 Meta-management's distinctive knowledge

In the cases we have reported above, meta-management's initiative has been triggered off by internal political processes in the company. However, management was not able to interpret these processes immediately, nor could it take action straight away on a basis of the tension generated. Only when tension is set in a broader context does it yield its full information content; only then can its causes be deciphered. It seems to me that the real mark of a meta-management is its ability not only to see the company as part of the task environment but also to envisage the company's task environment as part of an even larger system in society. Let us return to two of our examples.

● In order to draw the correct conclusions about the internal tension at the Industrial Gas Company, it was necessary to know someting about the trends and the general direction of thinking in the organization of the public sector as a whole—efforts to improve efficiency and coordination, for instance.

● When Heavy Conglomerates Ltd was reorganized to reflect the multiplicity of its feelers in new branches of industry, certain insights about the relevant branches were necessary: which were in a state of rapid development, and which were mature and stable and more difficult to penetrate?

It is a combination of the ability to understand internal political processes and a kind of fundamental understanding of the larger system which makes it possible for a meta-management to operate. The internal political system acts as a filter through which the great variety prevailing in the company's task environment passes and is translated into a manageable language relevant to the purposes of meta-management. But if the signals emitted are to be interpreted correctly, they must be illuminated by a thorough knowledge of what is going on at least in the industry and perhaps even in the whole community. The skilful statesman must be blessed with an acute sensitivity to political processes; he also has to be something of a social philosopher.*

11.4 Meta-management's distinctive practice

It is not meta-management's job to react directly to stimuli arising in the

*Thus the statesman must know something of the substance of his lines of business. Penrose (1959) and Drucker (1974), for example, both point out the importance of having some kind of common denominator even in multibusiness companies, and the era of the large American conglomerates which were supposed to build on 'professional leadership' and financial strategy alone soon proved short-lived.

task environment of a single operation; nor to take action aimed directly at influencing individual lines of business. Stimuli reach meta-management chiefly through the company's political system, and its actions follow the same indirect path; the statesman works by influencing the organizational structure.

Meta-management's intervention may concern the *power system* or the *conflict-resolving mechanisms*. It may be a question of supporting groups which represent the values and ideas that appear necessary and consonant with the company's new situation. In other cases it may be enough to provide arenas for conflict resolution and confrontation between diverging opinions, so as to integrate different kinds of knowledge or achieve some kind of synergy. In such cases a certain amount of direct influence on the company's *cognitive system* or *problem-solving resources* is also involved. These arenas for combined problem-solving and conflict resolution fulfil a double function: they make immediate problem-solving more efficient, and they influence the values and conceptual frameworks of the actors.

Meta-management may also act by making changes in the *control system*—perhaps by injecting new values into the reward system, or by adjusting the resource-allocation system so that the various lines of business are subjected to new demands and new conditions. But all its actions have one thing in common: meta-management does not intervene in the game itself; it exerts influence only *by changing the rules and the plan of the game*.

We can now summarize the qualities that an efficient meta-management should possess:

1. An acute sensitivity to internal political processes and tensions.

2. A thorough understanding of the basic structure (particularly any structural changes) of the social systems to which the company and the particular industry belong.

3. A language (or theory) to make possible the interpretation of the dynamics of the internal and external situation into meta-management practice.

4. Means to influence the organizational structure—in particular the power system, conflict-resolving mechanisms, cognitive system and control system—so as to change the company's growth culture.

Figure 11.2 illustrates how meta-management by means of a specific language (the central feature of this book) generates knowledge about the actual situation on the basis of its cognizance and experiences of internal political processes in relation to the larger systems. It also shows how meta-management, by working upon the organizational structure, changes the situation.

11.5 Growth culture and statesmanship—a summary

Those properties of a company which affect its pattern of growth and which lead to a certain way of dealing with growth problems and sometimes to the occurrence of certain growth maladies have been called here the *company's growth culture*. Statemanship is our name for the kind of leadership that aims at maintaining or changing the growth culture rather than at steering the individual exchange and growth processes.

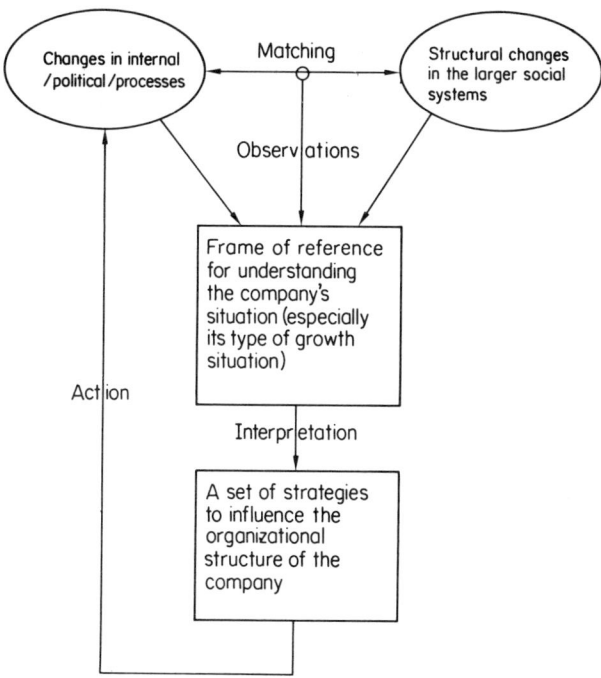

Figure 11.2. Major Ingredients in the Exercise of Statesmanship

The actual substance of the projects through which a company grows is shaped by a combination of the knowledge embedded in the company and the natural driving forces embodied in the environment and the technology. But the aptness of the company's structure to the discovery and generation of such projects, the selection of projects to be undertaken, the way in which they are undertaken—all these depend on various characteristics of the growth culture.

Thus the growth culture and the meta-management act as the watchmen at the gate: some values and ideas are encouraged and allowed to pass, others are turned away. But the watchmen must not remain passive. They must see that the gate lies on a reasonably busy path. If it doesn't, they must move it or somehow manipulate road planning or the pattern of the traffic. They can also try attaching a variety of conditions, sanctions and rewards to the right of entry.

Meta-management's job is to see that the idea system and structure of the company are adapted to the changing needs of the situation. We have seen that for the fulfilment of this task a highly developed capacity for identifying and interpreting internal political processes (particularly changes in the patterns of tension) is of fundamental importance, since it is these processes that translate changes in the company's situation into a language suitable for use in diagnosis and the exercise of 'meta-control'. Thus meta-management must have sensitive hearing, delicately attuned to what is 'in the air'.

But discovering tension is not necessarily the same as understanding it. What is 'in the air' is not always right; people don't always know what they want; the only thing that can be taken for granted is that *someting* lies behind their actions and reactions. Meta-management will only be able to interpret the tension correctly if its perceptions and understanding at a systems level are of a high quality, if it can understand the company in a wider context. As well as everything else, the statesman has to be something of a social philosopher too.

If the different processes in the company are to be understood and adequately supported, it is helpful to have representatives in meta-management of the different types of processes that are likely to occur. In the growth culture of a successful company, for example, we would expect to find a permanent built-in source of tension in the confrontation between learning values and exploitation values, both of which can be embodied in different meta-management roles. However, this basically fruitful tension often calls for some kind of regulatory balance, and this can also be embodied in meta-management in the person of a moderator. Another major role in a meta-management is occupied by the shield-maker. He is the protector of incipient ideas, even those that are generally regarded as illegitimate.

Finally, a set of instruments is included in meta-management's armoury. With these instruments meta-management can influence the crystallization of the company's dominating ideas.

Appendix

Clinical Research and Clinical Theory— Some Epistemological Premises

The search for a new approach

Since the material and the methods I have used in this study are both rather unconventional, at least in relation to the general run of research in business administration, I would like to try to explain a little more clearly why I have gone about things in the way I have. Part of the following explanation is really a kind of retrospective reconstruction: only recently have I been able to see and identify at all clearly the pattern in my method and in the type of theory it has generated.

The method I have used is closely linked to a graudally emerging view of reality, of the nature of knowledge, and of the way knowledge can be created and employed. It is therefore natural that my methodological approach has also developed as the project has proceeded. My main incentive has been a dissatisfaction with traditional positivist methods, but in the course of the project I have also become increasingly aware of my role as a change-oriented clinical consultant.

I have already described some of my attempts to find alternatives to a traditional positivist research method, in some short papers published in 1970 under the title 'A Personal Quest for Methodology'. The main subject of these papers is the importance of regarding *research as a genuine learning process* (in my view the design of the typical positivist study presupposes that the main learning activity has already taken place), and the importance of *developing a language* to help us to understand contexts and wholes or ensembles. I also touched upon another problem: how can the language used by the researcher be linked to the language used by the actors in the studied system, and how can these two languages be made to enrich one another in a combination process of research and change? About this second point, however, I have learnt a good deal more since I wrote that, partly because I am now more familiar with some of the orientations within the philosophy of science which provide alternatives to positivism (in particular the Frankfurt school) and also— perhaps mainly—because I now have much more experience as a clinical consultant.

Positivist research and clinical research—the underlying assumptions

What distinguishes the positivist view of science? Naturally, what we see in this view will depend on our premises, and what we are comparing it with. In the first place the positivist scientific approach supplies rules for the discovery and identification of regularities—invariances—in some sort of 'reality'. A researcher of the positivist school tries to find cause-and-effect relationships and to describe these in the form of laws. In the social sciences he is chiefly interested in the laws that describe the causes of various kinds of behaviour and the linkages between them, i.e. manifestations of the actions of individual people.

This type of theory-building, in which the theory consists of concepts (variables) and propositions or laws about relations between these concepts, has long dominated all research in the natural sciences. We can therefore call this kind of theory *naturalistic*. And it is in the natural sciences—mainly in physics—that the positivist school in the social sciences has found its scientific inspiration; it has tried to fit our knowledge of the structure and function of social systems into the confines of the naturalistic theory.

Positivistic studies of company growth and growth problems have tried to identify regularities in the relations between certain variables, for instance the age of the company, its organizational structure, the degree of bureaucracy in its structure, its goals, etc. And a positivistic method is well suited to studies whose aim is to find out, for example, how many companies in a given population are in a specific and clearly defined situation.

But we have had a different problem. We had to try to develop knowledge which would help us and other actors—in particular company managements—to understand and handle growth processes in companies in a more satisfactory way. We were interested in a theory of change and of effecting change. In fact we even wanted to go further than this; we needed a theory of change and of how to achieve change. Naturalistic theories based on positivist methods can be used to plot regularities between observable and already existing phenomena, but they provide an inadequate tool for any attempt to penetrate the dynamic world of social change (cf. Østerberg, 1971).

Thus we needed a scientific approach to help us to understand the actor operating in a system that he wants to change. A clinical theory must be concerned with the way *the actor improves his ability to deal with his situation*. A pivotal element in the theory must therefore concern the processes by which the actor develops his knowledge and ability. I have already explained that, as I see it, research can best be described as a learning process. I would now like to go further and claim that, to a great extent, clinical research is research *about* learning processes.

The actor system, the reality system and the research system

Subjective and social reality

Let us now make a fundamental assumption linked to the view of human nature on which my approach is based. People do not 'behave' because they have some 'motive' that compels them to do so. No, they 'act' in the light of the way they see reality (their frame of reference), which helps them to define their situation and provides them with general guidelines for suitable action (cf. also Argyris and Schön, 1974).

Thus, helping someone to deal better with his situation is ultimately the same as helping him to develop his frame of reference—his *subjective reality*. And understanding a person's behaviour means understanding how it agrees with his view of reality.

As soon as we look at a person in a context and start dealing with systems of actors, it is no longer only the individual person's subjective perceptions of reality that are relevant but also what we can call the *social reality*, i.e. the common perception of reality that emerges from the interaction between members of a group, of an organization or of a whole society. Much of this social reality is manifest in the language used in the social system, in the system's social and organizational structure, and in its institutions (Berger and Luckmann, 1967). The social, group-generated and group-sanctioned reality agrees in general, but never entirely, with the individual's subjective perceptions of reality. And the social reality differs between different groups in society: in a traditional society, where most people live under much the same conditions, it is relatively homogeneous; but in a pluralistic society it is in some ways extremely fragmented. Over and above the more or less shared everyday reality which most people experience, individual groups have their own specialized social reality which is contingent on their own particular situation. Nearly everybody can read and understand Agatha Christie, but the *Administrative Science Quarterly* or the professional journals of the medical profession are reserved for more limited circles.

Management as a professional group in society has its own social reality. It includes elements from many quarters—from everyday reality and from the management theories of the schools of business administration, for instance. And within this group each individual company also has a unique and somewhat divergent social reality, which embraces elements of the company's technology, the behaviour of competitors on the market, the education of the marketing director, the managing director's relations with his wife, etc.

Relation between the actor system and the reality system

For the individual actor or for the group of actors 'real life' exists in the form of the psycho-social reality we have been describing above. But the outside observer, for example the researcher, sees it in another way. He sees, on the one hand, an *actor system* and, on the other, some situation which the actor system is trying to handle. In the view of the observer, the actor and his social reality do not blend; from where he is standing he can see how the actor struggles with a system which, in relation to himself, is more or less exogenous and which we shall call the *reality system*. The actor's situation appears to have an inherent structure which can be analysed and revealed.

We need not assume here that this reality system—the actor's situation seen through the eyes of an outside observer—is either more or less 'real' than the social reality in the actor system. The only assumption that we make is that actors do in fact find themselves in situations which, in relation to their own actions and abilities, are exogenous ('given') and that these situations can be described and interpreted in different ways.

To the clinical researcher it is the relation between the actor system and the reality system which is interesting. How well do they agree? How is the actor system's knowledge of the reality system developed? Insofar as the clinical researcher has a therapeutic purpose, he will also be interested in methods of increasing the consonance between the reality system and the actor system and in constructing tools for increasing knowledge in the actor system.

Among clinically inclined social scientists a 'soft' school has recently emerged. This school tries to change the organization mainly or solely by studying and intervening in the interactions of the key actors, without attending to the concrete content of the interaction process or to the reality system in which the actors and their company are operating. However, it seems to me that this totally process-oriented school is wrong on one or two important counts. It is by no means unusual for actors to be ignorant of certain essential elements in their situation, and this ignorance may be a real obstacle to their problem-solving. But even more important is the way in which new approaches—new ways of 'seeing' the reality system and new concepts for describing the actors' relations with their situation, perhaps in the shape of action strategies—can play a major role in generating and effecting change.

It seems to me that, to be able to analyse the actors' language and the problem-solving process they use in handling their situation, the clinical consultant must also interest himself in the actors' situation. And the focus of interest lies in the tension between the actor system and the reality system. This means that the researcher must examine and learn about the reality system and the field of energy in which the actors operate.

Lack of consonance between a reality system and an actor system may have different causes. One kind of dissonance may arise simply because the actors have insufficient knowledge. Another depends on how relevant their knowledge is (as it is represented by the actor system's language and social reality). This relevance can always be questioned, particularly if there are competing perceptions of reality which distinguish different aspects of the reality system.

We are concerned here with a system of three components, namely, the reality system, the actor system and the researcher system. We return to the last of these below.

Research-guiding interests

Before we look more closely at the last of our three systems—the researcher system—we must digress briefly to say something about the researcher's values and *cognitive interests*. Following the Frankfurt philosophers, in parti-

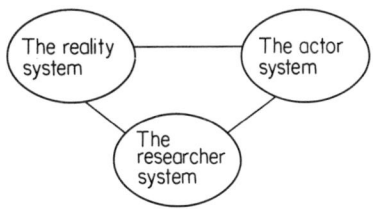

Figure A. 1. Three Related Subsystems

cular Habermas (1972), we can distinguish three cognitive interests (or 'types of research-motivating and research-guiding interests' (Radnitzky, 1968)):

1. A *technical* cognitive interest, according to which social and other systems are studied as objectified processes without direct reference to any actors, and with the aim of technical control. Positivist research is often regarded, consciously or unconsciously, as being based on a technical cognitive interest only.

2. A *practical* (or hermeneutic) cognitive interest governs hermeneutic inquiries aimed at understanding the actors and establishing a communication. This kind of research calls for quite different methods, replacing observation by the understanding of meaning.

3. An *emancipatory* cognitive interest governs a critical social science, which emphasizes the revelation, and possibly the elimination, of factors which bind the actor to a certain perception of reality and to a certain role. This has been described by Lowry, among others, in a new book which opens with the following words:

> Sociology is often at its best when it is myth breaking, when it turns its methodologies and theoretical perspectives to a critique of popular beliefs about human behavior that have obtained the force of dogma ...
>
> This book is a critical analysis of prevailing popular and scientific myths about contemporary social problems. It begins ... with a critique of popular American mythology which short-sightedly blames evil people, irrational behavior, the collapse of moral integrity, and the like, for the multitude of current world problems—from drug use, through sexual deviance, to war and pollution ...
>
> This situation is further complicated by the fact that although sociologists often debunk popular mythologies, they only infrequently turn their critical talents to a needed appraisal of their own misconceptions. As members of a social system, social scientists cannot escape the influence of accepted mythology. In addition, the theoretical perspectives they devise for analyzing and ordering the world study also frequently reflect historical biases and special misconceptions unique to the scientific community. (Lowry, 1974, pp. vi–vii)

It seems to me that these three cognitive interests can be described along a scale: that (or those) mentioned first must be to some extent fulfilled before that (or those) mentioned second can be fulfilled. In many respects it is clearly a practical or emancipatory cognitive interest which has permeated the present book; for instance, it has been important to us to try to understand how the dominating ideas in a company have arisen, and what restrictions and blockages make it difficult to change them. But this is not all we have done; we have also *constructed*: we have tried to develop new languages for describing reality systems—'the real situation'. These languages should, hopefully, be able to help people to deal more efficiently with the situations in which they find themselves, by enabling them to break away from the restrictions the situation has imposed.

Clearly, our ambition on this point agrees with the implications of Lindström's fourth cognitive interest, which he adds to Habermas' three. He calls this the *innovative* cognitive interest and describes its purpose as follows:

> ... to develop new perspectives and theories, constructions and 'inventions', and to 'improve our picture of the world'.
> (Lindström, 1973, p. 45, our translation)

Note on the relation between a cognitive interest and the diagnosis of a social system

In using a systems language to describe organizations in this book, I have often employed the concepts 'fit' and 'misfit' in describing relations between subsystems and in making my diagnoses. Naturally, what a researcher regards as a fit or a misfit will depend on the frame of reference and the cognitive interest that he applies. The clinical researcher finds that concepts such as 'sickness', 'health', etc., come readily to mind. But such concepts have no meaning unless the researcher has first described his point of reference. Although I have not used these medical analogies systematically, this is perhaps a suitable place to describe briefly the meta-theory which has guided my diagnoses.

The term 'misfit' can be motivated most simply when we operate entirely at the actor level: for example, where there is a clear lack of consonance between what an actor says he wants to achieve on the one hand, and the effects of his actions on the other; or where various different parts of the actor system function inconsistently.

But a state of misfit like this need not imply a state of 'sickness'. On the contrary, I have tried to show that, in certain situations, tension and misfits in the actor system may be desirable in terms of our overarching frame of reference (our 'ideal model'), and that they indicate a state far removed from any kind of 'sickness'. Rather than using the concepts 'sick' and 'healthy', I would prefer to use terms along the scale 'sick'–'not sick'–'beautiful'.

Insofar as we are clinically oriented—i.e. interested in the way the actors learn and the conditions under which their learning takes place—misfits cannot simply be regarded as symptoms of disease either in terms of the social reality or in terms of the researcher's theoretical language. First we have to know something about what the actor system is doing about the misfits. Only if the problem is left untreated, if the actor system is unable to learn or to diagnose and identify its situation, can we speak of a *sickness*.

According to the practical and emancipatory cognitive interests, we can then speak of a state of *non-sickness* if certain conditions are fulfilled, namely:

- the actor system is able to diagnose its situation and is able to learn
- the actor system is reasonably free from misconceptions about its own ability, about the driving forces behind its company's growth, and about the bases of its own behaviour
- the actor system is not a victim of circumstances but is involved in a real choice situation, i.e. it has consciously chosen a strategy and consciously excluded others.

But I am convinced that there is a sharp distinction between this state of non-sickness and certain other rarely encountered states, in which the actor system not only has a high learning ability and is free from misconceptions, but in which it is also truly innovative. We can call this state *beautiful* rather than healthy, since it is clearly distinct phenomenologically and existentially not only from the state of sickness but also from the state of non-sickness. At the same time there are no fixed criteria for what constitutes a beautiful state, since the degree of freedom is theoretically infinite once we have passed the non-sick stage.

The psychoanalytical situation as a paradigm of social science research

What are the implications of all this for the researcher system? Clearly the researcher must approach his problem from two directions. He must try to understand both the actors' world of ideas and their situation, and the mechanisms and restrictions on knowledge development in the actor system. The process of clinical research resembles in many ways what Apel (1972) has described as the process of knowledge development in the psychoanalytical situation. The essence of this process is that the researcher alternates between different levels of understanding and explanation and between different existential relations to his research object. He sometimes uses a humanistic, understanding-oriented method—what is termed '*verstehen*' in German literature—sometimes a naturalistic method in which he behaves more or less in accordance with positivist rules. Apel's model, which Radnitzky (1968) aptly calls a 'hermeneutic–dialectic' approach, can be described briefly in the following sequence:

1. In a first phase the analyst tries to understand the patient, i.e. to identify the ideas and rationality bases that lie behind his actions and words. The analyst's search for understanding assumes the shape of a *dialogue*, a conversa-

tion between equals. The dialogue takes place entirely in terms of the language represented by the patient's subjective reality. The analyst formulates continuously hypotheses—'good-reason essays'—about the patient's rationality bases.

2. The dialogue continues until the analyst finds some basic inconsistency in the patient, i.e. something in his behaviour for which the analyst can find no rational grounds or which does not agree with the hypotheses he has formulated about the patient's rationality base. At this point the analyst's existential relationship with the patient changes, and the latter is no longer regarded as an equal in the conversation but is now regarded as an object. The analyst leaves the world of ideas which up to then he and the patient have shared but which is obviously no longer adequate to explain the observations made, and proceeds to another world of ideas—*psychoanalytical theory*—to seek for explanations there. He no longer ascribes the patient's actions to different rationality bases, but seeks in the knowledge available to him (in the shape of psychoanalytical theory) for *motives* which can explain these actions. In this situation, if we disconnect it from preceding and succeeding stages, the analyst is acting exactly like a positivist, i.e. applying a naturalist theory with its propositions and laws about the relations between various phenomena. We can therefore speak of a 'naturalistic phase' in the process. But because this naturalistic phase is only part of a more complex process and is anyway subject to an emancipatory cognitive interest, it is usually described as 'quasi-naturalistic'.

3. The purpose of the psychoanalytical situation is to increase the patient's knowledge by increasing his self-awareness. The analyst must therefore be able to pass on his newly won knowledge about the patient so that the latter's self-awareness does in fact grow. It would probably be possible to do this directly, but it is generally done by means of an *historical explanation*. Among other things, I understand that there are pedagogical reasons for this. Together with his patient, the analyst tries to reconstruct when and how the 'motives' arose which have since given rise to the inconsistency in the patient's behaviour.

4. After the historical explanation, which increases the analyst's understanding and the patient's self-awareness, the dialogue is revived. The process starts again, but now at a higher level.

The limitations of this model for our purpose

There are many similarities between the situation described here, which is suggested by Apel as a paradigm for social science research, and the process which I have been using. I shall not comment here on the resemblances, which are fairly obvious, but will indicate instead some points at which the analogy does not altogether hold. I will also amplify the model a little.

1. The model deals mostly with the development of knowledge *about, and in, the individual client*, but not so much with the way the situation can be exploited to develop the analyst's 'naturalistic' theory.

2. The process is based on the assumption, or possibly on the cognitive interest, that the patient's self-awareness will lead to his 'liberation'. But for a study of whole organizations and social systems, the process has a serious drawback: in such cases the causal relationships and the techniques for achieving the desired state are often so complicated that insight alone cannot be expected to achieve results.

3. Also, the conditions for knowledge development are obviously more complicated in a system of actors than they are in a personal system, because in such cases the development of knowledge may also be affected by the value system, the social structure and the organizational structure in the actor system, and so on.

But allowing for the modifications that these objections require, Apel's model provides a good description of the method which I have tried to apply to the development of knowledge in and about the client (= management) and which I have presented as a kind of naturalistic theory of business management.

On the relation between our meta-theory and our clinical theory

This methodological appendix is mainly concerned with my overarching theory. I see an overarching theory or meta-theory as more or less the same thing as a philosophy of science, telling us something about what knowledge is relevant and how such relevant knowledge is created. The meta-theory is translated in any specific research problem into a concrete methodological approach which determines the data to be collected, how they are to be collected, how they are to be processed, and so on. The chosen method in turn has a decisive impact on the type of theory that it will be possible to develop. Thus there is a clear connection between meta-theory, method, and theory.

Given the meta-theory that I have suggested as the basis for clinical research, it would then be interesting to find out what type of theory can emerge from the research process. What is a clinical theory? According to Apel, even the knowledge which the analyst brings with him and creates as a psychoanalytical theory has the form of a naturalistic theory, i.e. in principle the same form as a positivist researcher's theory. The difference between a positivist theory and a clinical theory lies possibly in the way the theory is created, and certainly in the way it is used. But are there any other differences?

In practice it seems to me that the differences are very great. At the beginning of this appendix I said something about the nature of the positivist theories of company growth. The great difference between the positivist researcher and the clinical researcher lies in the way the latter *relates to the social reality in the studied systems*.

The basic data of the clinical researcher thus comprise *both* his descriptions and his analyses of the real-life system *and*—and this is particularly interesting in the present context—the language or the system of subjective and social meaning structures which he finds in the actor system. This second type of data is not used by the positivist researcher, at least not according to the rules.

Another set of basic data would produce a theory whose content, conceptual categories and relationships would also be different, even if the theory had a naturalistic form. I would like to suggest the following as the main elements to be found in a clinical theory:

1. Descriptions of reality *systems* and *types of situations*. Examples of these are to be found in Chapter 5, where we saw how exogenous and built-in driving forces in the situation tend to steer companies into particular growth situations.

2. *Models of actor systems* including types of roles, types of ideas and types of strategies. In this book, for instance, we have given several examples of different types of myths. A combination of this and point 1 gives us propositions about such things as 'types of actors in types of situations' (cf. Schutz, 1963).

3. *Process models* which describe processes whereby the actor system is changed or is not changed. For example, we have described some of the ways in which a system of dominating ideas can emerge in a company, and we have also looked at some of the obstacles and blockages that can inhibit changes in the system.

4. *Ideal-types* and tool concepts which are descriptive in the sense that they are based on an interpretation of empirical experience, but normative in the sense that on a basis of some kind of rationality criteria they appear to be more fruitful as descriptions of reality or of strategies than those at present prevailing in the relevant actor system and in other researcher systems. Our concepts of the business idea and the growth idea, our description of the different stages in a company's growth, and our description of meta-management and statesmanship are all examples of such ideal-types and tool concepts.

I find it difficult to pinpoint exactly the significance of these tool concepts in meta-theoretical terms. Obviously they do not represent explanatory variables; the examples mentioned cannot be the 'cause' of anything. Rather, they are abstractions of complex states or '*Gestalten*'. We could say that they can help the actors (and researchers) to structure complex situations in a new and fruitful way (they have something to do with the present 'state of the art'), since they transcend and establish a tension in relation to prevailing frames of reference and accepted theories, and, above all, that they can *serve as paradigms for the actions of actors (and researchers)*.*

5. *Intervention models*, which describe how the clinician can intervene in the knowledge-development process in the actor system. In this book I have made no systematic attempt to discuss this kind of intervention model, although I have given a few examples of intervention.

It is also obvious that the shape of the clinical theory will depend on the particular cognitive interest to which the researcher adheres. For example, category 4 above presupposes an innovative cognitive interest of the kind we described earlier.

*Cf. also Israel (1971).

Some consequences of the practical approach

My material consists mainly of clinical data collected over fairly long periods of time—from a few months up to three or four years or even longer—that I have spent attached to companies for the purpose of making an analysis in depth and aiding a process of change. I shall not go into detail here about the nature of the data or the way they were processed. I shall simply comment briefly on some basic principles.

In collecting and processing the data I was steered by certain meta-theoretical ideas about the researcher's relation to the studied system and about the classes of phenomena which constitute the ingredients of a clinical theory. Thus in the early stages of a project I was definitely seeking humanistic understanding by plotting the social reality and the rationality bases in the actor system. At the same time I also analysed the 'actual situation', or the reality system, using a variety of tools. The processes of knowledge development which lead to evolution and change in the social reality, the structure and the rationality bases of the actor system, came into the focus of attention quite early on in each individual project.

When a diagnosis had been made in theoretical terms, specifying in particular the degree of consonance between the actor system and the reality system and identifying the mechanisms for knowledge development in the actor system, a more active and constructive phase was launched. Its aim was to make the actor system more self-aware and to provide it with better instruments for analysing the prevailing situation and for steering the actions to be taken. In this phase we tried to help by improving the mechanisms for knowledge development, but in most cases we also engaged ourselves actively in the discovery of new and superior solutions.

I would like to make two points about the type of data that are suitable to the method I have outlined here, namely, the combination of very hard and very soft data, and the use of historical data.

The companies were all carefully studied with regard to a number of 'hard' features, such as product–market situation, financial structure and cost structure, production system, industrial structure, etc. This meant that, using our analytical models, we were able to diagnose the company's situation and compare this description with the actor system's perception of the same reality. But we also studied the actor system. We held long interviews with anything from about 20 to more than 100 people in the company concerned, and we tried to get some idea of the actors' view of reality—what did they think of the company's situation, for example, and which actions did they think led to which effects. We registered any tensions in the actor system and even helped to provoke situations which would reveal tension and the values from which it sprang.

After studying present and historical decisions and observing reactions to our own behaviour, we drew certain conclusions about the company's power system. We noted any special features of the language used in the company. We held interviews in depth with leading actors in the companies, from which we were able to derive a picture of their personal life situations, their driving forces, blockages, etc.

An historical approach was chosen for two reasons. First, it is well known that social systems and other systems generally reveal their fundamental and inherent nature at times of change or attempted change; by making an historical study of the companies and industries concerned, we were able to analyse many change processes which had persisted for periods far longer than the time we had available for making personal observations. Secondly, the historical approach satisfies our interest in the long-lasting process of knowledge development in actor systems. Here is how a psychoanalytically-minded researcher justifies his interest in historical material:

> Psychoanalysis, despite its preoccupation with a genetic or developmental frame of reference, despite the historicism of many of its theoretical formulations, is not a science of history but a science of the symbolizing activity of the mind.
> (Edelson, 1971, p. 58)

By studying historically the way the actor system operates—particularly in connection with critical events—we were able to identify the dominating ideas (many of which are not immediately obvious—it takes a crisis to show them up; cf. Garfinkel, 1967) and the learning mechanisms and blockages in the company and the actor system. We could then have a confrontation between the history of events and the history of ideas (cf. Vickers, 1965).

And this, systematically, has been my approach. A good theory of complex systems is a theory of patterns, not a theory of isolated relations between individual variables. A theory of patterns cannot be developed except by systematic confrontations between a frame of reference and empirical cases. The basic principle is to confront a *whole* frame of reference, on as many points and over as broad a front as possible, with new empirical real-life *ensembles* (= companies). Each such broad confrontation reveals weaknesses in the current frame of reference in the shape of false assumptions, irrelevant or unfruitful concepts, blank patches, etc. The frame of reference is then revised accordingly—in detail and as a whole—to be ready for the next confrontation.

Thus, through a series of direct confrontations between theoretical wholes (or ideal types) and empirical ensembles (actor systems in reality systems), the frame of reference successively evolves. I first came upon and defined the concept of the growth idea, for example, during the spring of 1974, but after testing it systematically in a number of cases, I gradually modified and elaborated it in many essential ways. Originally, for instance, I did not include the institutional strategy—the handling of the internal and external power systems—as a pivotal element in the growth idea; this aspect emerged gradually as I found that my original formulation couldn't satisfactorily explain the processes I had been studying during the past year.

When should these systematic confrontations be discontinued? The desirability of stopping is signalled by a kind of saturation point at which new cases no longer seem to add anything fresh or to deviate from the set of concepts already developed (Glaser and Strauss, 1968). According to this definition, I have not nearly finished. My latest observations, for example, suggest that my picture of role constellations and the impact of external factors on company learning, and my description of the company's growth idea, are still in need of considerable adjustment—to mention some of the most obvious examples only.

On validation

The problem of validation and testing is perhaps a little difficult to handle, given my meta-theory and my method. In positivist research, validation is usually reduced to a theoretically simple although technically complicated discussion of measurement problems. Individual hypotheses and laws are validated in a series of tests which measure the prediction value of the laws and similar factors.

Here, too, the problem of reliability as such—whether or not our observations can be trusted—is naturally important to the question of validation. But two other questions are of even greater interest. What is involved in *validating a whole language or paradigm*, as opposed to validating individual propositions? And: What special validation problems attach to the development of a *clinical* theory? This second question is even more complicated than it seems at first sight when we remember that we must naturally validate our innovations— the ideal types and our tool concepts—as well.

I am not sure that I have found really good answers to these questions yet. What is certain, however, is that validation is a complex multidimensional process. Thus we obviously cannot try to validate our approach by asking our clients (the actors) whether they 'feel any better', whether they are more self-aware, whether they understand their environment better after being exposed to a clinical process based on our theory, and so on. Equally obviously, a simple reliance on changes in share prices or profit-and-loss figures as a criterion of validity could give quite the wrong answers.

Although there is clearly something to be said for both these methods, we nevertheless need a more comprehensive validation than this. Any attempt to validate, in full, any action based on our theory would call for follow-up and control on a great many levels. Above all we would have to know whether, as clinical researchers, we can help the actors to function better—to make better diagnoses, to improve the efficiency of their knowledge-development processes, and to find better instruments for designing and implementing their strategies; but we must also find some way of assessing the ability of our analytical models to describe, for example, a company's external environment.

A practical problem is that validation often takes rather a long time, and that the researcher's learning cycle can also be lengthy. The result of this second process is often to reveal aspects that are incomplete rather than absolutely wrong. For instance, if I had been able to revise this report during 1976, I would have been able to evaluate the very interesting results, which are only just appearing, of the matrix organizations that I helped to install in various companies a few years ago. These results have considerably affected my ideas about the learning ability of matrix organizations and, consequently, about how these organizations should be designed.

In conclusion I would like to point out that the validation of a theory always presupposes that some external criteria are found—from a meta-theory that includes a value system. Thus validation is closely linked to the whole question of the researcher's cognitive interest. On account of certain peculiarities in social value systems, it tends to be more difficult to pinpoint these criteria the higher we are in a kind of value-system hierarchy—in other words, the further away we are from what is generally accepted.

Validation in the case of a technical cognitive interest is conducted in accordance with certain clear principles included in the positivist theory. Indeed, we have had no great difficulty in validating those parts of our theory referring to the healing of a 'sickness' in the sense we ascribed to this term above. In the same way it is often easy to validate *ex post* what a doctor has done to try to help a patient who was fatally ill.

In the case of a practical–emancipatory cognitive interest it is also possible to be relatively specific about the necessary validation criteria, as we saw when we discussed the state of 'non-sickness' in social systems.

The greatest problems arise when we consider the innovative cognitive interest—the 'beautiful' state. The range of states which can be described as beautiful is so great, and the possibly relevant value systems so complex, that a substantial elaboration of our meta-theory seems to be called for if we are to be able to tackle the question of validation satisfactorily. It is easy to see immediately and quite clearly whether a carpenter's work and the methods he has used have turned out well. Our value system does not supply equally clear criteria by which to judge the work of the artist.

References

Alderson, W., 1965, *Dynamic Marketing Behavior*, Homewood, Ill.: Irwin.
Alexander, C., 1964, *Notes on the Synthesis of Form*, Cambridge, Mass.: Harvard University Press.
Allen, J. A., 1967, *Studies in Innovation in the Steel and Chemical Industries*, Manchester: The University Press.
Ansoff, H. I., 1965, *Corporate Strategy*, New York: McGraw-Hill.
Apel, K-O., 1972, The *a priori* of communication and the foundation of the humanities, *Man and World*, No. 1, 3–37.
Argyris, C., 1972, *The Applicability of Organizational Sociology*, Cambridge, Mass.: Cambridge University Press.
Argyris, C., and Schön, D. A., 1974, *Theory in Practice: Increasing Professional Effectiveness*, San Francisco, Calif.: Jossey Bass.
Bateson, G., 1972, *Steps to an Ecology of Mind*, New York: Ballantine.
Bell, D., 1974, *The Coming of Post-industrial Society*, London: Heinemann.
Berger, P. L., and Luckmann, T., 1967, *The Social Construction of Reality*, Garden City: Doubleday/Anchor.
Boulding, K. E., 1956, *The Image*, Ann Arbor, Mich.: The University of Michigan Press.
Buchele, R. B., 1967, *Business Policy in Growing Firms. A Manual for Evaluation*, San Francisco: Chandler.
Buckley, W., 1967, *Sociology and Modern Systems Theory*, Englewood Cliffs, N. J.: Prentice-Hall.
Burns, T., 1961/62, Micropolitics: Mechanisms of institutional change, *Adm. Sci. Quarterly*, 257–281.
Burns, T., 1968, An enterprising future? Management system or innovating enterprise? *BP Shield*, 21–25.
Burns, T., and Stalker, G. M., 1961, *The Management of Innovation*, London: Tavistock.
Business Week, 1974, February 16.
Chandler, A. D., Jr., 1962, *Strategy and Structure*, Cambridge, Mass.: M.I.T. Press.
Chevalier, M., 1972, The strategy spectre behind your market share, *European Business*, Summer 1972, 63–71.
Collins, O. F., and Moore, D. G., 1964, *The Enterprising Man*, East Lansing, Mich.: MSU Business Studies.
Crozier, M., 1964, *The Bureaucratic Phenomenon*, Chicago: University of Chicago Press.
Cyert, R. M., and March, J. G., 1963, *A Behavioral Theory of the Firm*, Englewood Cliffs, N. J.: Prentice-Hall.
Dahlman, C., and Gärdborn, I., 1975, Utvecklingsproblem i Bygg-Sverige. En samhällsorganisatorisk studie av bostadsbygg nadssystemet, Stockholm: SIAR Dokumentation AB (SIAR-S-68).

202

Danielsson, C., 1974, Studier i företags tillväxtförlopp eller Historien om GOX, FOX, POX och de fyra telefondirektörerna, Stockholm: SIAR Dokumentation AB (SIAR-S-60).

Dessauer, J. H., 1971, *My Years with Xerox*. *The Billions Nobody Wanted*, New York: Doubleday.

Drucker, P. F., 1974, *Management. Tasks, Responsibilities, Practices*, London: Heinemann.

Dunn, E. S., Jr., 1971, *Economic and Social Development—A Process of Social Learning*, Baltimore: Johns Hopkins, for Resources for the Future Inc.

Edelson, M., 1971, *The Idea of a Mental Illness*, New Haven: Yale University Press.

Friend, J. K., and Jessop, W. N., 1969, *Local Government and Strategic Choice*, London: Tavistock.

Galbraith, J. K., 1967, *The New Industrial State*, Boston: Houghton Mifflin.

Garfinkel, H., 1967, *Studies in Ethnomethodology*, Englewood Cliffs, N. J.: Prentice-Hall.

Glaser, B. B., and Strauss, A. L., 1968, *The Discovery of Grounded Theory*. *Strategies for Qualitative Research*, London: Weidenfeld & Nicholson.

Greiner, L. E., 1972, Evolution and revolution as organizations grow, *Harv. Bus. Rev.*, July-August, 37–46.

Habermas, J., 1972, *Knowledge and Human Interests*, London:Heinemann.

Hampden-Turner, C., 1970, *Radical Man*, New York: Schenkman.

Hanan, M., 1972, *Life-styled Marketing*, New York: American Management Association.

Heller, R., 1974, *The Naked Manager*, London: Coronet.

Hirschman, A. O., and Lindblom, C. E., 1969, Economic development research and development policymaking: some converging views, in F. E., Emery, (Ed.), *Systems Thinking*, Harmondsworth: Penguin.

Hodgson, R. C., Levinson, D. J., and Zaleznik, A., 1965, *The Executive Role Constellation*, Boston: Harvard University Press.

Incentive's Annual Report, 1970, p. 5.

Israel, J., 1971, Postulates and construction in the social sciences (Mimeograph).

Koestler, A., 1969, *The Act of Creation*, London: Hutchinson.

Kuhn, T. S., 1962, *The Structure of Scientific Revolutions*, Chicago: University of Chicago Press.

Laing, R. D., 1961, *The Self and Others. Further Studies in Sanity and Madness*, London: Tavistock.

Lawrence, P. R., and Lorsch, J. W., 1967, *Organization and Environment. Managing Differentiation and Integration*, Boston: Harvard University Press.

Layton, C. (in collaboration with Harlow, C., and de Hoghton, C.), 1972, *Ten Innovations*, London: Allen & Unwin.

Levinson, H., 1968, *The Exceptional Executive*, Cambridge, Mass.: Harvard University Press.

Levitt, T., 1960, Marketing myopia, *Harv. Bus. Rev.*, **38**,1.

Levitt, T., 1969, *The Marketing Mode*, New York: McGraw-Hill.

Lindström, J., 1973, *Dialog och Förståelse*, Göteborgs Univ.: Pedagogiska inst. (PUMP-projektet).

Lowry, R. P., 1974, *Social Problems*, Lexington, Mass.: Heath.

March, J. G., and Simon, H. A., 1958, *Organizations*, New York: Wiley.

Marcuse, H., 1969, Repressive tolerance, In R. P. Wolff, B. Moore Jr. and H. Marcuse, 1969, *A Critique of Pure Tolerance*, London: Cape.

Maslow, A. H., 1962, *Toward a Psychology of Being*, Princeton, N. J.: van Nostrand.

Mead, G. H., 1934, *Mind, Self, and Society*, Chicago: University of Chicago Press.

Moose, S. O., and Zakon, A. J., 1971, Divestment—cleaning up your corporate portfolio, *European Business*, Autumn 1971, 19–26.

Nilsson, G., 1971, Företagsstrategier. En jämförelse mellan strategival inom nagra svenska branscher, Lund: Gleerups (SIAR-S-40).

Normann, R., 1970, A personal quest for methodology, Stockholm: SIAR Dokumentation AB (SIAR-E-19) (Mimeograph).

Normann, R., 1971, Organizational innovativeness: Product variation and reorientation, Stockholm: SIAR Dokumentation AB (SIAR-E-15) (Mimeograph). Also published in *Adm. Sci. Quarterly*, June 1971, 203–215.

Normann, R., 1972, Effektiv samhällsplanering eller kontrollerad slumpprocess? En systemstudie av bostadskvoteringen, Lund: Studentlitteratur (SIAR-S-42).

Normann, R., and Rhenman, E., 1975, Formulation of goals and measurement of effectiveness in the public administration, Stockholm: SIAR Dokumentation AB (SIAR-E-29) (Mimeograph).

Olivecrona, G., 1970, *De Nya Miljonärerna*, Stockholm: Wahlström & Widstrand.

Olofsson, C., 1969, Produktutveckling—Miljöförankring, Stockholm: SIAR Dokumentation AB (SIAR-S-22) (Mimeograph).

Penrose, E. T., 1959, *The Theory of the Growth of the Firm*, Oxford: Blackwell.

Polanyi, M., 1969, *Knowing and Being*, London: Routledge & Kegan Paul.

Price, D. J. de S., 1965, *Little Science, Big Science*, New York: Columbia University Press.

Radnitzky, G., 1968, *Contemporary Schools of Metascience*, Vol. II, *Continental School of Metascience*, Göteborg: Akademiförlaget (Scandinavian Univ. Books).

Rhenman, E., 1963, Research planning—a complex problem, Stockholm: SIAR Dokumentation AB (SIAR-E-4) (Mimeograph).

Rhenman, E., 1968, *Industrial Democracy and Industrial Management*, London: Tavistock (SIAR-E-8).

Rhenman, E., 1972, Långsiktsplanering inom kemisk industri, Stockholm: SIAR Dokumentation AB (SIAR-S-43) (Mimeograph).

Rhenman, E., 1973, *Organization Theory for Long-range Planning*, London: Wiley (SIAR-E-18).

Schon, D. A., 1963, *Displacement of Concepts*, London: Tavistock.

Schon, D. A., 1971, *Beyond the Stable State*, New York: Random House.

Schutz, A., 1944, The stranger: An essay in social psychology, *Am. J. of Sociology*, **XLIX**, 499–507.

Schutz, A., 1963, Concept and theory formation in the social sciences, In M. Natanson, (Ed.), *Philosophy of the Social Sciences*, New York: Random House, pp. 231–249.

Selznick, P., 1949, *TVA and the Grass Roots*, Berkeley, Calif.: University of California Press.

Selznick, P., 1957, *Leadership in Administration. A Sociological Interpretation*, New York: Harper & Row.

Simon, H. A., 1947, *Administrative Behavior*, New York: Macmillan.

Simon, H. A., 1968, Research for choice, In W. R., Ewald, Jr. (Ed.), *Environment and Policy. The Next Fifty Years*, Bloomington, Ind.: Ind. University Press.

Simpson, G. G., 1953, *The Major Features of Evolution*, New York: Columbia University Press.

Sloan, A. P., Jr., 1963, *My Years with General Motors*, New York: Doubleday.

Starbuck, W. H. (Ed.), 1971, *Organizational Growth and Development*, Harmondsworth: Penguin.

Stymne, B., 1970, Values and processes. A systems study of effectiveness in three organizations, Lund: Studentlitteratur (SIAR-E-17).

Thompson, J. D., 1967, *Organizations in Action*, New York: McGraw-Hill.

Thompson, J. D., 1974, Technology, polity, and societal development, *Adm. Sci. Quarterly*, March, 6–21.

Utblick No. 17, Stockholm: Frihets Förlag, p. 32.

Vickers, Sir G., 1965, *The Art of Judgment*, London: Chapman & Hall.

Vickers, Sir G., 1968, *Value Systems and Social Process*, London: Tavistock.

Woodward, J., 1965, *Industrial Organization: Theory and Practice*, London: Oxford University Press.

Zaleznik, A., 1966, *Human Dilemmas of Leadership*, New York: Harper & Row.

Østerberg, D., 1971, *Meta-sociologisk Essä*, Stockholm: Prisma.

Index